MW00438620

S OMETIMES treasures of unique value are unearthed while rummaging in the past. Charlotte Mason was a distinguished British educator at the turn of the century, whose work had a wide and lasting influence. At that time many of the upper-class children were educated at home, and Mason's insights changed their lives. Her ideas were also brought to life in many schools (mostly private), which gave the children an unusual and rich start in their education and development.

Nearly a hundred years later, a changing society often leaves us disappointed with its tangled, worn-out, and narrow practices in education. We chart a "falling capital" in the product that matters most: the life education and character of our children. Is it not the moment to look at some of the roots? To start again?

At last, after hundreds have searched for these original texts, these seminal books are back in print. Harvard University has Charlotte Mason's books; now, at last, you can too!

These writings will give important priorities and guidelines to parents, teachers, and schools. I believe that once again we need to think of all of life, our culture and heritage, so that our children may be nurtured with the nutrients of life and not sawdust. Welcome back, my dear valued mentor, Charlotte Mason! Our children need you as never before.

Susan Schaeffer Macaulay
director of L'Abri Fellowship, Switzerland, and
author of *For the Children's Sake: Foundations of Education for Home and School* (Crossway Books)

THE ORIGINAL HOME SCHOOLING SERIES

THE ORIGINAL HOME SCHOOLING SERIES

Formation of Character

CHARLOTTE M. MASON

Tyndale House
Publishers, Inc.
Wheaton, Illinois

This Tyndale House edition contains the
complete text of Charlotte Mason's original work.

Originally published as *Some Studies in the Formation of
Character* by Kegan Paul, Trench, Trubner and Co., Ltd.,
London, England, 1906

Library of Congress Catalog Card Number 89-51154
ISBN 0-8423-1359-1
Introduction copyright © 1989 by Dean Andreola
Foreword copyright © 1989 by John Thorley
All rights reserved
Printed in the United States of America

1 2 3 4 5 6 7 8 94 93 92 91 90 89

Introduction to the
Original Home Schooling Series

It was amidst a maze of opinions and conflicting points of view on child education that we were introduced to the life and work of Charlotte Mason.

While working for a literature mission in England, my wife, Karen, and I were home schooling our children. Child raising and schooling at home developed into a stressful and draining process for the whole family. Even after reading much on the subject of child raising and education we still seemed to lack direction. We discussed our dilemma with a coworker. She shared a book with us by Susan Schaeffer Macaulay called *For the Children's Sake*. This book hit close to home in many areas that concerned us. It was an introduction to the works of Charlotte Mason, and this whetted our appetites to learn more about Miss Mason's teachings.

Working in publishing, we thought it would be a simple matter to track down some of these books, especially in England where they were originally published many years ago. However, it took us many months searching secondhand bookshops, libraries, and book search services to find out that her books are not available anymore. They have not been published in a complete six volume set for over eighty years. When we had given up hope of finding them, we were informed about the Charlotte Mason College at Ambleside in the Lake District near Keswick, England. Through the kindness and cooperation of the principal, Dr. John Thorley, the college's copies of these rare books were loaned to us from their archives for this special edition of Charlotte Mason's Home Schooling Series.

This series is unique among other child-raising books because of its broad subject matter and amount of detailed study. Mason's teachings stress that both home and school education should be a learning and growing process for the child, parent, and teacher alike. Reading her works, we discover a great deal about ourselves and realize that we must continue to understand and educate ourselves if we wish to have success in educating our children.

Charlotte Mason is a bright light in the art of illuminating a child's mind. Her ideas are practical; they identify problems and offer well-tested and creative solutions. She gives us sweeping visions of what education could and should be and grave warnings about the neglect and abuse of our responsibility and authority.

Although she wrote generations ago, Mason boldly challenges us today. Many parents seem lost in their own homes, and many teachers and children are floundering in our educational systems. These systems are still seeking to educate our children without any parental and biblical influence; they prepare our youth for examinations and not *life!*

Recent books and magazine articles have referred to Charlotte Mason with information obtained from secondary sources. Now, to a new generation, Charlotte Mason speaks for herself in this brilliant, original series.

May these books offer hope and life to parents, teachers, and children, as Charlotte Mason said, "For the Children's Sake!"

Dean and Karen Andreola
Franklin, Tennessee

For information on future publications, products, newsletters, and curriculum (compatible with Miss Mason's principles), mail a S.A.S.E. to the address below. Please feel free to share your comments on Charlotte Mason, home schooling, and/or child raising.

Dean and Karen Andreola
Charlotte Mason Research and Supply Company
P.O. Box 172
Stanton, NJ 08885

Foreword to the
Original Home Schooling Series

Charlotte Mason founded her "House of Education" in Ambleside, in the heart of the English Lake District, in 1892. "It is far from London," she wrote at the time, "but in view of that fact there is much to be said in its favour. Students will be impressed with the great natural beauty around them, will find a country rich in flowers, mosses and ferns. They will learn to know and love the individuality of great natural features—mountain pass, valley, lake and waterfall." The "House of Education" is now the principal's house, "Springfield," and I am writing this foreword in the room that was Charlotte Mason's own living room. I look out of the window and can confirm all its attractions.

Charlotte Mason came to Ambleside when she was nearly fifty, and the college was to be the main focus of her life's work from then until her death in 1923. Hers was no simple success story. Her early childhood is obscure, and she seems never to have wished to elucidate it. She was probably brought up by her father, a Liverpool merchant who, it seems, went bankrupt and then died when Charlotte was still in her teens. Aided by friends of her family, Charlotte became a pupil teacher in Birkenhead and then attended a training college for teachers in London from 1860 to 1861. After qualifying, she taught in an infant school in Worthing, Sussex, until 1873. She then obtained a post on the staff of Bishop Otter Teacher Training College, Chichester, where she lectured in elementary school teaching method. The college was in the forefront of educational thinking in its dedication to the principle of education for all—including girls. W. E. Forster's Education Act of 1870, which provided for elementary schools to be set up across the country, was still fresh and needed trained teachers to implement the promises. The Bishop Otter College certainly influenced Charlotte Mason's thinking, but, for reasons that are difficult now to disentangle, in 1878 Charlotte felt dissatisfied with her work, left the college, and went to live with friends in Bradford in Yorkshire.

Apparently with financial help from these friends (she was certainly never rich), Charlotte began to write. In 1880 she published a series of books on the geography of England, which were well received. But it was her book *Home Education*, published in 1886, that sparked off the most interest. In it one can certainly see the influence of other educational thinkers of the nineteenth century, particularly the child-centered views of Pestalozzi and the artistic ideas of John Ruskin. What Charlotte Mason added was a practical, down-to-earth perspective that showed how one could actually set about and *do* it. Her style and her exposition were homely, both in the sense that she wrote in an easy, intelligible way, and in the sense that she stressed the influence and responsibility of the home. She also wrote from a firmly held evangelical perspective.

The book turned out to be a kind of educational "Dr. Spock" avidly bought by women anxious to ensure the best possible upbringing for their offspring. The need was real, especially among middle-class women of modest means. Education was a subject of much debate and discussion, which had led to the Education Act of 1870, though the reality of primary education all too often was but the palest reflection of Pestalozzi, Ruskin, or even W. E. Forster. Many concerned parents, perhaps more particularly concerned mothers, were looking for something better. Charlotte Mason's *Home Education* offered it. It explained how parents could—and should—provide their children with a broad, stimulating, even exciting education, far removed from the common diet of so many elementary schools of the day.

The book sold well and in influential circles. Very soon the Parents National Education Union (PNEU) was established, with the bishop of London as its first president. Miss Beale, a formidable protagonist in the fight for women's education, was an early member of the organization, as was Anne Clough, the founder of Newnham College, Cambridge. Branches were set up in many major towns and cities, and by 1890 the organization had its own monthly magazine, "The Parents Review," edited by Charlotte Mason herself. Charlotte had quickly become a leading authority on early childhood.

In 1891 Charlotte came to live in Ambleside. A friend of her student days, Selina Healey, had lived in Ambleside, and Charlotte had visited her and had gotten to know the Lake District well. She loved the area, particularly the quiet town of Ambleside. When she moved into Springfield, she was sure she had found the ideal place to train governesses for young children.

So, in January 1892, the House of Education was established. There were four students. Two years later, with thirteen students, the college moved into Scale how, a beautiful Georgian house across the main road from Springfield on a hill amid the trees with fine views of the town and of Loughrigg across the Rothay valley.

Charlotte saw children as thinking, feeling human beings, as spirits to be kindled and not as vessels to be filled. And she demonstrated how it could be done. She believed all children were entitled to a liberal education based upon good literature and the arts. These were in her own day radical thoughts and practices, certainly not just confined to Charlotte Mason, but few of her contemporaries had the sheer practicality that she displayed. The practicing school attached to the House of Education took in local children with no payment; Charlotte firmly believed that her liberal education ideas were applicable to all children regardless of class, status, or ability, and she put her ideas into practice, as she always did.

The college flourished, never larger than fifty students in Charlotte's own lifetime but with a reputation out of proportion to its size. By the 1920s the PNEU had established several schools as well as a correspondence school, run from Ambleside, which sent out lesson notes and advice on educational matters to parents and governesses.

Charlotte died on January 16, 1923; by then she was the object of deep veneration within the movement. She was buried in the churchyard at Ambleside, close to the graves of W. E. Forster and the Arnold family. Educationists flourished—and died—in Ambleside.

The college and the correspondence school continued on the same site until 1966, when the PNEU (now with the added title of "World Education Service") moved to new premises in London and absorbed the correspondence school. PNEU/WES has continued to provide full syllabuses and educational advice to PNEU affiliated schools in the UK and in many countries abroad where English-medium schools have been established. But much of its work is still with parents, mainly with those parents living abroad who need to educate their children at home. The principles established by Charlotte Mason over a hundred years ago are still the guiding principles of all the work of PNEU/WES. They have proved themselves through the many changes in syllabus content and educational demands of the twentieth century.

Meanwhile, the college has undergone its own development. Until 1960 it continued as an independent teacher training institution, but then transferred to the control of the then Westmorland Local Education Authority, and at the same time took over the Kelsick site on Stockghyll Lane, the town's former secondary school. In 1968 the college changed its validating university from Manchester to the newly founded University of Lancaster, some thirty-five miles from Ambleside. Local government reorganization in 1970 resulted in the absorption of Westmorland into the new county of Cumbria. On April 1, 1989, after fifteen years of fruitful partnership with Cumbria, the college became an independent corporation.

John Thorley
Principal
Charlotte Mason College

Preface to the 'Home Education' Series

THE educational outlook is rather misty and depressing both at home and abroad. That science should be a staple of education, that the teaching of Latin, of modern languages, of mathematics, must be reformed, that nature and handicrafts should be pressed into service for the training of the eye and hand, that boys and girls must learn to write English and therefore must know something of history and literature; and, on the other hand, that education must be made more technical and utilitarian—these, and such as these, are the cries of expedience with which we take the field. But we have no unifying principle, no definite aim; in fact, no philosophy of education. As a stream can rise no higher than its source, so it is probable that no educational effort can rise above the whole scheme of thought which gives it birth; and perhaps this is the reason of all the 'fallings from us, vanishings,' failures, and disappointments which mark our educational records.

Those of us, who have spent many years in pursuing the benign and elusive vision of Education, perceive that her approaches are regulated by a law, and that this law has yet to be evoked. We can discern its outlines, but no more. We know that it is pervasive; there is no part of a child's home-life or school-work which the law does not penetrate. It is illuminating, too, showing the value, or lack of value, of a thousand systems and expedients. It is not only a light, but a measure, providing a standard whereby all things, small and great, belonging to educational work must be tested. The law is liberal, taking in whatsoever things are true, honest, and of good report, and offering no limitation or hindrance save where excess should injure. And the path indicated by the law is continuous and progressive, with no transition stage from the cradle to the grave, except that maturity takes up the regular self-direction to which immaturity has been trained. We shall doubtless find, when we apprehend the law, that certain German thinkers—Kant, Herbart, Lotze, Froebel — are justified ; that, as they say, it is 'necessary' to believe in God; that, therefore, the knowledge of God is the principal knowledge, and the chief end of education. By one more character shall we be able to recognise this perfect law of educational liberty when it shall be made evident. It has been said that 'The best idea which we can form of absolute truth is that it is able to meet every condition by which it can be tested.' This we shall expect of our law—that it shall meet every test of experiment and every test of rational investigation.

Not having received the tables of our law, we

fall back upon Froebel or upon Herbart; or, if we belong to another School, upon Locke or Spencer; but we are not satisfied. A discontent, is it a divine discontent? is upon us; and assuredly we should hail a workable, effectual philosophy of education as a deliverance from much perplexity. Before this great deliverance comes to us it is probable that many tentative efforts will be put forth, having more or less of the characters of a philosophy; notably, having a central idea, a body of thought with various members working in vital harmony.

Such a theory of education, which need not be careful to call itself a system of psychology, must be in harmony with the thought movements of the age; must regard education, not as a shut-off compartment, but as being as much a part of life as birth or growth, marriage or work; and it must leave the pupil attached to the world at many points of contact. It is true that educationalists are already eager to establish such contact in several directions, but their efforts rest upon an axiom here and an idea there, and there is no broad unifying basis of thought to support the whole.

Fools rush in where angels fear to tread; and the hope that there may be many tentative efforts towards a philosophy of education, and that all of them will bring us nearer to the *magnum opus*, encourages me to launch one such attempt. The central thought, or rather body of thought, upon which I found, is the somewhat obvious fact that the child is a *person* with all the possibilities and powers included in personality. Some of the members which develop from this nucleus have been exploited from time to time by educational thinkers, and exist vaguely in the general common sense, a notion here, another there. One thesis, which is, perhaps, new, that *Education is the Science of Relations*, appears to me to solve the question of a curriculum, as showing that the object of education is to put a child in living touch with as much as may be of the life of Nature and of thought. Add to this one or two keys to self-knowledge, and the educated youth goes forth with some idea of self-management, with some pursuits, and many vital interests. My excuse for venturing to offer a solution, however tentative and passing, to the problem of education is twofold. For between thirty and forty years I have laboured without pause to establish a working and philosophic theory of education; and in the next place, each article of the educational faith I offer has been arrived at by inductive processes; and has, I think, been verified by a long and wide series of experiments. It is, however, with sincere diffidence that I venture to offer the results of this long labour; because I know that in this field there are many labourers far more able and expert than I — the 'angels' who fear to tread, so precarious is the footing!

But, if only *pour encourager les autres*, I append a short synopsis of the educational theory advanced in the volumes of the 'Home Education Series.' The treatment is not methodic, but incidental ; here a little, there a little, as seemed to me most likely to meet the occasions of parents and teachers. I should add that in the course of a number of years the various essays have been prepared for the use of the Parents' Educational Union in the hope that that Society might witness for a more or less coherent body of educational thought.

> "The consequence of truth is great ; therefore the judgment of it must not be negligent."
>
> WHICHCOTE.

1. Children are born *persons*.

2. They are not born either good or bad, but with possibilities for good and evil.

3. The principles of authority on the one hand and obedience on the other, are natural, necessary and fundamental ; but—

4. These principles are limited by the respect due to the personality of children, which must not be encroached upon, whether by fear or love, suggestion or influence, or undue play upon any one natural desire.

5. Therefore we are limited to three educational instruments—the atmosphere of environment, the discipline of habit, and the presentation of living ideas.

6. By the saying, EDUCATION IS AN ATMO-SPHERE, it is not meant that a child should be isolated in what may be called a 'child environment,'

especially adapted and prepared; but that we should take into account the educational value of his natural home atmosphere, both as regards persons and things, and should let him live freely among his proper conditions. It stultifies a child to bring down his world to the 'child's' level.

7. By EDUCATION IS A DISCIPLINE, is meant the discipline of habits formed definitely and thoughtfully, whether habits of mind or body. Physiologists tell us of the adaptation of brain structure to habitual lines of thought—*i.e.*, to our habits.

8. In the saying that EDUCATION IS A LIFE, the need of intellectual and moral as well as of physical sustenance is implied. The mind feeds on ideas, and therefore children should have a generous curriculum.

9. But the mind is not a receptacle into which ideas must be dropped, each idea adding to an 'apperception mass' of its like, the theory upon which the Herbartian doctrine of interest rests.

10. On the contrary, a child's mind is no mere *sac* to hold ideas; but is rather, if the figure may be allowed, a spiritual *organism*, with an appetite for all knowledge. This is its proper diet, with which it is prepared to deal, and which it can digest and assimilate as the body does foodstuffs.

11. This difference is not a verbal quibble. The Herbartian doctrine lays the stress of education— the preparation of knowledge in enticing morsels, presented in due order—upon the teacher. Children

taught upon this principle are in danger of receiving much teaching with little knowledge; and the teacher's axiom is, 'What a child learns matters less than how he learns it.'

12. But, believing that the normal child has powers of mind that fit him to deal with all knowledge proper to him, we must give him a full and generous curriculum; taking care, only, that the knowledge offered to him is vital — that is, that facts are not presented without their informing ideas. Out of this conception comes the principle that,—

13. EDUCATION IS THE SCIENCE OF RELATIONS; that is, that a child has natural relations with a vast number of things and thoughts: so we must train him upon physical exercises, nature, handicrafts, science and art, and upon *many living* books; for we know that our business is, not to teach him all about anything, but to help him to make valid as many as may be of—

> 'Those first-born affinities
> That fit our new existence to existing things.'

14. There are also two secrets of moral and intellectual self-management which should be offered to children; these we may call the Way of the Will and the Way of the Reason.

15. *The Way of the Will.*—Children should be taught—

(*a*) To distinguish between 'I want' and 'I will.'

(*b*) That the way to will effectively is to turn our

thoughts from that which we desire but do not will.

(*c*) That the best way to turn our thoughts is to think of or do some quite different thing, entertaining or interesting.

(*d*) That, after a little rest in this way, the will returns to its work with new vigour.

(This adjunct of the will is familiar to us as *diversion*, whose office it is to ease us for a time from will effort, that we may 'will' again with added power. The use of suggestion— even self-suggestion—as an aid to the will, is to be deprecated, as tending to stultify and stereotype character. It would seem that spontaneity is a condition of development, and that human nature needs the discipline of failure as well as of success.)

16. *The Way of the Reason.* — We should teach children, too, not to 'lean' (too confidently) 'unto their own understanding,' because the function of reason is, to give logical demonstration (*a*) of mathematical truth; and (*b*) of an initial idea, accepted by the will. In the former case reason is, perhaps, an infallible guide, but in the second it is not always a safe one; for whether that initial idea be right or wrong, reason will confirm it by irrefragable proofs.

17. Therefore children should be taught, as they become mature enough to understand such teaching, that the chief responsibility which rests on them as persons is the acceptance or rejection of initial ideas.

To help them in this choice we should give them principles of conduct and a wide range of the knowledge fitted for them.

These three principles (15, 16 and 17) should save children from some of the loose thinking and heedless action which cause most of us to live at a lower level than we need.

18. We should allow no separation to grow up between the intellectual and 'spiritual' life of children; but should teach them that the divine Spirit has constant access to their spirits, and is their continual helper in all the interests, duties and joys of life.

The 'Home Education' Series is so called from the title of the first volume, and not as dealing, wholly or principally, with 'Home' as opposed to 'School' education.

Preface

IN editing *Home Education* and *Parents and Children* for the 'Home Education' Series, the introduction of much new matter made it necessary to transfer a considerable part of the contents of those two members of the series to this volume, *Some Studies in the Formation of Character*.

I have used the current phrase 'formation of character' because it *is* current, and therefore convenient; but, to show that I recognise the fallacy it contains, I venture to quote the following (very inadequate) definition:—" His character—the efflorescence of the man wherein the fruit of his life is a-preparing—character is original disposition, modified, directed, expanded by education, by circumstances; later, by self-control and self-culture; above all, by the supreme agency of the Holy Spirit, even when that agency is little suspected and as little solicited ";[1] that is to say, character is not the outcome of a formative educational process; but inherent tendencies are played upon, more or less incidentally, and the outcome is character.

I should like to urge that this incidental play of education and circumstances upon personality is our

[1] *Parents and Children.*

only legitimate course. We may not make character our conscious objective. Provide a child with what he needs in the way of instruction, opportunity, and wholesome occupation, and his character will take care of itself: for normal children are persons of good will, with honest desires toward right thinking and right living. All we can do further is to help a child to get rid of some hindrance—a bad temper, for example—likely to spoil his life. In our attempts to do this, our action should, I think, be most guarded. We may not interfere with his psychological development, because we recognise that children are persons, and personality should be far more inviolable in our eyes than property. We may use direct teaching and command, but *not* indirect suggestion, or even the old-fashioned 'influence.' Influence will act, of course, but it must not be consciously brought to bear.

But we may make use of certain physiological laws without encroaching on personality, because, in so doing, we should affect the instrument and not the agent. The laws of habit and, again, the tendency of will-power to rhythmic operation should be of use to us, because these are affected by brain-conditions and belong to the outworks of personality. The little studies in Part I. indicate ways of helping a child to cure himself of tiresome faults.

I am diffident about offering Part IV. of this volume, because, though the public is wonderfully patient with writers who 'adorn the tale,'—half the books we read are about other books,—I am not sure of equal forbearance towards an attempt to 'point the moral.' But, indeed, we read in such a hurry, are satisfied with such slight and general impressions, that the leisurely investigation of educational hints thrown out by great authors might well be of use to us. If, in the few following studies, the reader fail to find what Wordsworth calls the "authentic comment," why, he will be provoked into making the right comment for himself, and so the end will be gained.

I should like, in this fifth volume of the 'Home Education' Series, to acknowledge my indebtedness to Miss Elsie Kitching for the constant interest she has thrown into the work, and her always intelligent collaboration as amanuensis.

CHARLOTTE M. MASON.

AMBLESIDE,
October 1906.

Contents

PART I

SOME STUDIES IN TREATMENT

(*WEISSALL'S FOLLOWING*)

CONTENTS

PART II

PARENTS IN COUNCIL

PART III

CONCERNING YOUTHS AND MAIDENS

CONTENTS

PART IV

"It is written"

SOME STUDIES IN THE EVOLUTION
OF CHARACTER

CONTENTS

APPENDIX

Part I

Some Studies in Treatment

(Weissall's Following)

I

THE PHILOSOPHER AT HOME

" HE has *such* a temper, ma'am ! "

And there, hot, flurried, and generally at her wits' end, stood the poor nurse at the door of her mistress's room. The terrific bellowing which filled the house was enough to account for the girl's distress. Mrs Belmont looked worried. She went up wearily to what she well knew was a weary task. A quarter of an hour ago life had looked very bright—the sun shining, sparrows chirping, lilac and laburnum making a gay show in the suburban gardens about; she thought of her three nestlings in the nursery, and her heart was like a singing-bird giving out chirps of thanks and praise. But that was all changed. The outside world was as bright as ever, but she was under a cloud. She knew too well how those screams from the nursery would spoil her day.

There the boy lay, beating the ground with fists and feet; emitting one prodigious roar after another, features convulsed, eyes protruding, in the unrestrained rage of a wild creature, so transfigured by passion that even his mother doubted if the noble countenance and lovely smile of her son had any existence beyond her fond imagination. He eyed

3

his mother askance through his tumbled, yellow hair,
but her presence seemed only to aggravate the demon
in possession. The screams became more violent;
the beating of the ground more than ever like a
maniac's rage.

"Get up, Guy."

Renewed screams; more violent action of the
limbs!

"Did you hear me, Guy?" in tones of enforced
calmness.

The uproar subsided a little; but when Mrs Belmont laid her hand on his shoulder to raise him, the
boy sprang to his feet, ran into her head-foremost,
like a young bull, kicked her, beat her with his fists,
tore her dress with his teeth, and would no doubt
have ended by overthrowing his delicate mother, but
that Mr Belmont, no longer able to endure the dis-
turbance, came up in time to disengage the raging
child and carry him off to his mother's room. Once
in, the key was turned upon him, and Guy was left
to "subside at his leisure," said his father.

Breakfast was not a cheerful meal, either upstairs
or down. Nurse was put out; snapped up little Flo,
shook baby for being tiresome, until she had them
both in tears. In the dining-room, Mr Belmont read
the *Times* with a frown which last night's debate did
not warrant; sharp words were at his tongue's end,
but, in turning the paper, he caught sight of his wife's
pale face and untasted breakfast. He said nothing,
but she knew and suffered under his thoughts fully
as much as if they had been uttered. Meantime, two
closed doors and the wide space between the rooms
hardly served to dull the ear-torturing sounds that
came from the prisoner.

All at once there was a lull, a sudden and complete cessation of sound. Was the child in a fit?

"Excuse me a minute, Edward;" and Mrs Belmont flew upstairs, followed shortly by her husband. What was her surprise to see Guy with composed features contemplating himself in the glass! He held in his hand a proof of his own photograph which had just come from the photographers. The boy had been greatly interested in the process; and here was the picture arrived, and Guy was solemnly comparing it with that image of himself which the looking-glass presented.

Nothing more was said on the subject; Mr. Belmont went to the City, and his wife went about her household affairs with a lighter heart than she had expected to carry that day. Guy was released, and allowed to return to the nursery for his breakfast, which his mother found him eating in much content and with the sweetest face in the world; there was no more trace of passion than a June day bears when the sun comes out after a thunderstorm. Guy was, indeed, delightful; attentive and obedient to Harriet, full of charming play to amuse the two little ones, and very docile and sweet with his mother, saying from time to time the quaintest things. You would have thought he had been trying to make up for the morning's fracas, had he not looked quite unconscious of wrong-doing.

This sort of thing had gone on since the child's infancy. Now, a frantic outburst of passion, to be so instantly followed by a sweet April-day face and a sunshiny temper that the resolutions his parents made about punishing or endeavouring to reform him passed away like hoar-frost before the child's genial mood.

A sunshiny day followed this stormy morning; the next day passed in peace and gladness, but, the next, some hair astray, some crumpled rose-leaf under him, brought on another of Guy's furious outbursts. Once again the same dreary routine was gone through; and, once again, the tempestuous morning was forgotten in the sunshine of the child's day.

Not by the father, though: at last, Mr Belmont was roused to give his full attention to the mischief which had been going on under his eyes for nearly the five years of Guy's short life. It dawned upon him—other people had seen it for years—that his wife's nervous headaches and general want of tone might well be due to this constantly recurring distress. He was a man of reading and intelligence, in touch with the scientific thought of the day, and especially interested in what may be called the physical basis of character—the interaction which is ever taking place between the material brain and the immaterial thought and feeling of which it is the organ. He had even made little observations and experiments, declared to be valuable by his friend and ally, Dr Weissall, the head physician of the county hospital.

For a whole month he spread crumbs on the window-sill every morning at five minutes to eight; the birds gathered as punctually, and by eight o'clock the "table" was cleared and not a crumb remained. So far, the experiment was a great delight to the children, Guy and Flo, who were all agog to know how the birds knew the time.

After a month of free breakfasts: "You shall see now whether or no the birds come because they see the crumbs." The prospect was delightful, but, alas!

this stage of the experiment was very much otherwise to the pitiful childish hearts.

"Oh, father, *please* let us put out crumbs for the poor little birds, they are so hungry!" a prayer seconded by Mrs Belmont, met with very ready acceptance. The best of us have our moments of weakness.

"Very interesting;" said the two savants; "nothing could show more clearly the readiness with which a habit is formed in even the less intelligent of the creatures."

"Yes, and more than that, it shows the automatic nature of the action once the habit is formed. Observe, the birds came punctually and regularly when there were no longer crumbs for them. They did not come, look for their breakfast, and take sudden flight when it was not there, but they settled as before, stayed as long as before, and then flew off without any sign of disappointment. That is, they came, as we set one foot before another in walking, just out of habit, without any looking for crumbs, or conscious intention of any sort—a mere automatic or machine-like action with which conscious thought has nothing to do."

Of another little experiment Mr Belmont was especially proud, because it brought down, as it were, two quarries at a stroke; touched heredity and automatic action in one little series of observations. Rover, the family dog, appeared in the first place as a miserable puppy saved from drowning. He was of no breed to speak of, but care and good living agreed with him. He developed a handsome shaggy white coat, a quiet, well-featured face, and betrayed his low origin only by one inveterate habit; carts he took no notice of, but never a carriage, small or

great, appeared in sight but he ran yelping at the
heels of the horses in an intolerable way, contriving
at the same time to dodge the whip like any street
Arab. Oddly enough, it came out through the milk-
man that Rover came of a mother who met with her
death through this very peccadillo.

Here was an opportunity. The point was, to prove
not only that the barking was automatic, but that the
most inveterate habit, even an inherited habit, is open
to cure.

Mr Belmont devoted himself to the experiment:
he gave orders that, for a month, Rover should go
out with no one but himself. Two pairs of ears
were on the alert for wheels; two, distinguished
between carriage and cart. Now Rover was the
master of an accomplishment of which he and the
family were proud: he could carry a newspaper in
his mouth. Wheels in the distance, then, "Hi!
Rover!" and Rover trotted along, the proud bearer
of the *Times*. This went on daily for a month, until
at last the association between wheels and newspaper
was established, and a distant rumble would bring
him up—a demand in his eyes. Rover was cured.
By-and-by the paper was unnecessary, and "To heel!
good dog!" was enough when an ominous falling of
the jaw threatened a return of the old habit.

It is extraordinary how wide is the gap between
theory and practice in most of our lives. "The man
who knows the power of habit has a key wherewith
to regulate his own life and the lives of his household, down to that of the cat sitting at his hearth."
(*Applause.*) Thus, Mr Belmont at a scientific gathering. But only this morning did it dawn upon him
that, with this key between his fingers, he was letting

his wife's health, his child's life, be ruined by a habit fatal alike to present peace, and to the hope of manly self-control in the future. Poor man! he had a bad half-hour that morning on his way Citywards. He was not given to introspection, but, when it was forced upon him, he dealt honestly.

"I must see Weissall to-night, and talk the whole thing out with him."

. . . . . .

"Ah, so; the dear Guy! And how long is it, do you say, since the boy has thus out-broken?"

"All his life, for anything I know—certainly it began in his infancy."

"And do you think, my good friend"—here the Doctor laid a hand on his friend's arm, and peered at him with twinkling eyes and gravely set mouth—"do you think it possible that he has—er—*inherited* this little weakness? A grandfather, perhaps?"

"You mean me, I know; yes, it's a fact. And I got it from my father, and he, from his. We're not a good stock. I know I'm an irascible fellow, and it has stood in my way all through life."

"Fair and softly, my dear fellow! go not so fast. I cannot let you say bad things of my best friend. But this I allow; there are thorns, bristles all over; and they come out at a touch. How much better for you and for Science had the father cured all that!"

"As I must for Guy! Yes, and how much happier for wife, children, and servants; how much pleasanter for friends. Well, Guy is the question now. What do you advise?"

The two sat far into the night discussing a problem on the solution of which depended the future of a noble boy, the happiness of a family. No wonder they found the subject so profoundly interesting that 'two' by the church clock startled them into a hasty separation. Both Mrs Belmont and Mrs Weissall resented this dereliction on the part of their several lords; but these ladies would have been meeker than Sarah herself had they known that, not science, not politics, but the bringing up of the children, was the engrossing topic.

Breakfast-time three days later. Scene, the dining-room.
NURSE *in presence of* MASTER *and* MISTRESS.

"You have been a faithful servant and good friend, both to us and the children, Harriet, but we blame you a little for Guy's passionate outbreaks. Do not be offended, we blame ourselves more. Your share of blame is that you have worshipped him from his babyhood, and have allowed him to have his own way in everything. Now, your part of the cure is, to do exactly as we desire. At present, I shall only ask you to remember that, Prevention is better than cure. The thing for all of us is to take precautions against even one more of these outbreaks.

"Keep your eye upon Guy; if you notice—no matter what the cause—flushed cheeks, pouting lips, flashing eye, frowning forehead, with two little upright lines between the eyebrows, limbs held stiffly, hands, perhaps, closed, head thrown slightly back; if you notice any or all of these signs, the boy is on the verge of an outbreak. Do not stop to ask questions, or soothe him, or make peace, or threaten. Change his thoughts. That is the one hope. Say quite naturally and pleasantly, as if you saw nothing, 'Your father wants you to garden with him,' or, 'for a game of dominoes'; or, 'Your mother wants you to help her in the store-room,' or, 'to tidy her work-box.' Be ruled by the time of the day, and how you know we are employed.   And be quite sure we *do* want the boy."

"But, sir, please excuse me, is it any good to save him from breaking out when the passion is there in his heart?"

"Yes, Harriet, all the good in the world.   Your master thinks that Guy's passions have become a habit, and that the way to cure him is to keep him a long time, a month or two, without a single outbreak; if we can manage that, the trouble will be over. As for the passion in his heart, that comes with the outer signs, and both will be cured together.   Do, Harriet, like a good woman, help us in this matter, and your master and I will always be grateful to you!"

"I'm sure, ma'am," with a sob (Harriet was a soft-hearted woman, and was very much touched to be taken thus into the confidence of her master and mistress), "I'm sure I'll do my best, especially as I've had a hand in it; but I'm sure I never meant to, and, if I forget, I hope you'll kindly forgive me."

"No, Harriet, you must not forget any more than you'd forget to snatch a sharp knife from the baby. This is almost a matter of life and death."

"Very well, sir, I'll remember; and thank you for telling me."

.   .   .   .   .   .

Breakfast time was unlucky; the very morning after the above talk, Nurse had her opportunity. Flo, for some inscrutable reason, preferred to eat her porridge with her brother's spoon. Behold, quick as a flash, flushed cheeks, puckered brow, rigid frame!

"Master Guy, dear," in a quite easy, friendly tone (Harriet had mastered her lesson), "run down to your father; he wants you to help him in the garden."

Instantly the flash in the eye became a sparkle of delight, the rigid limbs were all active and eager; out of his chair, out of the room, downstairs, by his father's side, in less time than it takes to tell. And the face—joyous, sparkling, full of eager expectation —surely Nurse had been mistaken this time? But no; both parents knew how quickly Guy emerged from the shadow of a cloud, and they trusted Harriet's discretion.

"Well, boy, so you've come to help me garden? But I've not done breakfast. Have you finished yours?"

"No, father," with a dropping lip.

"Well, I'll tell you what. You run up and eat your porridge and come down as soon as you're ready; I shall make haste, too, and we shall get a good half-hour in the garden before I go out."

Up again went Guy with hasty, willing feet.

"Nurse" (breathless hurry and importance), "I must make haste with my porridge. Father wants me *directly* to help him in the garden."

Nurse winked hard at the fact that the porridge was gobbled. The happy little boy trotted off to one of the greatest treats he knew, and that day passed without calamity.

. . . . . .

"I can see it will answer, and life will be another thing without Guy's passions; but do you think, Edward, it's *right* to give the child pleasures when he's naughty—in fact, to put a premium upon naughtiness, for it amounts to that?"

"You're not quite right there. The child does not know he is naughty; the emotions of 'naughtiness' are there; he is in a physical tumult, but wilfulness has not set in; he does not yet *mean* to be naughty, and all is gained if we avert the set of the will towards wrong-doing. He has not had time to recognise that he is naughty, and his thoughts are changed so suddenly that he is not in the least aware of what was going on in him before. The new thing comes to him as naturally and graciously as do all the joys of the childish day. The question of desert does not occur."

. . . . . .

For a week all went well. Nurse was on the alert, was quick to note the ruddy storm-signal in the fair little face; she never failed to despatch Guy instantly, and with a quiet unconscious manner, on some errand to father or mother; nay, she improved on her instructions; when father and mother were out of the way, she herself invented some pleasant errand to cook about the pudding for dinner; to get fresh water for Dickie, or to see if Rover had had his breakfast. Nurse was really clever in inventing expedients, in hitting instantly on something to be done novel and amusing enough to fill the child's fancy. A mistake in this direction would, experience told her, be fatal; propose what was stale, and not only would Guy decline to give up the immediate gratification of a passionate outbreak—for it *is* a gratification, that must be borne in mind—but he would begin to look suspiciously on the "something else" which so often came in the way of this gratification.

Security has its own risks. A morning came when Nurse was not on the alert. Baby was teething and

fractious, Nurse was overdone, and the nursery was
not a cheerful place. Guy, very sensitive to the moral
atmosphere about him, got, in Nurse's phrase, out
of sorts. He relieved himself by drumming on the
table with a couple of ninepins, just as Nurse was
getting baby off after a wakeful night.

"Stop that noise this minute, you naughty boy!
Don't you see your poor little brother is going to
sleep?" in a loud whisper. The noise was redoubled,
and assisted by kicks on chair-rungs and table-legs.
Sleep vanished and baby broke into a piteous wail.
This was too much; the Nurse laid down the child,
seized the young culprit, chair and all, carried him
to the farthest corner, and, desiring him not to move
till she gave him leave, set him down with a vigorous
shaking. There were days when Guy would stand
this style of treatment cheerfully, but this was not
one. Before Harriet had even noted the danger
signals, the storm had broken out. For half an hour
the nursery was a scene of frantic uproar, baby assist-
ing, and even little Flo. Half an hour is nothing
to speak of; in pleasant chat, over an amusing book,
the thirty minutes fly like five; but half an hour in
struggle with a raging child is a day and a night in
length. Mr and Mrs Belmont were out, so Harriet
had it all to herself, and it was contrary to orders
that she should attempt to place the child in confine-
ment; solitude and locked doors involved risks that
the parents would, rightly, allow no one but themselves to run. At last the tempest subsided, spent,
apparently, by its own force.

A child cannot bear estrangement, disapproval; he
must needs live in the light of a countenance smiling
upon him. His passion over, Guy set himself labo-

riously to be good, keeping watch out of the corner of his eye to see how Nurse took it. She was too much vexed to respond in any way, even by a smile. But her heart was touched; and though, by-and-by when Mrs Belmont came in, she did say—"Master Guy has been in one of his worst tempers again, ma'am: screaming for better than half an hour"— yet she did not tell her tale with the *empressement* necessary to show what a very bad half-hour they had had. His mother looked with grave reproof at the delinquent, but she was not proof against his coaxing ways.

After dinner she remarked to her husband, "You will be sorry to hear that Guy has had one of his worst bouts again. Nurse said he screamed steadily for more than half an hour."

"What did you do?"

"I was out at the time doing some shopping. But when I came back, after letting him know how grieved I was, I did as you say, changed his thoughts and did my best to give him a happy day."

"How did you let him know you were grieved?"

"I looked at him in a way he quite understood, and you should have seen the deliciously coaxing, half-ashamed look he shot up at me. What eyes he has!"

"Yes, the little monkey! and no doubt he measured their effect on his mother; you must allow me to say that my theory certainly is *not* to give him a happy day after an outbreak of this sort."

"Why, I thought your whole plan was to change his thoughts, to keep him so well occupied with pleasant things that he does not dwell on what agitated him."

"Yes, but did you not tell me the passion was over when you found him?"

"Quite over; he was as good as gold."

"Well, the thing we settled on was to *avert* a threatened outbreak by a pleasant change of thought; and to do so in order that, at last, the *habit* of these outbreaks may be broken. Don't you see, that is a very different thing from pampering him with a pleasant day when he has already pampered himself with the full indulgence of his passion?"

"Pampered himself! Why, you surely don't think those terrible scenes give the poor child any pleasure. I always thought he was a deal more to be pitied than we."

"Indeed I do. Pleasure is perhaps hardly the word; but that the display of temper is a form of self-indulgence, there is no doubt at all. You, my dear, are too amiable to know what a relief it is to us irritable people to have a good storm and clear the air."

"Nonsense, Edward! But what should I have done? What is the best course *after* the child has given way?"

"I think we must, as you once suggested, consider how we ourselves are governed. Estrangement, isolation are the immediate consequences of sin, even of what may seem a small sin of harshness or selfishness."

"Oh, but don't you think that is our delusion? that God is loving us all the time, and it is *we* who estrange ourselves?"

"Without doubt; and we are aware of the love all the time, but, also, we are aware of a cloud between it and ourselves; we know we are out of favour.

We know, too, that there is only one way back, through the fire. It is common to speak of repentance as a light thing, rather pleasant than otherwise; but it is searching and bitter: so much so, that the Christian soul dreads to sin, even the sin of coldness, from an almost cowardly dread of the anguish of repentance, purging fire though it be."

Mrs Belmont could not clear her throat to answer for a minute. She had never before had such a glimpse into her husband's soul. Here were deeper things in the spiritual life than any of which she yet knew.

"Well then, dear, about Guy; must he feel this estrangement, go through this fire?"

"I think so, in his small degree; but he must never doubt our love. He must see and feel that it is always there, though under a cloud of sorrow which he only can break through."

.   .   .   .   .   .

Guy's lapse prepared the way for further lapses. Not two days passed before he was again in a passion. The boy, his outbreak over, was ready at once to emerge into the sunshine. Not so his mother. His most bewitching arts met only with sad looks and silence.

He told his small scraps of nursery news, looking in vain for the customary answering smile and merry words. He sidled up to his mother, and stroked her cheek; that did not do, so he stroked her hand; then her gown; no answering touch, no smile, no word; nothing but sorrowful eyes when he ventured to raise his own. Poor little fellow! The iron was beginning to enter; he moved a step or two away from his mother, and raised to hers eyes full of piteous doubt and pleading. He saw love, which could not reach him, and sorrow, which he was just beginning to comprehend. But his mother could bear it no longer: she got up hastily and left the room. Then the little boy, keeping close to the wall, as if even that were something to interpose between him and this new sense of desolation, edged off to the farthest corner of the room, and sinking on the floor with a sad, new quietness, sobbed in his loneliness; Nurse had had her lesson, and although she too was crying for her boy, nobody went near him but Flo. A little arm was passed round his neck; a hot little cheek pressed against his curls:

" Don't cry, Guy!" two or three times, and when the sobs came all the thicker, there was nothing for it but that Flo must cry too; poor little outcasts!

At last bedtime came, and his mother; but her face had still that sad far-away look, and Guy could see she had been crying. How he longed to spring up and hug her and kiss her as he would have done yesterday. But somehow he dared not; and she never smiled nor spoke, and yet never before had Guy known how his mother loved him.

She sat in her accustomed chair by the little white bed, and beckoned the little boy in his nightgown to come and say his prayers. He knelt at his mother's knee as usual, and then she laid her hands upon his.

" 'Our Father'—oh, mother, mo—o—ther, mother!" and a torrent of tears drowned the rest, and Guy was again in his mother's arms, and she was raining kisses upon him, and crying with him.

Next morning his father received him with open arms.

"So my poor little boy had a bad day yesterday!"
Guy hung his head and said nothing.

"Would you like me to tell you how you may help
ever having quite such another bad day?"

"Oh yes, please, father; I thought I couldn't help."

"Can you tell when the 'Cross-man' is coming?"

Guy hesitated. "Sometimes, I think. I get all hot."

"Well, the minute you find he's coming, even if
you have begun to cry, say, 'Please excuse me, Nurse,'
and run downstairs, and then four times round the
paddock as fast as you can, without stopping to take
breath!"

"What a good way! Shall I try it now?"

"Why, the 'Cross-man' isn't there now. But I'll
tell you a secret: he always goes away if you begin
to do something else as hard as you can; and if
you can remember to run away from him round the
garden, you'll find he won't run after you; at the
very worst, he won't run after you more than *once*
round!"

"Oh, father, I'll try! What fun! See if I don't
beat him! Won't I just give Mr 'Cross-man' a race!
He shall be quite out of breath before we get round
the fourth time."

The vivid imagination of the boy personified the
foe, and the father jumped with his humour. Guy
was eager for the fray; the parents had found an
ally in their boy; the final victory was surely within
appreciable distance.

.   .   .   .   .   .

"This is glorious, Edward; and it's as interesting
as painting a picture or writing a book! What a
capital device the race with 'Mr Cross-man' is! It's
like 'Sintram.' He'll be so busy looking out for

'Cross-man' that he'll forget to be cross. The only danger I see is that of many false alarms. He'll try the race, in all good faith, when there is no foe in pursuit."

"That's very likely; but it will do no harm. He is getting the habit of running away from the evil, and may for that be the more ready to run when it's at his heels; this, of running away from temptation, is the right principle, and may be useful to him in a thousand ways."

"Indeed, it may be a safeguard to him through life. How did you get the idea?"

"Do you remember how Rover was cured of barking after carriages? There were two stages to the cure; the habit of barking was stopped, and a new habit was put in its place; I worked upon the recognised law of association of ideas, and got Rover to associate the rumble of wheels with a newspaper in his mouth. I tried at the time to explain how it was possible to act thus on the 'mind' of a dog."

"I recollect quite well; you said that the stuff—nervous tissue, you called it—of which the brain is made is shaped in the same sort of way—at least so I understood—by the thoughts that are in it, as the cover of a tart is shaped by the plums below. And then, when there's a place ready for them in the brain, the same sort of thoughts always come to fill it."

"I did not intend to say precisely that," said Mr Belmont, laughing, "especially the plum part. However, it will do. Pray go on with your metaphor. It is decided that plums are not wholesome eating. You put in your thumb, and pick out a plum; and that the place may be filled, and well filled, you pop in a —a—figures fail me—a peach!"

" I see! I see! Guy's screaming fits are the un-wholesome plum which we are picking out, and the running away from Cross-man the peach to be got in instead. (I don't see why it should be a peach though, unpractical man!) His brain is to grow to the shape of the peach, and behold, the place is filled. No more room for the plum." [1]

" You have it; you have put, in a light way, a most interesting law, and I take much blame to myself that I never thought until now of applying it to Guy's case. But now I think we are making way; we have made provision for dislodging the old habit and set-ting a new one in its place."

" Don't you think the child will be a hero in a very small way, when he makes himself run away from his temper?"

" Not in a small way at all; the child will be a hero. But we cannot be heroes all the time. In sudden gusts of temptation, God grant him grace to play the hero, if only through hasty flight; but in what are called besetting sins, there is nothing safe but the contrary besetting good habit. And here is where parents have immense power over the future of their children."

" Don't think me superstitious and stupid; but somehow this scientific training, good as I see it is, seems to me to undervalue the help we get from above in times of difficulty and temptation."

" Let me say that it is you who undervalue the

[1] To state the case more accurately, certain cell connections appear to be established by habitual traffic in certain thoughts ; but there is so much danger in over-stating or in localising mental operations, that perhaps it is safer to convey the practical outcome of this line of research in a more or less figurative way—as, the wearing of a field-path ; the making of a bridge ; a railway, etc.

virtue, and limit the scope of the Divine action. Whose are the laws Science labours to reveal? Whose are the works, body or brain, or what you like, upon which these laws act?"

"How foolish of me! But one gets into a way of thinking that God cares only for what we call spiritual things. Let me ask you one more question. I do see that all this watchful training is necessary, and do not wish to be idle or cowardly about it. But don't you think Guy would grow out of these violent tempers naturally, as he gets older?"

"Well, he would not, as youth or man, fling himself on the ground and roar; but no doubt he would grow up touchy, fiery, open at any minute to a sudden storm of rage. The man who has too much self-respect for an open exhibition may, as you know well enough, poor wife, indulge in continual irritability, suffer himself to be annoyed by trifling matters. No, there is nothing for it but to look upon an irate habit as one to be displaced by a contrary habit. Who knows what cheerful days we may yet have, and whether in curing Guy I may not cure myself? The thing can be done; only one is so lazy about one's own habits. Suppose you take me in hand?"

"Oh, I couldn't! and yet it's your only fault."

"*Only* fault! well, we'll see. In the meantime there's another thing I wish we could do for Guy— stop him in the midst of an outbreak. Do you remember the morning we found him admiring himself in the glass?"

"Yes, with the photograph in his hand."

"That was it; perhaps the Cross-man race will answer even in the middle of a tempest. If not, we must try something else."

" It won't work."

" Why not ? "

"Guy will have no more rages; how then can he be stopped in mid-tempest ? "

"Most hopeful of women! But don't deceive yourself. Our work is only well begun, but that, let us hope, is half done."

.   .   .   .   .   .

His father was right. Opportunities to check him in mid-career occurred; and Guy answered to the rein. Mr Cross-man worked wonders. A record of outbreaks was kept; now a month intervened; two months; a year; two years; and at last his parents forgot their early troubles with their sweet-tempered, frank-natured boy.

II

INCONSTANT KITTY

"But now for the real object of this letter—does it take your breath away to get four sheets? We want you to help us about Kitty. My husband and I are at our wits' end, and would most thankfully take your wise head and kind heart into counsel. I fear we have been laying up trouble for ourselves and for our little girl. The ways of nature are, there is no denying it, very attractive in all young creatures, and it is so delightful to see a child do as ''tis its nature to,' that you forget that Nature, left to herself, produces a waste, be it never so lovely. Our little Kitty's might so easily become a wasted life.

"But not to prose any more, let me tell you the history of Kitty's yesterday—one of her days is like the rest, and you will be able to see where we want your help.

"Figure to yourself the three little heads bent over 'copy-books' in our cheery schoolroom. Before a line is done, up starts Kitty.

"'Oh, mother, may I write the next copy—s h e l l? "Shell" is so much nicer than—k n o w, and I'm so tired of it.'

"'How much have you done?'

" ' I have written it three whole times, mother, and I really *can't* do it any more! I think I could do—s h e l l. "Shell" is so pretty ! '

" By-and-by we read ; but Kitty cannot read—can't even spell the words (don't scold us, we know it is quite wrong to spell in a reading lesson), because all the time her eyes are on a smutty sparrow on the topmost twig of the poplar ; so she reads, 'W i t h, birdie ! ' We do sums ; a short line of addition is to poor Kitty a hopeless and an endless task. 'Five and three make—nineteen,' is her last effort, though she knows quite well how to add up figures. Half a scale on the piano, and then—eyes and ears for everybody's business but her own. Three stitches of hemming, and idle fingers plait up the hem or fold the duster in a dozen shapes. I am in the midst of a thrilling history talk : 'So the Black Prince——' 'Oh, mother, do you think we shall go to the sea this year? My pail is quite ready, all but the handle, but I can't find my spade *anywhere !* '

" And thus we go on, pulling Kitty through her lessons somehow ; but it is a weariness to herself and to all of us, and I doubt if the child learns anything except by bright flashes. But you have no notion how quick the little monkey is. After idling through a lesson she will overtake us at a bound at the last moment, and thus escape the wholesome shame of being shown up as the dunce of our little party.

" Kitty's dawdling ways, her restless desire for change of occupation, her always wandering thoughts, lead to a good deal of friction, and spoil our school-room party, which is a pity, for I want the children to enjoy their lessons from the very first. What do you think the child said to me yesterday in the most coaxing pretty way? 'There are so many things nicer than lessons! Don't you think so, mother?' Yes, dear aunt, I see you put your finger on those unlucky words 'coaxing, pretty way,' and you look, if you do not say, that awful sentence of yours about sin being bred of allowance. Isn't that it? It is quite true; we are in fault. Those butterfly ways of Kitty's were delicious to behold until we thought it time to set her to work, and then we found that we should have been training her from her babyhood. Well,

> " 'If you break your plaything yourself, dear,
>   Don't you cry for it all the same?
> I don't think it is such a comfort
>   To have only oneself to blame.'

So, like a dear, kind aunt, don't scold us, but help us to do better. Is Kitty constant to anything? you ask. Does she stick to any of the '*many* things so much nicer than lessons'? I am afraid that here, too, our little girl is 'unstable as water.' And the worst of it is, she is all agog to be at a thing, and then, when you think her settled to half an hour's pleasant play, off she is like any butterfly. She says her, 'How doth the little busy bee,' dutifully; but when I tell her she is not a bit like a busy bee, but rather like a foolish, flitting butterfly, I'm afraid she rather likes it, and makes up to the butterflies as if they were akin to her, and were having just the good time she would prefer. But you must come and see the child to understand how volatile she is.

" 'Oh, mother, *please* let me have a good doll's wash this afternoon; I'm quite unhappy about poor Peggy! I really think she *likes* to be dirty!'

" Great preparations follow in the way of little tub,

and soap, and big apron; the little laundress sits down, greatly pleased with herself, to undress her dirty Peggy; but hardly is the second arm out of its sleeve, than, *presto!* a new idea; off goes Kitty to clean out her doll's house, deaf to all Nurse's remonstrances about 'nice hot water,' and 'poor dirty Peggy.'

"I'm afraid the child is no more constant to her loves than to her play; she is a loving little soul, as you know, and is always adoring somebody. Now it's her father, now Juno, now me, now Hugh; and the rain of warm kisses, the soft clasping arms, the nestling head, are delicious, whether to dog or man. But, alas! Kitty's blandishments are a whistle you must pay for; to-morrow it is somebody else's turn, and the bad part is that she has only room for one at a time. If we could get a little visit from you, now, Kitty would be in your pocket all day long; and we, even Peggy, would be left out in the cold. But do not flatter yourself it would last; I think none of Kitty's attachments has been known to last longer than two days.

"If the chief business of parents is to train *character* in their children, we have done nothing for Kitty; at six years old the child has no more power of application, no more habit of attention, is no more able to make herself do the thing she ought to do, indeed, has no more desire to do the right thing than she had at six months old. We are getting very unhappy about it. My husband feels strongly that parents should labour at character as the Hindoo gold-beater labours at his vase; that *character* is the one thing we are called upon to effect. And what have we done for Kitty? We have turned out a 'fine animal,' and are glad and thankful for that; but that is all; the

child is as wayward, as unsteady, as a young colt.
Do help us, dear aunt. Think our little girl's case
over; if you can get at the source of the mischief,
send us a few hints for our guidance, and we shall be
yours gratefully evermore."

.　　　.　　　.　　　.　　　.　　　.

"And now for my poor little great-niece! Her
mother piles up charges against her, but how interesting and amusing and like the free world of fairy-land
it would all be were it not for the *tendencies* which, in
these days, we talk much about and watch little
against. We bring up our children in the easiest,
happy-go-lucky way, and all the time talk solemnly
in big words about the momentous importance of
every influence brought to bear upon them. But it is
true; these naughty, winsome ways of Kitty's will
end in her growing up like half the 'girls'—that is,
young women—one meets. They talk glibly on
many subjects; but test them, and they know nothing
of any; they are ready to undertake anything, but
they carry nothing through. This week, So-and-so is
their most particular friend; next week, such another;
even their amusements, their one real interest, fail
and flag; but then, there is some useful thing to be
learnt—how to set tiles or play the banjo! And, all
the time, there is no denying, as you say, that this
very fickleness has a charm, so long as the glamour
of youth lasts, and the wayward girl has bright smiles
and winning, graceful ways to disarm you with. But
youth does not last; and the poor girl who began as
a butterfly ends as a grub, tied to the earth by the
duties she never learnt how to fulfil; that is,
supposing she is a girl with a conscience; wanting
that, she dances through life whatever befalls—

children, husband, home, must take their chance.
'What a giddy old grandmother the Peterfields
have!' remarked a pert young man of my acquaintance. But, indeed, the 'giddy old grandmother' is
not an unknown quantity.

"Are you saying to yourself, a prosy old 'great-
aunt' is as bad as a 'giddy old grandmother'? I
really have prosed abominably, but Kitty has been on
my mind all the time, and it is quite true, you must
take her in hand.

"First, as to her lessons: you *must* help her to
gain the power of attention; that should have been
done long ago, but better late than never, and an aunt
who has given her mind to these matters takes blame
to herself for not having seen the want sooner. 'But,'
I fancy you are saying, 'if the child has no faculty of
attention, how can we give it to her? It's just a
natural defect.' Not a bit of it! Attention is not a
faculty at all, though I believe it is worth more than
all the so-called faculties put together; this, at any
rate, is true, that no talent, no genius, is worth much
without the power of attention; and this is the power
which makes men or women successful in life. (I talk
like a book without scruple, because you know my
light is borrowed; Professor Weissall is our luminary.)

"Attention is no more than this—the power of
giving your mind to what you are about—the bigger
the better so far as the mind goes, and great minds
do great things; but have you never known a person
with a great mind, 'real genius,' his friends say, who
goes through life without accomplishing anything?
It is just because he wants the power to 'turn on,' so
to speak, the whole of his great mind; he is unable
to bring the whole of his power to bear on the subject

in hand. 'But Kitty?' Yes, Kitty must get this power of 'turning on.' She must be taught to give her mind to sums and reading, and even to dusters. Go slowly; a little to-day and a little more to-morrow. In the first place, her lessons must be made *interesting*. Do not let her scramble through a page of 'reading,' for instance, spelling every third word and then waiting to be told what it spells, but let every day bring the complete mastery of a few new words, as well as the keeping up of the old ones.

"But do not let the lesson last more than ten minutes, and insist, with brisk, bright determination, on the child's full concentrated attention of eye and mind for the whole ten minutes. Do not allow a moment's dawdling at lessons.

"I should not give her rows of figures to add yet; use dominoes or the domino cards prepared for the purpose, the point being to add or subtract the dots on the two halves in a twinkling. You will find that the three can work together at this as at the reading, and the children will find it as exciting and delightful as 'old soldier.' Kitty will be all alive here, and will take her share of work merrily; and this is a point gained. Do not, if you can help it, single the little maid out from the rest and throw her on her own responsibility. 'Tis 'a heavy and a weary weight' for the bravest of us, and the little back will get a trick of bending under life if you do not train her to carry it lightly, as an Eastern woman her pitcher.

"Then, vary the lessons; now head, and now hands; now tripping feet and tuneful tongue; but in every lesson let Kitty and the other two carry away the joyous sense of—

"'Something attempted, something done.'

"Allow of no droning wearily over the old stale work—which must be kept up all the time, it is true, but rather by way of an exciting game than as the lesson of the day, which should always be a distinct *step* that the children can recognise.

"You have no notion, until you try, how the 'now-or-never' feeling about a lesson quickens the attention of even the most volatile child; what you can drone through all day, you will; what *must* be done, is done. Then, there is a by-the-way gain besides that of quickened attention. I once heard a wise man say that, if he must choose between the two, he would rather his child should learn the meaning of 'must' than inherit a fortune. And here you will be able to bring moral force to bear on wayward Kitty. Every lesson must have its own time, and no other time in this world is there for it. The sense of the precious-ness of time, of the irreparable loss when a ten minutes' lesson is thrown away, must be brought home.

"Let your own unaffected distress at the loss of 'golden minutes' be felt by the children, and also be visited upon them by the loss of some small childish pleasure which the day should have held. It is a sad thing to let a child dawdle through a day and be let off scot-free. You see, I am talking of the chil-dren, and not of Kitty alone, because it is so much easier to be good in company; and what is good for her will be good for the trio.

"But there are other charges; poor Kitty is neither steady in play nor steadfast in love! May not the *habit* of attending to her lessons help her to stick to her play? Then, encourage her. 'What! The doll's tea-party over! That's not the way grown-up ladies have tea ; they sit and talk for a long time. See if you can make your tea-party last twenty minutes by my watch!' This failing of Kitty's is just a case where a little gentle ridicule might do a great deal of good. It is a weapon to be handled warily, for one child may resent, and another take pleasure in being laughed at ; but managed with tact I do believe it's good for children and grown-ups to see the comic side of their doings.

"I think we err in not enough holding up certain virtues for our children's admiration. Put a premium of praise on every finished thing, if it be only a house of cards. Steadiness in work is a step on the way towards steadfastness in love. Here, too, the praise of constancy might very well go with good-humoured family 'chaff,' not about the new loves, which are lawful, whether of kitten or playmate, but about the discarded old loves. Let Kitty and all of them grow up to glory in their constancy to every friend.

"There, I am sending you a notable preachment instead of the few delicate hints I meant to offer ; but never mount a woman on her hobby—who knows when she will get off again ? "

III

UNDER A CLOUD

You wish me to tell you the story of my little girl? Well, to begin at the beginning. In looking back through the pages of my journal I find many scattered notices of Agnes, and I always write of her, I find, as "poor Agnes." Now, I wonder why? The child is certainly neither unhealthy nor unhappy—at least, not with any reason; but again and again I find this sort of entry:—

"Agnes displeased with her porridge; says nothing, but looks black all day."

"Harry upset his sister's work-basket—by accident, I truly believe; but she can't get over it—speaks to no one, and looks as if under a cloud."

I need not go on; the fact is, the child is sensible of many injuries heaped upon her; I think there is no ground for the feeling, for she is really very sweet when she has not, as the children say, the black dog on her back.

It is quite plain to me, and to others also, I think that we have let this sort of thing go on too long without dealing with it. We must take the matter in hand. Please God, our little Agnes must not grow up in this sullen habit, for all our sakes, but chiefly for

her own, poor child. I felt that in this matter I might
be of more use than Edward, who simply does not
understand a temper less sunny and open than his
own. I pondered and pondered, and, at last, some
light broke in upon me. I thought I should get hold
of one principle at a time, work that out thoroughly,
and then take up the next, and so on, until all the
springs of sullenness were exhausted, and all supplies
from without stopped. I was beginning to suspect
that the laws of habit worked here as elsewhere, and
that, if I could get our dear child to pass, say, six
weeks without a "fallen countenance," she might lose
this distressing failing for life.

I meant at first to take most of the trouble of this
experiment upon myself; but I think men have clearer
heads than we women—that is, they can see *both* sides
of a question and are not carried away by the one side
presented to them. So I said—

"Well, Edward, our little Agnes does not get over
her sulky fits; in fact, they last longer, and are harder
to get out of than ever!"

"Poor little girl! It is unhappy for her and for all
of us. But don't you think it is a sort of childish
malaise she will soon grow out of?"

"Now, have you not said, again and again, that a
childish fault, left to itself, can do no other than
strengthen?"

"True; I suppose the fact is I am slow to realise
the fault. But you are right. From the point of
view of *habit* we are pledged to deal with it. Have
you made any plans?"

"Yes; I have been trying to work the thing out
on Professor Weissall's lines. We must watch the
rise of the sullen cloud, and change her thoughts

before she has time to realise that the black fit is coming."

"You are right; if we can keep the child for only a week without this settling of the cloud, the mere habit would be somewhat broken."

We had not to wait for our opportunity. At breakfast next day—whether Harry's porridge looked more inviting than her own, or whether he should not have been helped first, or whether the child had a little pain of which she was hardly aware—suddenly, her eyes fell, brows dropped, lips pouted, the whole face became slightly paler than before, the figure limp, limbs lax, hands nerveless—and our gentle child was transformed, become entirely unlovable. So far, her feelings were in the emotional stage; her injury, whatever it was, had not yet taken shape in her thoughts; she could not have told you what was the matter, because she did not know; but very soon the thinking brain would come to the aid of the quick emotions, and then she would be sulky of fixed purpose. Her father saw the symptoms rise and knew what they would lead to, and, with the promptness which has often saved us, he cried out—

"Agnes, come here, and hold up your pinafore!" and Agnes trotted up to his side, her pinafore held up very much to receive the morning dole of crumbs for the birds; presently, she came back radiant with the joy of having given the birds a good breakfast, and we had no more sulky fits that day. This went on for a fortnight or so with fair but not perfect success. Whenever her father or I was present, we caught the emotion before the child was conscious of it, and succeeded in turning her thoughts into some pleasant channel. But poor nurse has had bad hours with

Agnes; there would sit the child, pale and silent, for hours together, doing nothing because she liked to do it, but only because she must. And, once the fit had settled down, thick and steady as a London fog, neither her father nor I could help in the least. Oh, the inconceivable settled cloudiness and irresponsiveness of that child face!

Our tactics were at fault. No doubt they helped so far as they went. We managed to secure bright days that might otherwise have been cloudy when we happened to be present at the first rise of the sullen mood. But it seemed impossible to bring about so long an abstinence from sullen fits as would nullify the *habit*. We pictured to ourselves the dreary life that lay before our pretty little girl; the distrust of her sweetness, to which even one such sullen fit would give rise; worse, the isolation which accompanies this sort of temper, and the anguish of repentance to follow. And then, I know, madness is often bred of this strong sense of injured personality.

It is not a pleasant thing to look an evil in the face. Whether or no "a little knowledge is a dangerous," certainly, it is a trying thing. If we could only have contented ourselves with, "Oh, she'll grow out of it by-and-by," we could have put up with even a daily cloud. But these forecasts of our little girl's future made the saving of the child at *any* cost our most anxious care.

"I'll tell you what, Helen; we must strike out a new line. In a general way, I do believe it's best to deal with a child's faults without making him aware that he has them. It fills the little beings with a ridiculous sense of importance to have anything belonging to *them*, even a fault. But in this case, I think, we shall have to strike home and deal with *the cause* at least as much as with *the effects*, and that, chiefly, because we have not effects entirely under our control."

"But, what if there is no cure? What if this odious temper were *hereditary*—our child's inheritance from those who should have brought her only good?"

"The question is not 'How has it come?' but 'How are we to deal with it?'—equally, you and I. Poor things! It's but a very half-and-half kind of matrimony if each is to pick out his or her own particular bundle of failings, and deal with it single-handed. This poor man finds the prospect too much for him! As a matter of fact, though, I believe that failings of mind, body, temper, and what not, are matters of inheritance, and that each parent's particular business in life is to pass his family forward freed from that particular vicious tendency which has been his own bane—or hers, if you prefer it."

"Well, do as you will; I can trust you. What it would be in these days of greater insight to be married to a man who would say, 'There, that boy may thank his mother' for this or the other failure! Of course, the thing is done now, but more often than not as a random guess."

"To return to Agnes. I think we shall have to show her to herself in this matter, to rake up the ugly feeling, however involuntary, and let her see how hateful it is. Yes, I do not wonder you shrink from this. So do I. It will destroy the child's unconsciousness."

"Oh, Edward, how I dread to poke into the little

wounded heart, and bring up worse things to startle her!"

"I am sorry for you, but I think it must be done; and don't you think you are the person to do it? While they have a mother I don't think I could presume to pry too much into the secrets of the children's hearts."

"I'll try; but if I get into a mess you must help me through."

The opportunity came soon enough. It was pears this time. Harry would never have known whether he had the biggest or the least. But we had told Nurse to be especially careful in this matter. "Each of the children must have the biggest or best as often as one another, but there must be no fuss, no taking turns, about such trifles. Therefore, very rightly, you gave Harry the bigger and Agnes the smaller pear."

Agnes's pear was not touched; there the child sat, without word or sob, but all gathered into herself, like a sea-anemone whose tentacles have been touched. The stillness, whiteness, and brooding sullenness of the face, the limp figure and desolate attitude, would have made me take the little girl in my arms if I had not too often failed to reach her in that way. This went on all day, all of us suffering; and in the evening, when I went to hear the children's prayers before bed, I meant to have it out.

We were both frozen up with sadness, and the weary child was ready to creep into her mother's arms again. But I must not let her yet.

"So my poor Agnes has had a very sad day?"

"Yes, mother," with a sob.

"And do you know we have all had a very sad day

—father, mother, your little brother, Nurse—every one of us has felt as if a black curtain had been hung up to shut out the sunshine?"

The child was sympathetic, and shivered at the sight of the black curtain and the warm sunshine shut out.

"And do you know who has put us all out in the dark and the cold? Our little girl drew the curtain, because she would not speak to any of us, or be kind to any of us, or love any of us all the day long; so we could not get into the sunshine, and have been shivering and sad in the cold."

"Mother, mother!" with gasping sobs; "*not* you and father?"

"Ah! I thought my little girl would be sorry. Now let us try to find out how it all happened. Is it possible that Agnes noticed that her brother's pear was larger than her own?"

"Oh, mother, how could I?" The poor little face was hidden in her mother's breast, and the outbreak of sobs that followed was very painful. I feared it might mean actual illness for the sensitive child. I think it was the right thing to do; but I had barely courage enough to leave the results in more loving hands.

"Never mind; don't cry any more, darling, and we will ask 'Our Father' to forgive and forget all about it. Mother knows that her dear little Agnes will try not to love herself best any more. And then the black curtain will never fall, and we shall never again be a whole long day standing sadly out in the cold. Good-night from mother, and another good-night from father."

The treatment seems to answer. On the slightest

return of the old sullen symptoms we show our little girl what they mean. The grief that follows is so painful that I'm afraid we could not go on with it for the sake of the child's health; but, happily, we very rarely see a sulky face now; and when we do we turn and look upon our child, and the look melts her into gentleness and penitence.

IV

DOROTHY ELMORE'S ACHIEVEMENT

CHAPTER I

I KNOW of no happier moment for parents than that
when their eldest daughter returns from school to
take her place finally by her mother's side. It was
two years that very day since we had seen Dorothy,
when her father set out for Lausanne to bring her
home; and how the children and I got through the
few days of his absence, I don't know. The last
touches had been put many times over to her rooms
—not the plain little room she had left, but a dainty
bower for our young maiden, a little sitting-room
opening into a pure nest of a bedroom. Our eyes
met, her father's and mine, and moistened as we
conjured up I don't know what visions of pure young
life to be lived there, of the virginal prayers to be
offered at the little prayer table, the gaiety of heart
that should, from this nook, bubble over the house;
and, who knows, by-and-by, the dreams of young
love which should come to glorify the two little
rooms.

Two or three times already had the children put
fresh flowers into everything that would hold a
flower. Pretty frocks and sweet faces, bright hair

and bright eyes had been ready this long time to meet sister Dorothy.

At last, a telegram from Dover—" Home by five "—and our restlessness subsided into a hush of expectation.

Wheels sounded on the gravel, and we flew to the hall door and stood in two files, children and maids, Rover and Floss, waiting to welcome the child of the house. Then, a lovely face, glad to tears, looking out of a nest of furs; then, a light leap, almost before the carriage drew up, and I had her in my arms, my Dorothy, the child of my heart! The order of the day was "high tea," to which every one, down to baby May, sat up. We two, her father and I, gave her up to the children, only exchanging notes by the species of telegraphy married folk understand.

" Indubitably lovely! " said her father's eyes. " And what grace—what an elegant girl she is! " answered mine. " And do but see what tact she shows with the little ones—" " And notice the way she has with us, as if her heart were brimming with reverence and affection." Thus, we two with our eyes. For a week or more we could not settle down. As it was the Christmas holidays, we had not Miss Grimshaw to keep us in order, and so it happened that wherever Dorothy ran—no, she went with a quick noiseless step, but never ran—about the house to find out the old dear nooks, we all followed, a troop of children with their mother in the rear; their father too, if he happened to be in. Truly we were a ridiculous family, and did our best to turn the child's head. Every much has its more-so. Dorothy's two special partisans were Elsie, our girl of fifteen years,

fast treading in her sister's steps, and Herbert, our
eldest son, soon to go to college. Elsie would come
to my room and discourse by the hour, her text being
ever, "Dorothy says." And as for Herbs, it was
pleasant to see his budding manhood express itself in
all sorts of little attentions to his lovely sister.

For lovely she was; there could not be two
opinions on that point. A lily maid, tall and graceful,
without a trace of awkwardness or self-consciousness ;
the exquisite complexion of the Elmores (they are a
Devonshire family), warm, lovely rose on creamy white,
no hint of brunette colouring ; a smile which meant
spring and love and other good things ; and deep
blue eyes reflecting the light of her smile—this was
Dorothy.

Never, not even during the raptures of early
married life, have I known a month of such joyous
exhilaration as that which followed Dorothy's return,
and I think her father would own as much.

What a month it was! There was the pleasant
earthly joy of going to town to get frocks for Dorothy ;
then, the bewilderment of not being able to find out
what suited her best.

"Anything becomes her!" exclaims Mdme. la
Modiste; "that figure, that complexion, may wear
anything."

And then, how pleasant it was to enter a room
where all eyes were bent upon us in kindliness—our
dear old friends hurrying forward to make much of
the child. The deference and gentleness of her
manner to these, and the warmth with which she was
received by her compeers, both maidens and men ;
her grace in the dance; her simplicity in conversation ;
the perfection of her manner, which was not manner

at all but her own nature, in every situation — all these added to our delight. After all, she liked best to be at home, and was more amiable and lovely with father and mother, brothers and sisters, than with the most fascinating strangers. Our good child! We had grown a little shy of speaking to her about the best things, but we knew she said her prayers: how else this outflow of sweet maiden life upon us all?

I can imagine these ramblings of mine falling into the hands of a young pair whose life is in each other: "Oh, only the outpourings of a doting mother;" and they toss the pages aside. But never believe, young people, that yours are the only ecstatic moments, yours the only experiences worth recording; wait and see.

CHAPTER II

THESE happy days had lasted for a month or more, when, one bright day in February, I remember it well, a little cloud arose. This is how it was: Dorothy had promised Elsie that she would drive her in the pony-carriage to Banford to choose a doll for May's birthday. Now, it happened that I wanted the little carriage to take to my "Mothers" at Ditchling the clothing I had bought in London with their club money. My errand could not be deferred; it must be done that day or a week later. But I did not see why the children's commission would not do as well to-morrow; and so I said, in good faith, as I was stepping into the carriage, hardly noticing the silence with which my remark was received.

I came home tired, after a long afternoon, looking forward to the welcome of the girls. The two seniors were sitting in the firelight, bright enough just then to show me Dorothy, limp and pale, in a low chair, and Elsie watching her with a perplexed and anxious expression. Dorothy did look up to say, " Are you tired, mother?" but only her eyes looked, there was nothing behind them.

" *You* look tired and cold enough, my dear; what has been the matter?"

" Oh, I'm very well, thank you ; but I am tired, I think I'll go to bed." And she held up a cold cheek for the mother's kiss for which she offered no return.

Elsie and I gazed at one another in consternation ; our fairy princess, our idol—was it indeed so?—what had come to her?

" What is the matter with Dorothy? Has she a headache?"

" Oh, mother, I don't know," said the poor child, on the verge of tears. " She has been like this ever since you went, saying ' Yes,' and ' No,' and ' No, thank you,' quite kindly, but never saying a word of herself. Has any one been grieving our Dorothy, or is she going to be ill? Oh, mother, mother!"

" Nay, child, don't cry. Dorothy is overdone; you know she has been out twice this week, and three times last, and late hours don't suit her. We must take better care of her, that's all."

Elsie was comforted, but not so her mother. I believed every word I had said to the child ; but all the time there was a stir in my heart like the rustling of a snake in the grass. But I put it from me.

It was with a hidden fear that I came down to

breakfast. Dorothy was in the room already, doing the little duties of the breakfast table. But she was pale and still; her hands moved, her figure hung, in the limp way I had noticed the night before. Her cheek, a cold "Good-morning, mother," and a smile on her lips that brought no light to her eyes, was all the morning salutation I got. Breakfast was an uncomfortable, constrained meal. The children wondered what was the matter, and nobody knew. Her father got on best with Dorothy, for he knew nothing of the evening's history, so he petted her as usual, making all the more of her for her pale looks.

For a whole week this went on, and never once was I allowed to meet Dorothy eye to eye. The children were hardly better served, for they, too, had noticed something amiss; only her father could win any of the old friendliness, because he treated her as the Dorothy who had come home to us, only a little done up.

"We must have the doctor for that child, wife. Don't you see she is beginning to lose flesh, and how the roses she brought home are fading! She has no appetite and no spirits. But, why, you surely don't think our dainty moth has singed her wings already? There's nobody here, unless it's young Gardiner, and she would never waste herself on a gawky lad like that!"

This was a new idea, and I stopped a moment to consider, for I knew of at least half-a-dozen young men who had been attentive to Dorothy, all to be preferred to this hobbledehoy young Gardiner. But, no! I could trace the change from the moment of my return from Ditchling. But I jumped at the notion of the doctor; it would, at any rate, take her out of herself, and—we should see.

The doctor came; said she wanted tone; advised, not physic, but fresh air, exercise, and early hours. So we all laid ourselves out to obey his directions that day, but with no success to speak of.

But the next was one of those glorious February days when every twig is holding itself stiffly in the pride of coming leafage, and the snowdrops in the garden beds lift dainty heads out of the brown earth. The joy of the spring did it. We found her in the breakfast-room, snowdrops at her throat, rosy, beaming, joyous; a greeting, sweet and tender, for each; and never had we known her talk so sparkling, her air so full of dainty freshness. There was no relapse after this sudden cure. Our good friend Dr Evans called again, to find her in such flourishing health that ten minutes' raillery of "my poor patient" was the only attention he thought necessary. But, "H'm! Mighty sudden cure!" as he was going out, showed that he, too, found something odd in this sudden change.

In a day or two we had forgotten all about our bad week. All went well for awhile. At the end of five weeks, however, we were again pulled up—another attack of sudden indisposition, so outsiders thought. What did I think? Well, my thoughts were not enviable.

"Father, I wish you would call at Walker's and choose me some flowers for this evening." It was the evening of the Brisbanes' dance, and I had half an idea that Arthur Brisbane had made some impression on Dorothy. *His* state of mind was evident enough. But, without thinking twice, I interrupted with—

"Don't you think what we have in the 'house' will do, dear? Nothing could make up better than stephanotis and maidenhair."

Dorothy made no answer, and her father, thinking all was right, went off at once; he was already rather late. We thought no more of the matter for a minute or two, when, at the same moment, Elsie and I found our eyes fixed upon Dorothy. The former symptoms followed—days of pallor and indisposition, which were, at the same time, days of estrangement from us all. Again we had in Dr Evans, "just to look at her," and this time I noticed—not without a foolish mother's resentment—that his greeting was other than cordial. "Well, young lady, and what's gone amiss this time?" he said, knitting his bushy brows, and gazing steadily at her out of the eyes which could be keen as well as kind. Dorothy flushed and fidgeted under his gaze, but gave only the cold unsatisfactory replies we had been favoured with. The prescription was as before; but again the recovery was sudden, and without apparent cause.

CHAPTER III

To make a long story short, this sort of thing went on, at longer or shorter intervals, through all that winter and summer and winter again. My husband, in the simplicity of his nature, could see nothing but—

"The child is out of sorts; we must take her abroad for a month or two; she wants change of air and scene."

The children were quicker-eyed; children are always quick to resent unevenness of temper in those about them. A single angry outbreak, harsh word, and you may lay yourself out to please them for months before they will believe in you again. George was the first to let the cat out of the bag.

"Dorothy is in a sulky fit again, mother; I wish she wouldn't!"

Elsie, who has her father's quick temper, was in the room.

"You naughty, ungrateful little boy, you! How can you say such a thing of Dorothy? Didn't she sit all yesterday morning making sails for your boat?"

"Yes," said George, a little mollified; "but why need she be sulky to-day? We all liked her yesterday, and I'm sure I want to, to-day!"

Now that the mask was fallen and even the children could see what was amiss, I felt that the task before me must not be put off. I had had great misgivings since the first exhibition of Dorothy's sullen temper; now I saw what must be done, and braced myself for a heavy task. But I could not act alone; I must take my husband into my confidence, and that was the worst of it.

"George, how do you account for Dorothy's fits of wretchedness?"

"Why, my dear, haven't I told you? The child is out of sorts, and must have change. We'll have a little trip up the Rhine, and perhaps into Switzerland, as soon as the weather is fit. It will be worth something to see her face light up at some things I mean to show her!"

"I doubt if there is anything the matter with her health; remember how perfectly well and happy she is between these fits of depression."

"What is it, then? You don't think she's in love, do you?"

" Not a bit of it; her heart is untouched, and her dearest loves are home loves."

My husband blew his nose, with a " Bless the little girl! I could find it in my heart to wish it might always be so with her. But what is your notion? I can see you have got to the bottom of the little mystery. Trust you women for seeing through a stone wall!"

" Each attack of what we have called 'poorliness' has been a fit of sullenness, lasting sometimes for days, sometimes for more than a week, and passing off as suddenly as it came."

My dear husband's face clouded with serious displeasure; never before had it worn such an expression for me. I had a sense of separation from him, as if we two, who had so long been one, were two once more.

" This is an extraordinary charge for a mother to bring against her child. How have you come to this conclusion?"

Already was my husband become my judge. He did not see that I was ill, agitated, still standing, and hardly able to keep my feet. And there was worse to come: how was I to go through with it?

" What causes for resentment can Dorothy conceivably have?" he repeated, in the same cold judicial tone.

" It is possible to feel resentment, it is possible to nurse resentment, to let it hang as a heavy cloud-curtain between you and all you love the best, without any adequate cause, without any cause, that you can see yourself when the fit is over!"

My voice sounded strange and distant in my own ears: I held by the back of a chair to steady myself, but I was not fainting; I was acutely alive to all that was passing in my husband's mind. He looked at me curiously, inquisitively, but not as if I belonged to him and were part and parcel of his life.

"You seem to be curiously familiar with a state of feeling which I should have judged to be the last a Christian lady would know anything about."

"Oh, husband, don't you see you are hurting me? I am not going through this anguish for nothing. I *do* know what it is. And if Dorothy, my poor child, suffers, it is all my fault! There is nothing bad in her but what she has got from me."

George was moved; he put his arm round me in time to save me. But I was not surprised, a few days later, to find my first grey hairs. If that hour were to be repeated, I think I could not bear it.

"Poor wife! I see; it is to yourself you have been savagely cruel, and not to our little girl. Forgive me, dear, that I did not understand at once; but we men are slow and dull. I suppose you are putting yourself (and me too) to all this pain because there is something to be gained by it. You see some way out of the difficulty, if there is one!"

"Don't say 'if there is one.' How could I go through this pain if I did not think some way of helping our daughter would come out of it?"

"Ah! appearances were against you, but I knew you loved the child all the time. Clumsy wretch that I am, how could I doubt it? But, to my mind, there are two difficulties: First, I cannot believe that you ever cherished a thought of resentment; and next, who could associate such a feeling with our child's angelic countenance? Believe me, you are suffering under a morbid fancy; it is you, and not

Dorothy, who need entire change of scene and thought."

How should I convince him? And how again run the risk of his even momentary aversion? But if Dorothy were to be saved, the thing must be done. And, oh, how could he for a moment suppose that I should deal unlovingly with my firstborn?

" Be patient with me, George. I want to tell you everything from the beginning. Do you remember when you wooed me in the shady paths of our old rectory garden, how I tried hard to show you that I was not the loved and lovely home-daughter you pictured? I told you how I was cross about this and that; how little things put me out for days, so that I was under a cloud, and really *couldn't* speak to, or care about anybody; how, not I, but (forgive the word) my plain sister Esther, was the beloved child of the house, adored by the children, by my parents, by all the folk of the village, who must in one way or other have dealings with the parson's daughters. Do you recollect any of this?"

" Yes; but what of it? I have never for a moment rued my choice, nor wished that it had fallen on our good Esther, kindest of friends to us and ours."

" And you, dear heart, put all I said down to generosity and humility ; every effort I made to show you the truth was put down to the count of some beautiful virtue, until at last I gave it up; you *would* only think the more of me, and think the less kindly of my dear home people, because, indeed, they didn't ' appreciate ' me. How I hated the word. I'm not sure I was sorry to give up the effort to show you myself as I was. The fact is, your love made me all it believed me to be, and I thought the old things had passed away."

"Well, and wasn't I right? Have we had a single cloud upon our married life?"

"Ah, dear man, little you know what the first two years of married life were to me. If you read your newspaper, I resented it; if you spent half an hour in your smoking den, or an hour with a friend, if you admired another woman, I resented each and all, kept sulky silence for days, even for weeks. And you, all the time, thought no evil, but were sorry for your poor 'little wife,' made much of her, and loved her all the more, the more sullen and resentful she became. She was 'out of sorts,' you said, and planned a little foreign tour, as you are now doing for Dorothy. I do believe you loved me out of it at last. The time came when I felt myself hunted down by these sullen rages. I ran away, took immense walks, read voraciously, but could not help myself till our first child came; God's gift, our little Dorothy. Her baby fingers healed me as not even your love could do. But, oh, George, don't you see?"

"My poor Mary! Yes, I see; your healing was bought at the little child's expense, and the plague you felt within you was passed on to her. This, I see, is your idea; but I still believe it is a morbid fancy, and I still think my little trip will cure both mother and daughter."

"You say well, mother and daughter. The proverb should run, not, 'a burnt child dreads the fire,' but 'a burnt child will soonest catch fire!' I feel that all my old misery will come back upon me if I am to see the same thing repeated in Dorothy."

George sat musing for a minute or two, but my

fear of him was gone; his face was full of tenderness for both of us.

"Do you know, Mary, I doubt if I'm right to treat this effort of yours with a high hand, and prescribe for evils I don't understand. Should you mind very much our calling our old friend, Dr Evans, into council? I believe, after all, it will turn out to be an affair for him rather than for me."

This was worse than all. Were the miseries of this day to know no end? Should we, my Dorothy and her mother, end our days in a madhouse? I looked at my husband, and he understood.

"Nonsense, wife, not that! Now you really are absurd, and must allow me the relief of laughing at you. There, I feel better now, but I understand; a few years ago a doctor was never consulted about this kind of thing unless it was supposed to denote insanity. But we have changed all that, and you're as mad as a hatter to get the notion. You've no idea how interesting it is to hear Evans talk of the mutual relations between thought and brain, and on the other hand, between thought and character. Homely an air as he has, he is up to all that's going on. You know he went through a course of study at Leipsic, where they know more than we about the brain and its behaviour, and then, he runs across every year to keep himself abreast with the times. It isn't every country town that is blessed with such a man."

I thought I was being let down gently to the everyday level, and answered as we answer remarks about the weather, until George said—

"Well, when shall we send for Evans? The sooner we get more light on this matter, the better for all of us."

"Very well, send for him to-morrow; tell him all I have told you, and, if you like, I shall be here to answer further questions."

CHAPTER IV

"MRS ELMORE is quite right; this is no morbid fancy of hers. I have observed your pretty Miss Dorothy, and had my own speculations. Now, the whole thing lies in a nutshell."

"Can you deal with our trouble, doctor?" I cried out.

"Deal with it, my dear madam? Of course I can. I am not a pupil of Weissall's for nothing. Your Dorothy is a good girl, and will yield herself to treatment. As to that, you don't want me. The doctor is only useful on the principle that lookers-on see most of the game. Once understand the thing, and it is with you the cure must lie."

"Please explain; you will find me very obedient."

"I'm not so sure of that; you know the whole of my mental property has not been gathered in Midlington. You ladies look very meek; but directly one begins to air one's theories—which are not theories, by the way, but fixed principles of belief and conduct —you scent all manner of heterodoxy, and because a valuable line of scientific thought and discovery is new to you, you take up arms, with the notion that it flies in the face of the Bible. When, as a matter of fact, every new advance in science is a further revelation, growing out, naturally, from that we already have."

"Try me, doctor; your 'doxy shall be my 'doxy

if you will only take us in hand, and I shall be ready enough to believe that your science is by revelation."

"Well, here goes. In for a penny, in for a pound. In the first place, I want to do away with the sense of moral responsibility, both for yourself and Dorothy, which is wearing you out. Or, rather, I want to circumscribe its area and intensify its force. Dorothy has, perhaps, and conceivably her mother has also, inherited her peculiar temperament; but you are not immediately responsible for that. She, again, has fostered this inherited trait, but neither is she immediately responsible for the fact."

"How do you mean, doctor? That we can't help it, and must take our nature as we find it? But that is worse than ever. No; I cannot believe it. Certainly my husband has done a great deal to cure me."

"No doubt he has. And how he has done it—without intention, I dare say—I hope by-and-by to show you. Perhaps you now and then remark, What creatures of habit we are!"

"And what of that? No one can help being struck now and then with the fact; especially, no mother."

"Well, and what does this force of habit amount to? and how do you account for it?"

"Why, I suppose it amounts to this, that you can do almost anything once you get into the way of it. Why, I don't know; I suppose it's the natural constitution of the mind."

"The 'natural constitution of the mind' is a conversational counter with whose value I am not acquainted. That you can get into the way of doing almost anything, is simple fact; but you must add, of thinking anything, of feeling anything, before you begin to limit the force of habit."

"I think I begin to see what you mean. We, my child and I, are not so much to blame now for our sullen and resentful feelings, because we have got the habit of them. But surely habits may be cured?"

"Ah, once we begin to see that, we are to blame for them. We must ask, How are we to set about the cure? What's to be *done*? What hopeless idiots we are, the best of us, not to see that the very existence of an evil is a demand for its cure, and that, in the moral world, there's a dock for every nettle!"

"And then, surely, the sins of the fathers visited upon the children, is a bitter law. How could Dorothy help what she inherited?"

"Dorothy could not help it, but you could; and what have you two excellent parents been about to defer until the child is budding into womanhood this cure which should have been achieved in her infancy? Surely, seventeen years ago at least, you must have seen indications of the failing which must needs be shown up now, to the poor girl's discredit."

I grew hot all over under this home thrust, while George looked half dubious, half repentant, not being quite sure where his offence lay.

"It is doubly my fault, doctor; I see it all now. When Dorothy was a child I *would* not face the fact. It was too awful to think my child would be as I still was. So we had many little fictions that both nurse and mother saw through: the child was poorly, was getting her second teeth, was overdone. The same thing, only more so, went on during her schoolroom life. Dorothy was delicate, wanted stamina, must have a tonic. And this, though we had a governess who tried to convince me that it was temper and not delicacy that ailed my little girl. The worst of deceiving yourself is that you get to believe the lie. I saw much less of the schoolroom, than of the nursery party, and firmly believed in Dorothy's frequent attacks of indisposition."

"But, supposing you had faced the truth, what would you have done?"

"There is my excuse; I had no idea that anything could be done."

"Now, please, don't write me down a pagan if I try to show you what might have been done, and may yet be done."

"Doctor Evans!"

"Oh, yes, 'tis a fact; you good women are convinced that the setting of a broken limb is a work for human skill, but that the cure of a fault of disposition is for Providence alone to effect, and you say your prayers and do nothing, looking down from great heights upon us who believe that skill and knowledge come in here too, and are meant to do so in the divine scheme of things. It's startling when you come to think of it, that every pair of parents has so largely the *making* of their child!"

"But what of *inherited* failings—such cases as this of ours?"

"Precisely a case in point. Don't you see, such a case is just a problem set before parents with a, 'See, how will you work out this so as to pass your family on free from taint?'"

"That's a noble thought of yours, Evans. It gives every parent a share in working out the salvation of the world, even to thousands of generations.—Come, Mary, we're on our promotion! To pass on our children free from the blemishes they get from us is a thing worth living for."

"Indeed it is. But don't think me narrow-minded, doctor, nor that I should presume to think hard things of you men of science, if I confess that I still think the ills of the flesh fall within the province of man, but the evils of the spirit within the province of God."

"I'm not sure but that I'm of your mind; where we differ is as to the boundary-line between flesh and spirit. Now, every fault of disposition and temper, though it may have begun in error of the spirit in ourselves or in some ancestor, by the time it becomes a fault of character is *a failing of the flesh*, and is to be dealt with as such—that is, by appropriate treatment. Observe, I am not speaking of occasional and sudden temptations and falls, or of as sudden impulses towards good, and the reaching of heights undreamed of before. These things are of the spiritual world, and are to be spiritually discerned. But the failing or the virtue which has become habitual to us is flesh of our flesh, and must be treated on that basis whether it is to be uprooted or fostered."

"I confess I don't follow: this line of argument should make the work of redemption gratuitous. According to this theory, every parent can save his child, and every man can save himself."

"No, my dear; there you're wrong. I agree with Evans. It is we who lose the efficacy of the great Redemption by failing to see what it *has* accomplished. That we have still to engage in a spiritual warfare, enabled by spiritual aids, Dr Evans allows. His point is, as I understand it, why embarrass ourselves with these less material ills of the flesh which are open to treatment on the same lines, barring the drugs, as a broken limb or a disordered stomach. Don't you see how it works? We fall, and fret, and repent, and fall again; and are so over-busy with our own internal affairs, that we have no time to get that knowledge of God which is the life of the living soul?"

"All this is beyond me. I confess it is neither the creed nor the practice in which I was brought up. Meantime, how is it to affect Dorothy? That is the practical question."

Dr Evans threw a smiling "I told you so" glance at my husband, which was a little annoying; however, he went on:—

"To be sure; that is the point. Poor Dorothy is just now the occasional victim of a troop of sullen, resentful thoughts and feelings, which wear her out, shut out the sunshine, and are as a curtain between her and all she loves. Does she want these thoughts? No; she hates and deplores them on her knees, we need not doubt; resolves against them; goes through much spiritual conflict. She is a good girl, and we may be sure of all this. Now we must bring physical science to her aid. How those thoughts began we need not ask, but there they are; they go patter, patter, to and fro, to and fro, in the nervous tissue of the brain until—here is the curious point of contact between the material and the immaterial, we see by results that there is such point of contact, but how or why it is so we have not even a guess to offer—until the nervous tissue is modified under the continued traffic in the same order of thoughts. Now, these thoughts become automatic; they come of themselves, and spread and flow as a river makes and enlarges its bed. Such habit of thought is set up, and must go on indefinitely, in spite of struggles, unless—and here is the word of hope—a contrary habit is set up, diverting the thoughts into some quite new channel. Keep the thoughts running briskly in the new channel, and, behold, the old connections are broken, whilst a new growth of brain substance is perpetually taking place. The old thoughts return, and there is no place for them, and Dorothy has time to make herself think of other things before they ean establish again the old links. There is, shortly, the philosophy of ordering our thoughts—the first duty of us all."

"That is deeply interesting, and should help us. Thank you very much; I had no idea that our *thoughts* were part and parcel, as it were, of any substance. But I am not sure yet how this is to apply to Dorothy. It seems to me that it will be very difficult for her, poor child, to bring all this to bear on herself. It will be like being put into trigonometry before you are out of subtraction."

"You are right, Mrs Elmore, it will be a difficult piece of work, to which she will have to give herself up for two or three months. If I am not mistaken in my estimate of her, by that time we shall have a cure. But if you had done the work in her childhood, a month or two would have effected it, and the child herself would have been unconscious of effort."

"How sorry I am. Do tell me what I should have done."

"The tendency was there, we will allow; but you should never have allowed the *habit* of this sort of feeling to be set up. You should have been on the watch for the outward signs—the same then as now, some degree of pallor, with general limpness of attitude, and more or less dropping of the lips and eyes. The moment one such sign appeared, you should have been at hand to seize the child out of the cloud she was entering, and to let her bask for an hour or two in love and light, forcing her to meet you eye to eye, and to find love and gaiety in yours. Every sullen attack averted is so much against setting up the habit; and habit, as you know, is a chief factor in character."

"And can we do nothing for her now?"

"Certainly you can. Ignore the sullen humours; let gay life go on as if she was not there, only drawing her into it now and then by an appeal for her opinion, or for her laugh at a joke. Above all, when good manners compel her to look up, let her meet unclouded eyes, full of pleasure in her; for, believe, whatever cause of offence she gives to you, she is far more deeply offensive to herself. And you should do this all the more because, poor girl, the brunt of the battle will fall upon her."

"I see you are right; all along, her sullenness has given away before her father's delight in her, and indeed it is in this way that my husband has so far cured me. I suppose you would say he had broken the habit. But won't you see her and talk to her? I know you can help her most."

"Well, to tell you the truth, I was going to ask you if I might; her sensitive nature must be gently handled; and, just because she has no such love for me as for her parents, I run less risk of wounding her. Besides, I have a secret to tell which should help her in the management of herself."

"Thank you, Evans; we are more grateful than I can say. Will you strike while the iron's hot? Shall we go away and send her to you, letting her suppose it is a mere medical call?"

CHAPTER V

"GOOD-MORNING, Miss Dorothy; do you know I think it's quite time this state of things should come to an end. We are both tired of the humbug of treating you for want of health when you are quite strong and well."

Dorothy looked up with flushed face (I had it all later from both Dr Evans and Dorothy herself), and eyes half relieved, half doubtful, but not resentful, and stood quietly waiting.

"All the same, I think you are in a bad way, and are in great need of help. Will you bear with me while I tell you what is the matter, and how you may be cured?"

Dorothy was past speaking, and gave a silent assent.

"Don't be frightened, poor child; I don't speak to hurt you, but to help. A considerable part of a life which should be all innocent gaiety of heart, is spent in gloom and miserable isolation. Some one fails to dot his i's, and you resent it, not in words or manner, being too well brought up; but the light within you is darkened by a flight of black thoughts. 'He (or she) shouldn't have done it! It's too bad! They don't care how they hurt me! I should never have done so to her!'—and so on without end. Presently you find yourself swathed in a sort of invisible shroud;

you cannot reach out a living hand to anybody, nor speak in living tones, nor meet your dear ones eye to eye with a living and loving glance. There you sit, like a dead man at the feast. By this time you have forgotten the first offence, and would give the world to get out of this death-in-life. You cry, you say your prayers, beg to be forgiven and restored, but your eyes are fixed upon yourself as a hateful person, and you are still wrapped in the cloud; until, suddenly (no doubt in answer to your prayers), a hug from little May, the first primrose of the year, a lark, filling the world with his gladness, and, presto! the key is turned, the enchanted princess liberated, glad as the lark, sweet as the flower, and gay as the bright child!"

No answer: Dorothy's arms were on the table, and her face hidden upon them. At last she said in a choked voice—"Please go on, doctor!"

"All this may be helped" (she looked up), "may, within two or three months, be completely cured, become a horrid memory and nothing more!" Dorothy raised streaming eyes, where the light of hope was struggling with fear and shame.

"This is very trying for you, dear child! But I must get on with my task, and when I have done, it's my belief you'll forget the pain for joy. In the first place, you are not a very wicked girl because these ugly thoughts master you; I don't say, mind you, that you will be without offence once you get the key between your fingers; but as it is, you need not sit in judgment on yourself any more."

Then Dr Evans went on to make clear to Dorothy what he had already made clear to us of the interaction of thought and brain; how that Thought, Brain & Co. were such close allies that nobody could tell which of the two did what: that they even ran a business of their own, independently of *Ego*, who was supposed to be the active head of the firm, and so on.

Dorothy listened with absorbed intentness, as if every word were saving; but the light of hope died slowly out.

"I think I see what you mean; these black thoughts come and rampage even against the desire of the *Ego*, I, myself: but, oh doctor, don't you see, that's all the worse for me?"

"Stop a bit, stop a bit, my dear young lady, I have not done yet. *Ego* sees things are going wrong and asserts himself; sets up new thoughts in a new course, and stops the old traffic; and in course of time, and a very short time too, the old nerve connections are broken, and the old way under tillage; no more opening for traffic there. Have you got it?"

"I think so. I'm to think of something else, and soon there will be no room in the brain for the ugly thoughts which distress me. But that's just the thing I can't do!"

"But that is exactly the only thing you have power to do! Have you any idea what the will is, and what are its functions?"

"I don't know much about it. I suppose your will should make you able to do the right thing when you feel you can't! You should say, 'I *will*,' and go and do it. But you don't know how weak I am. It makes no difference to me to say, I will!"

"Well, now, to own up honestly, I don't think it ever made much difference to anybody outside of the story-books. All the same, Will is a mighty fellow in his own way, but he goes with a sling and a stone, and not with the sword of Goliath. He attacks the giant with what seems a child's plaything, and the giant is slain. This is how it works. When ill thoughts *begin* to molest you, turn away your mind with a vigorous turn, and *think of something else.* I don't mean think good forgiving thoughts, perhaps you are not ready for that yet ; but think of something interesting and pleasant ; the new dress you must plan, the friend you like best, the book you are reading; best of all, fill heart and mind suddenly with some capital plan for giving pleasure to some poor body whose days are dull. The more exciting the thing you think of, the safer you are. Never mind about fighting the evil thought. This is the one thing you have to do; for this is, perhaps, the sole power the will has. It enables you to change your thoughts ; to turn yourself round from gloomy thoughts to cheerful ones. Then you will find that your prayers will be answered, for you will know what to ask for, and will not turn your back on the answer when it comes. There, child, I have told you the best secret I know—given to me by a man I revere—and have put into your hands the key of self-government and a happy life. Now you know how to be better than he that taketh a city."

"Thank you a thousand times for your precious secret. You have lifted my feet out of the slough. I *will* change my thoughts (may I say that?). You shall find that your key does not rust for want of use. I trust I may be helped never to enter that cloud again."

It is five years since Dorothy had that talk in the library with Dr Evans (he died within the year, to our exceeding regret). What battles she fought we never heard; never again was the subject alluded to. For two years she was our joyous home daughter; for three, she has been Arthur Brisbane's happy wife; and her little sunbeam of an Elsie—no fear that she will ever enter the cloud in which mother and grandmother were so nearly lost.

V

CONSEQUENCES

HAVE you ever played at "Consequences," dear reader? This is how it goes. He said to her, "It's a cold day." She said to him, "I like chocolates." The consequence was, they were both put to death, and the world said, "It serves them right."

Just so exquisitely inconsequent is the game of "consequences" in real life, at which many a child is an unwilling player, and just so arbitrary their distribution. We are all born heirs to all the Russias if a certain aptness at autocratic government can be construed into a title. Watch the children in the street play at keeping school; how the schoolmistress lavishes "handers," how she corners and canes her scholars! And the make-believe scholars enter into the game. They would do the same if they had the chance, and their turn will come.

How does it work in real life, this turn for autocracy, which, you may observe, gives zest to most of the children's games?

Little Nancy is inclined to be fretful; her nurse happens to be particularly busy this morning looking out the children's summer clothing. She is a kind-hearted woman, and fond of Nancy, but, "Why does the child whine so?" And a hasty box on the little ear emphasises the indignant query. There is mischief already, which is the cause of the whining; and, by that concussion, Nancy is "put to death," like the people in the game; not for a year or two, though, and nobody associates nurse with the family sorrow; and she, for her part, never thinks again of that hasty blow. But, you object, nurse is ignorant, though kind; with the child's parents, it is otherwise. Yes, but not entirely otherwise. Mr Lindsay, who is a book-lover, goes into his den to find his little boy of four, making "card-houses," with some choice volumes he has clambered after; down they go, bump, and the corners are turned, and the books unsightly objects evermore. "What are you doing here, child? Go to the nursery, and don't let me see you here again!" Ah, me! Does he know how deep it cuts? Does he know that the ten minutes' romp with "father" in his room is the supreme joy of the day for little Dick? And does he know that everything is for ever and ever to a little child, whose experience has not yet taught him the trick of hoping when things look dark? But, "It is for the child's good." Is it? Dick does not yet know what is wrong. "Never touch books which are not given you to play with," would have instructed him, and hindered similar mischief in the future.

How is it that devoted nurse and affectionate father cause injurious "concussions," moral and physical, to a child's tender nature? A good deal is to be set down to ignorance or thoughtlessness; they do not know, or they do not consider, how this and that must affect a child. But the curious thing is, that grown-up people nearly always err on the same lines.

The arbitrary exercise of authority on the part of parent, nurse, governess, whoever is set in authority over him, is the real stone of stumbling and rock of offence in the way of many a child.

Nor is there room for the tender indulgent mother to congratulate herself and say, "I always thought Mrs Naybor was too hard on her children," for the most ruinous exercise of arbitrary authority is when the mother makes herself a law unto her child, with power to excuse him from his duties, and to grant him (more than papal) indulgences. This sort of tender parent is most tenacious of her authority, no one is permitted to interfere with her rule—for rule it is, though her children are notably unruly. She answers all advice and expostulation with one formula: "My children shall never have it to say that their mother refused them anything it was in her power to give."

"*In her power.*" This mother errs in believing that her children are hers—in her power, body and soul. Can she not do what she likes with her own?

It is worth while to look to the springs of conduct in human nature for the source of this common cause of the mismanagement of children. There must be some unsuspected reason for the fact that persons of weak and of strong nature should err in the same direction.

In every human being there are implanted, as we know, certain so-called primary or natural desires, which are among the springs or principles out of which his action or conduct flows. These desires are neither virtuous nor vicious in themselves: they are quite involuntary: they have place equally in the savage and the savant: he who makes his appeal to any one of those primary desires is certain of a hearing. Thus, every man has an innate desire for companionship: every man wants to *know*, however little worthy the objects of his curiosity: we all want to stand well with our neighbours, however fatuously we lay ourselves out for esteem: we would, each of us, fain be the best at some one thing, if it be only a game of chance which excites our emulation; and we would all have rule, have authority, even if our ambition has no greater scope than the rule of a dog or a child affords. These desires being primary or natural, the absence of any one of them in a human being makes that person, so far, unnatural. The man who hates society is a misanthrope; he who has no curiosity is a clod. But, seeing that a man may make shipwreck of his character and his destiny by the excessive indulgence of any one of these desires, the regulating, balancing, and due ordering of these springs of action is an important part of that wise self-government which is the duty of every man.

It is not that the primary desires are the only springs of action; we all know that the affections, the appetites, the emotions, play their part, and that reason and conscience are the appointed regulators of machinery which may be set in motion by a hundred impulses. But the subject for our consideration is the punishments inflicted on children; and we shall not arrive at any safe conclusion unless we regard these punishments from the point of view of the punisher as well as from that of the punished.

Now every one of the primary desires, as well as of the affections and appetites, has a tendency to run riot if its object be well within its grasp. The desire for society undirected and unregulated may lead to endless gadding about and herding together. The fine principle of curiosity may issue in an inordinate love of gossip, and of poor disconnected morsels of knowledge served up in scraps, which are of the nature of gossip. Ambition, the desire of power, comes into play when we have a live thing to order; and we rule child and servant, horse and dog. And it is well that we should. The person who is (comparatively) without ambition has no capacity to rule. Have you a nurse who "manages" children well? She is an ambitious woman, and her ambition finds delightful scope in the government of the nursery. At the same time, the love of power, unless it be duly and carefully regulated and controlled, leads to arbitrary behaviour—that is, to lawless, injurious behaviour —towards those under our rule. Nay, we may be so carried away, intoxicated, by a fierce lust of power that we do some terrible, irrevocable deed of cruelty to a tender child-body or soul, and wake up to neverending remorse. We meant no harm; we meant to teach obedience, and, good God! we have killed a child.

Within the last few years tales have been told in the newspapers of the savage abuse of power, free for the time being from external control; tales, which, be they true or not, should make us all commune with our hearts and be still. For, we may believe it, they who have done these things are no worse than we could be; they had opportunity to do ill deeds, and they did them. We have not been so far left to ourselves. But let us look ourselves in the face; let us recognise that the principle which has betrayed others into the madness of crime is inherent in us also, and that whether it shall lead us to heights of noble living or to criminal cruelty is not a matter to be left to the chapter of accidents. We have need of the divine grace to prevent and follow us, and we have need to

seek consciously, and diligently use, this grace to keep
us who are in authority in the spirit of meekness,
remembering always that the One who is entrusted
with the rod of iron is meek and lowly of heart.

In proportion as we keep ourselves fully alive to our
tendency in this matter of authority may we trust
ourselves to administer the law to creatures so tender
in body and soul as are the little children. We shall
remember that a word may wound, that a look may
strike as a blow. It may indeed be necessary to
wound in order to heal, but we shall examine ourselves well before we use the knife. There will be no
hasty dealing out of reproof and punishment, reward
and praise, according to the manner of mood we are in.
We shall not only be aware that our own authority
is deputed, and to be used with the meekness of
wisdom; but we shall be very careful indeed in our
choice of the persons in whose charge we place our
children. It is not enough that they be good Christian
people. We all know good Christian persons of an
arbitrary turn who venture to wield that rod of iron
which is safe in the hands of One alone. Let them be
good Christian persons of culture and self-knowledge;
not the morbid self-knowledge that comes of introspection, but that wider, humbler cognisance of self
that comes of a study of the guiding principles and
springs of action common to us all as human beings,
and which brings with it the certainty that—"I am
just such an one as the rest, and might even be as
the worst, were it not for the grace of God and careful walking."

It is no doubt much easier to lay down our
authority and let the children follow their own lead,
or be kept in order by another, than to exercise

constant watchfulness in the exercise of our calling. But this is not in our option; we *must rule* with diligence. It is necessary for the children that we should; but we must keep ourselves continually in check, and see that our innate love of power finds lawful outlet in the building up of a child's character, and not in the rude rebuff, the jibe and sneer, the short answer and hasty slap which none of us older people could conceivably endure ourselves, and yet practise freely on the children "for their good."

"To this day," says an American author,[1] "the old tingling pain burns my cheeks as I recall certain rude and contemptuous words which were said to me when I was very young, and stamped on my memory for ever. I was once called 'a stupid child' in the presence of strangers. I had brought the wrong book from my father's study. Nothing could be said to me to-day which would give me a tenth part of the hopeless sense of degradation which came from those words. Another time, on the arrival of an unexpected guest to dinner, I was sent, in a great hurry, away from the table to make room, with the remark that 'it was not of the least consequence about the child; she could just as well have her dinner afterward.' 'The child' would have been only too happy to help in the hospitality of the sudden emergency if the thing had been differently put; but the sting of having it put that way I never forgot. Yet, in both these instances, the rudeness was so small in comparison with what we habitually see that it would be too trivial to mention, except for the bearing of the fact that the pain it gave has lasted until now."

[1] *Bits of Talk about Home Matters*, by Helen Hunt Jackson.

"What, is it severity in these maudlin days to call a child 'stupid'? A pretty idiot he'll make of himself when the world comes to bandy names with him if he's to be brought up on nothing but the butter and honey of soft speeches." This is a discordant protest, not at all in harmony with the notions of perfect child-living with which we are amusing ourselves in these days; but we cannot afford to turn a deaf ear to it. "Don't make a fool of the child," was the warning young mothers used to get from their elders. But we have changed all that, and a child's paradise must be prepared for the little feet to walk in. "He's so happy at school," we are told, and we ask no more. We have reversed the old order; it used to be, "If he's good, he will be happy"; now we say, "If he's happy, he will be good." Goodness and happiness are regarded as convertible terms, only we like best to put "happy" as the cause, and "good" as the consequent. And the child brought up on these lines is both happy and good without much moral effort of self-compelling on his own part, while our care is to surround him with happy-making circumstances until he has got into the trick, as it were, of being good.

But there's something rotten in the state of Denmark. Once upon a time there was a young mother who conceived that every mother might be the means of gracing her offspring with fine teeth: "For," said she, "it stands to reason that for every year of wear and grind you save the child's teeth, the man will have a fine set a year the longer." "Nonsense, my dear madam," said the doctor, "you are ruining the child's teeth with all this pappy food; they'll be no stronger than egg-shells Give him plenty of hard crusts to crunch, a bone to gnaw; he must have something to harden his teeth upon." Just so, of the moral "teeth" by means of which the child must carve out a place for himself in this full world. He must endure hardness if you would make a man of him. Blame as well as praise, tears as well as smiles, are of human nature's daily food; pungent speech is a tool of the tongue not to be altogether eschewed in the building of character; let us call a spade a spade, and the child who brings the wrong book "stupid," whether before strangers or behind them. Much better, this, than a chamber-conference with "Mother" about every trifle, which latter is apt to lead to a habit of morbid introspection.

We are, in truth, between Scylla and Charybdis: on this side, the six-headed, many-toothed monster of our own unbridled love of power; on that, the whirlpool which would engulf the manly virtues of our poor little Ulysses. If we must choose, let it be Scylla rather than Charybdis; better lose something through the monster with the teeth, than lose ourselves in the whirlpool. But is there not a better way?

> Weigh his estate and thine; accustom'd, he,
> To all sweet courtly usage that obtains
> Where dwells the King. How, with thy utmost pains,
> Canst thou produce what shall full worthy be?
> One, 'greatest in the kingdom,' is with thee,
> Whose being yet discerns the Father's face,
> And, thence replenish'd, glows with constant grace:
> Take fearful heed lest he despised be!
> Order thy goings softly, as before
> A Prince; nor let thee out unmannerly
> In thy rude moods and irritable: more,
> Beware lest round him wind of words rave free.
> Refrain thee; see thy speech be sweet and rare:
> Thy ways, consider'd; and thine aspect, fair.

VI

MRS SEDLEY'S TALE

IT is strange how a moral weakness in her child gives a mother the same sense of yearning pity that she has for a bad bodily infirmity. I wonder if that is how God feels for us when we go on year by year doing the thing we hate? I think a mother gets to understand many things about the dealings of God that are not plain to others. For instance, how it helps me to say, " I believe in the forgiveness of sins," when I think of my poor little Fanny's ugly fault. Though there is some return of it nearly every day, what could I do but forgive?

But forgiveness that does not heal is like the wretched ointments with which poor people dress their wounds. In one thing I know I have not done well; I have hardly said a word to John about the poor little girl's failing, though it has troubled me constantly for nearly a year. But I think he suspects there is something wrong ; we never talk quite freely about our shy, pretty Fanny. Perhaps that is one reason for it. She is such a nervous, timid little being, and looks so bewitching when the long lashes droop, the tender mouth quivers, and the colour comes and goes in her soft cheek, that we are shy of exposing, even to each other, the faults we see in our graceful, fragile little girl. Perhaps neither of us quite trusts the other to deal with Fanny and to use the knife sparingly.

But this state of things must not go on: it is a miserable thing to write down, but I cannot believe a word the child says! And the evil is increasing. Only now and then used Fanny to be detected in what we called a fib, but now the doubt lest that little mouth may be at any moment uttering a lie takes the delight out of life, and accounts for the pale looks which give my husband much concern.

For example, only within the last day or two I have noticed the following and other such examples :—

"Fanny, did you remember to give my message to cook?"

"Yes, mother."

"And what did she say?"

"That she wouldn't be able to make any jam to-day, because the fruit had not come."

I went into the kitchen shortly after, and found cook stirring the contents of a brass pan, and, sad to say, I asked no questions. It was one of Fanny's circumstantial statements of the kind I have had most reason to doubt. Did she lie because she was afraid to own that she had forgotten? Hardly so: knowing the child's sensitive nature, we have always been careful not to visit her small misdemeanours with any punishment whenever she "owned up." And then, cowardice would hardly cause her to invent so reasonable an answer for cook. Again :—

"Did you meet Mrs Fleming's children?"

"Oh yes, mother! and Berty was so rude! He pushed Dotty off the curb-stone!"

Nurse, who was sitting by the fire with baby, raised her eyebrows in surprise, and I saw the whole thing was an invention. Another more extraordinary instance :—

"Mother, when we were in the park we met Miss Butler, just by the fountain, you know; and she kissed me, and asked me how my mother was";—said *apropos* of nothing, in the most quiet, easy way.

I met Miss Butler this morning, and thanked her for the kind inquiries she had been making through my little girl; and—"Do you think Fanny grown?"

Miss Butler looked perplexed; Fanny was a great favourite of hers, perhaps because of the loveliness of which her parents cannot pretend to be unaware.

"It is more than a month since I have seen the little maid, but I shall look in soon, and gladden her mother's heart with all the praises my sweet Fan deserves!"

Little she knew that shame, and not pride, dyed my cheek; but I could not disclose my Fanny's sad secret to even so near a friend.

But to talk it out with John is a different matter. He ought to know. There had I been thinking for months in a desultory kind of way as to the why and wherefore of this ingrained want of truthfulness in the child, and yet I was no nearer the solution, when a new departure in the way of lying made me at last break the ice with John; indeed, this was the only subject about which we had ever had reserves.

"Mother, Hugh was so naughty at lessons this morning! He went close up to Miss Clare while she was writing, nudged her elbow on purpose, and made her spill the ink all over the table-cloth."

I chanced to meet Miss Clare in the hall, and remarked that I heard she had found Hugh troublesome this morning.

"Troublesome? Not at all; he was quite industrious and obedient."

I said nothing about the ink, but went straight to the schoolroom, to find the table neat, as Miss Clare always leaves it, and no sign of even a fresh ink-spot. What possessed the child? This inveterate and inventive untruthfulness was like a form of mania. I sat in dismay for an hour or more, not thinking, but stunned by this new idea—that the child was not responsible for her words; and yet, could it be so? Not one of our children was so merry at play, so intelligent at lessons. Well, I would talk it over with her father without the loss of another day.

.   .   .   .   .   .

"John, I am miserable about Fanny. Do you know the child tells fibs constantly?"

"Call them lies; an ugly thing deserves an ugly name. What sort of lies? What tempts her to lie?"

John did not seem surprised. Perhaps he knew more of this misery than I supposed.

"That's the thing! Her fi—lies are so uncalled-for, so unreasonable, that I do not know how to trust her."

"Unreasonable? You mean her tales don't hang together; that's a common case with liars. You know the saying—'Liars should have good memories'?"

"Don't call the poor child a liar, John; I believe she is more to be pitied than blamed. What I mean is, you can't find rhyme or reason for the lies she tells." And I gave my husband a few instances like those I have written above.

"Very extraordinary! There's a hint of malice in

the Hugh and the ink-bottle tale, and a hint of cowardice in that about the jam; but for the rest, they are inventions pure and simple, with neither rhyme nor reason, as you say."

"I don't believe a bit in the malice. I was going to correct her for telling an unkind tale about Hugh, but you know how she hangs on her brother; and she told her tale with the most innocent face. I am convinced there was no thought of harming him."

"Are you equally sure that she never says what is false to cover a fault; in fact, out of cowardice?"

"No; I think I have found her out more than once in ingenious subterfuges; you know what a painfully nervous child she is. For instance, I found the other day a blue cup off that cabinet, with handle gone, hidden behind the woodwork. Fanny happened to come in at the moment, and I asked her if she knew who had broken it.

"'No, mother, I don't know, but I think it was Mary, when she was dusting the cabinet; indeed, I'm nearly sure I heard a crash.'

"But the child could not meet my eye, and there was a sort of blenching as of fear about her."

"But, as a rule, you do not notice these symptoms?"

"As a rule, poor Fanny's tarradiddles come out in the most quiet, easy way, with all the boldness of innocence; and even when she is found out, and the lie brought home to her, she looks bewildered rather than convicted."

"I wish you would banish the whole tribe of foolish and harmful expressions whose tendency is to make light of sin. Call a spade a spade. A 'tarradiddle' is a thing to make merry over; a fib you smile and wink at; but a *lie*—why, the soul is very far gone from original righteousness that can endure the name, even while guilty of the thing."

"That's just it; I cannot endure to apply so black a name to the failings of our child; for, do you know, I begin to suspect that poor little Fanny does it un-awares—does not know in the least that she has departed from the fact. I have had a horrible dread upon me from time to time that her defect is a mental, and not a moral one: that she has not the clear perception of true and false with which most of us are blessed."

"Whe—ew!" from John; but his surprise was feigned. I could see now that he had known what was going on all the time, and had said nothing, because he had nothing to say; in his heart he agreed with me about our pretty child. The defect arose from a clouded intelligence, which showed itself in this way only, now; but how dare we look forward? Now I saw why poor John was so anxious to have the offence called by the blackest moral name. He wished to save us from the suspicion of an evil— worse, because less open to cure. We looked blankly at each other, he trying to carry the matter off with a light air, but his attempt failed.

I forgot to say that my sister Emma was staying with us, the 'clever woman of the family,' who was "going in" for all sorts of things, to come out, we believed, at the top of her profession as a lady doctor. She had taken no part in the talk about Fanny— which was rather tiresome of her, as I wanted to know what she thought; but now, while we were vainly trying to hide our dismay, she broke out into a long laugh, which seemed a little unfeeling.

"Oh, you absurd parents! You are too good and

earnest, and altogether too droll! Why in the world, instead of sitting there with blank eyes—conjuring up bogeys to frighten each other—why don't you look the thing in the face, and find out by the light of modern thought what really ails Fan? Poor pet! 'Save me from my parents!' is a rendering which might be forgiven her."

"Then you don't think there's any mental trouble?" we cried in a breath, feeling already as if a burden were lifted, and we could straighten our backs and walk abroad.

"'Mental trouble?' What nonsense! But there, I believe all you parents are alike. Each pair thinks their own experiences entirely new; their own children the first of the kind born into the world. Now, a mind that had had any scientific training would see at once that poor Fanny's lies—if I must use John's terrible bad word—inventions, I should have called them, are symptomatic, as you rightly guessed, Annie, of certain brain conditions; but of brain disease—oh, no! Why, foolish people, don't you see you are entertaining an angel unawares? This vice of 'lying' you are mourning over is the very quality that goes to the making of poets!"

"Poets and angels are well in their places," said John, rather crossly, "but my child must speak the truth. What she states for a fact, I must know to be a fact, according to the poor common-sense view of benighted parents."

"And there is your work as parents. Teach her truth, as you would teach her French or sums—a little to-day, a little more to-morrow, and every day a lesson. Only as you teach her the nature of truth will the gift she has be effectual. But

I really should like to know what is your notion about truth—are we born with it, or educated up to it?"

"I am not sure that we care to be experimented upon, and held up to the world as blundering parents," said I; "perhaps we had better keep our crude notions to ourselves." I spoke rather tartly, I know, for I was more vexed for John than for myself. That he should be held up to ridicule in his own house—by a sister of mine, too!

"Now I have vexed you both. How horrid I am! And all the time, as I watch you with the children, I don't feel good enough to tie your shoes. Don't I say to myself twenty times a day, 'After all, the insight and love parents get from above is worth a thousandfold more than all science has to teach'?"

"Nay, Emma, it is we who have to apologise for being jealous of science—that's the fact—and quick to take offence. Make it up, there's a good girl! and let Annie and me have the benefit of your advice about our little girl, for truly we are in a fog."

"Well, I think you were both right in considering that her failing had two sources: moral cowardice the first; she does something wrong, or wrong in her eyes, and does not tell—why?"

"Aye, there's the difficulty; why is she afraid to tell the truth? I may say that we have never punished her, or ever looked coldly on her for any fault but this of prevarication. The child is so timid that we feared severe measures might make truth-telling the more difficult."

"There I think you are right. And we have our finger on one of the weak places: Fanny tells lies out of sheer fear—moral weakness; causeless it may be, but there it is. And I'm not so sure that it is cause-less; she is always in favour for good behaviour, gentleness, obedience, and that kind of thing; indeed, this want of veracity seems to me her one fault. Now, don't you think the fear of having her parents look coldly on her and think less well of her may be, to such a timid, clinging child, a great temptation to hide a fault?"

"Very likely; but one does not see how to act. Would you pass over her faults altogether without inquiry or notice?"

"I'm afraid you must use the knife there boldly, for that is the tenderest way in the end. Show little Fan your love—that there is *no* fault you cannot forgive in her, but that the one fault which hurts you most is, not to hear the exact truth."

"I see. Suppose she has broken a valuable vase and hides the fact, I am to unearth her secret—not, as I am very much inclined to do, let it lie buried for fear of involving her in worse falsehood, but show her the vase and tax her with hiding it."

"And her immediate impulse will be to say, 'I didn't.' No; make sure of your ground, then show her the pieces; say the vase was precious, but you do not mind about that; the thing that hurts you is that she could not trust her mother. I can imagine one of the lovely scenes you mothers have with your children, too good for outsiders to look in upon."

The tears came into my eyes, for I could imagine the scene too. I could see the way to draw my child closer and closer by *always* forgiving, always compre-hending and loving her, and always protesting against the falsehood which *would* rise between us. I was lost in a happy reverie—how I might sometime come to show her that her mother's ever-ready forgive-ness was but a faint picture of what someone calls the "all-forgiving gentleness of God," when I heard John break in :—

"Yes, I can see that if we both make a point of free and tender forgiveness of every fault, on condition that she owns up, we may in time cure her of lying out of sheer fear. But I don't see that she gets the principle of truth any more. The purely inventive lies go on as before, and the child is not to be trusted."

"'Purely inventive,' there you have it. Don't you see? The child is full of imagination, and figures to herself endless scenes, evolved like the German student's camel. The thousand and one things which *might* happen are so real to her that the child is, as you said, bewildered ; hardly able to distingush the one which has happened. Now, it's perfect nonsense to lament over this as a moral failing—it is a want of mental balance ; not that any quality is deficient, but that her conceptive power runs away with her percep-tive ; she sees the many things that might be more readily than the thing that is. Doesn't she delight in fairy tales?"

"Well, to tell the truth, I have thought them likely to foster her failing, and have kept her a good deal on a diet of facts."

"I shouldn't wonder if you are wrong there. An imperious imagination like Fanny's demands its proper nourishment. Let her have her daily meal: 'The Babes in the Wood,' 'The Little Match-Girl,' 'The Snow-Maiden,' tales and legends half-historic ; above all, the lovely stories of the Bible; whatever she can figure to herself and live over and over ; but *not* twad-dling tales of the daily doings of children like herself,

whether funny or serious. The child wants an opening
into the larger world where all things are possible and
where beautiful things are always happening. Give
her in some form this necessary food, and her mind
will be so full of delightful imaginings that she will be
under no temptation to invent about the commonplaces
of everyday life."

My husband laughed: "My dear Emma, you must
let us do our best with the disease; the cure is too
wild! 'Behold, this dreamer cometh!'—think of sending the child through life with that label."

"Your quotation is unfortunate, and you have not
heard me out. I do believe that to starve her
imagination would be to do real wrong to the child.
But, at the same time, you must diligently cultivate
the knowledge and the love of the truth. Now, the
truth is no more than the fact as it is; and it is my
belief that Fanny's falsehoods come entirely from
want of perception of the fact through pre-occupation
of mind."

"Well, what must we do?"

"Why, give her daily, or half-a-dozen times a day,
lessons in truth. Send her to the window: 'Look
out, Fanny, and tell me what you see.' She comes
back, having seen a cow where there is a horse. She
looks again and brings a true report, and you teach
her that it is not true to say the thing which is not.
You send a long message to the cook, requiring the
latter to write it down as she receives it and send you
up the slate; if it is all right, the kiss Fanny gets is
for speaking the truth: gradually, she comes to revere
truth, and distinguishes between the facts of life where
truth is all in all, and the wide realms of make-believe,
where fancy may have free play."

"I do believe you are right, Emma; most of Fanny's falsehoods seem to be told in such pure innocence, I should not wonder if they do come out of the kingdom of make-believe. At any rate, we'll try Emma's specific—shall we, John?"

"Indeed, yes; and carefully, too. It seems to me to be reasonable, the more so, as we don't find any trace of malice in Fanny's misleading statements."

"Oh, if there were, the treatment would be less simple; first, you should deal with the malice, and then *teach* the love of truth in daily lessons. That is the mistake so many people make. They think their children are capable of loving and understanding *truth* by nature, which they are not. The best parents have to be on the watch to hinder all opportunities of misstatement."

"And now, that you may see how much we owe you, let me tell you of the painful example always before our eyes, which has done more than anything to make me dread Fanny's failing. It is an open secret, I fear, but do not let it go further out of this house. You know Mrs Casterton, our neighbour's wife? It is a miserable thing to say, but you cannot trust a word she utters. She tells you, Miss So-and-So has a bad kind of scarlet fever, and even while she is speaking you know it to be false; husband, children, servants, neighbours, none can be blind to the distressing fact, and she has acquired the sort of simpering manner a woman gets when she loses respect and self-respect. What if Fanny had grown up like her?"

"Poor woman! and this shame might have been spared her, had her parents been alive to their duty."

VII

ABILITY

"BE *sure* you call at Mrs Milner's, Fred, for the address of her laundress."

"All right, mother!" And Fred was half-way down the path before his mother had time to add a second injunction. A second? Nay, a seventh, for this was already the sixth time of asking; and Mrs Bruce's half-troubled expression showed she placed little faith in her son's "All right."

"I don't know what to do with Fred, doctor; I am not in the least sure he will do my message. Indeed, to speak honestly, I am sure he will not. This is a trifling matter; but when the same thing happens twenty times a day—when his rule is to forget everything he is desired to remember—it makes us anxious about the boy's future."

Dr Maclehose drummed meditatively on the table, and put his lips into form for a whistle. This remark of Mrs Bruce's was "nuts" to him. He had assisted, professionally, at the appearance of the nine young Bruces, and the family had no more esteemed friend and general confidant. For his part, he liked the Bruces. Who could help it? The parents, intelligent and genial, the young folk well looking, well grown, and open-hearted, they were just the family to make friends. All the same, the doctor found in the Bruces occasion to mount his pet hobby :—" My Utopia is the land where the family doctor has leave to play schoolmaster to the parents. To think of a fine brood like the young Bruces running to waste in half-a-dozen different ways through the invincible ignorance of father and mother! Nice people, too!"

For seventeen years, Dr Maclehose had been deep in the family counsels, yet never till now had he seen the way to put in his oar anent any question of the bringing up of the children. Wherefore he drummed on the table, and pondered :—" Fair and softly, my good fellow; fair and softly! Make a mess of it now, and it's your last chance; hit the nail on the head, and, who knows?"

"Does the same sort of thing go on about his school work?"

"Precisely; he is always in arrears. He has forgotten to take a book, or to write an exercise, or learn a lesson ; in fact, his school life is a record of forgets and penalties."

"Worse than that Dean of Canterbury, whose wife *would* make him keep account of his expenditure ; and thus stood the entries for one week :—' Gloves, 5s.; Forgets, £4, 15s.' His writing was none too legible, so his wife, looking over his shoulder, cried, ' Faggots! Faggots! What in the world! Have you been buying wood?' 'No, my dear; those are *forgets* :'—his wife gave it up."

"A capital story ; but what is amusing in a Dean won't help a boy to get through the world, and we are both uneasy about Fred."

"He is one of the ' School Eleven,' isn't he?"

"Oh yes, and is wild about it: and there, I grant you, he never forgets. It's, 'Mother, get cook to give us an early dinner: we must be on the field by two!' 'Don't forget to have my flannels clean for Friday, will you, mumsy?' he knows when to coax. 'Subscription is due on Thursday, mother!' and this, every day till he gets the money."

"I congratulate you, my dear friend; there's nothing seriously amiss with the boy's brain."

"Good heavens, doctor! Whoever thought there was? You take my breath away!"

"Well, well, I didn't mean to frighten you, but, don't you see, it comes to this: either it's a case of chronic disease, open only to medical treatment, if to any; or it is just a case of defective education, a piece of mischief bred of allowance which his parents cannot too soon set themselves to cure."

Mrs Bruce was the least in the world nettled at this serious view of the case. It was one thing for *her* to write down hard things of her eldest boy, the pride of her heart, but a different matter for another to take her *au sérieux*.

"But, my dear doctor, are you not taking a common fault of youth too seriously? It's tiresome that he should forget so, but give him a year or two, and he will grow out of it, you'll see. Time will steady him. It's just the volatility of youth, and for my part I don't like to see a boy with a man's head on his shoulders." The doctor resumed his drumming on the table. He had put his foot in it already, and confounded his own foolhardiness.

"Well, I daresay you are right in allowing something on the score of youthful volatility; but we old doctors, whose business it is to study the close connection between mind and matter, see our way to only one conclusion, that any failing of mind or body, left to itself, can do no other than strengthen."

" Have another cup of tea, doctor? I am not sure I understand. I know nothing about science. You mean that Fred will become more forgetful and less dependable the older he gets?"

" I don't know that I should have ventured to put it so baldly, but that's about the fact. But, of course, circumstances may give him a bent in the other direction, and Fred may develop into such a careful old sobersides that his mother will be ashamed of him."

" Don't laugh at me, doctor; you make the whole thing too serious for a laughing matter." To which there was no answer, and there was silence in the room for the space of fully three minutes, while the two pondered.

" You say," in an imperious tone, " that 'a fault left to itself must strengthen.' What are we to do? His father and I wish, at any rate, to do our duty." Her ruffled maternal plumage notwithstanding, Mrs Bruce was in earnest, all her wits on the alert. "Come, I've scored one!" thought the doctor; and then, with respectful gravity, which should soothe any woman's *amour propre,*—

" You ask a question not quite easy to answer. But allow me, first, to try and make the principle plain to you : that done, the question of what to do settles itself. Fred never forgets his cricket or other pleasure engagements? No? And why not? Because his interest is excited ; therefore his whole attention is fixed on the fact to be remembered. Now, as a matter of fact, what you have regarded with full attention, it is next to impossible to forget. First, get Fred to fix his attention on the matter in hand, and you may be sure he won't forget it."

"That may be very true; but how can I make a message to Mrs Milner as interesting to him as the affairs of his club?"

"Ah! There you have me. Had you begun with Fred at a year old the thing would have settled itself. The *habit* would have been formed."

To the rescue, Mrs Bruce's woman's wit:—"I see; he must have the *habit* of paying attention, so that he will naturally take heed to what he is told, whether he cares about the matter or not."

"My dear madam, you've hit it; all except the word ' naturally.' At present Fred is in a delightful state of nature in this and a few other respects. But the educational use of *habit* is to correct nature. If parents would only see this fact, the world would become a huge reformatory, and the next generation, or, at any rate, the third, would dwell in the kingdom of heaven as a regular thing, and not by fits and starts, and here and there, which is the best that happens to us."

"I'm not sure I see what you mean; but," said this persistent woman, "to return to this habit of attention which is to reform my Fred—do try and tell me what to do. You gentlemen are so fond of going off into general principles, while we poor women can grasp no more than a practical hint or two to go on with. My boy would be cut up to know how little his fast friend, ' the doctor,' thinks of him!"

"' Poor women,' truly! and already you have thrown me with two staggering buffets. My theories have no practical outcome, and I think little of Fred,

who has been my choice chum ever since he left off
draperies! It remains for the vanquished to 'behave
pretty.' Pray, ma'am, what would you like me to say
next?"

"To 'habit,' doctor, to 'habit'; and don't talk nonsense while the precious time is going. We'll suppose
that Fred is just twelve months old to-day. Now,
if you please, tell me how I'm to make him *begin* to
pay attention. And, by the way, why in the world
didn't you talk to me about it when the child really
was young?"

"I don't remember that you asked me; and who
would be pert enough to think of schooling a young
mother? Not I, at any rate. Don't I know that
every mother of a first child is infallible, and knows
more about children than all the old doctors in creation? But, supposing you had asked me, I should
have said—Get him each day to occupy himself a
little longer with one plaything than he did the day
before. He plucks a daisy, gurgles over it with glee,
and then in an instant it drops from the nerveless
grasp. Then you take it up, and with the sweet
coaxings you mothers know how to employ, get him
to examine it, in his infant fashion, for a minute, two
minutes, three whole minutes at a time."

"I see; fix his thoughts on one thing at a time,
and for as long as you can, whether on what he sees
or what he hears. You think if you go on with that
sort of thing with a child from his infancy he gets
accustomed to pay attention?"

"Not a doubt of it; and you may rely on it that
what is called *ability*—a different thing from genius,
mind you, or even talent—ability is simply the power
of fixing the attention steadily on the matter in hand,

and success in life turns upon this cultivated power far more than on any natural faculty. Lay a case before a successful barrister, an able man of business, notice how he absorbs all you say; tell your tale as ill as you like, he keeps the thread, straightens the tangle, and by the time you have finished, has the whole matter spread out in order under his mind's eye. Now comes in talent, or genius, or what you will, to deal with the facts he has taken in. But attention is the attribute of the trained intellect, without which genius makes shots in the dark."

"But, don't you think attention itself is a natural faculty, or talent, or whatever we should call it?"

"Not a bit of it; it is entirely the result of training. A man may be born with some faculty or talent for figures, or drawing, or music, but attention is a different matter; it is simply the power of bending such powers as one has to the work in hand; it is a key to success within the reach of every one, but the skill to turn it comes of training. Circumstances may compel a man to train himself, but he does so at the cost of great effort, and the chances are ten to one against his making the effort. For the child, on the other hand, who has been trained by his parents to fix his thoughts, all is plain sailing. He will succeed, not a doubt of it."

"But I thought school-work, Latin and mathematics, and that sort of thing, should give this kind of intellectual training?"

"They should; but it's the merest chance whether the right spring is touched, and from what you say of Fred's school-work, I should say it has not been touched in his case. It is incredible how much solid learning a boy will contrive to let slip by him instead of into him! No; I'm afraid you must tackle the difficulty yourself. It would be a thousand pities to let a fine fellow like Fred run to waste."

"What can I do?"

"Well, we must begin where we are; Fred *can* attend, and therefore remember: and he remembers what interests him. Now, to return to your question. How are you to make a message to Mrs Milner as interesting to him as the affairs of his cricket club? There is no interest in the thing itself; you must put interest into it from without. There are a hundred ways of doing this: try one, and when that is used up, turn to another. Only, with a boy of Fred's age, you cannot form the habit of attention as you could with a child. You can only aid and abet; give the impulse; the training he must do for himself."

"Make it a little plainer, doctor; I have not yet reduced your remarks to the practical level of something I can do."

"No? Well, Fred must train himself, and you must feed him with motives. Run over with him what we have been saying about attention. Let him know how the land lies; that you cannot help him, but that if he wants to make a man of himself he must *make* himself attend and remember. Tell him it will be a stand-up fight, for this habit is contrary to nature. He will like that; it is boy nature to show fight, and the bigger and blacker you make the other side, the more will he like to pitch in. When I was a boy I had to fight this very battle for myself, and I'll tell you what I did. I stuck up a card every week, divided down the middle. One side was for 'Remembers'; the other side for 'Forgets.' I took myself to task every night—the very effort was a help—and put a stroke for every 'Remember' and 'Forget' of the day. *I* scored for every 'Remember,' and 't'other fellow' for every 'Forget.' You don't know how exciting it got. If by Thursday I had thirty-three 'Remembers' and he thirty-six 'Forgets,' it behoved me to look alive; it was not only that 'Forget' might win the game, which was up on Saturday night, but unless 'Remember' scored ten in advance, the game was 'drawn'—hardly a remove from lost."

"That's delightful! But I wish, doctor, you would speak to Fred yourself. A word from you would go a long way."

"I'll look out for a chance, but an outsider cannot do much; everything rests with the boy himself, and his parents."

VIII

POOR MRS JUMEAU!

" Now, young people, when I go out, let there be no
noise in the house; your mother is ill, so let her little
folk be thoughtful for her!"

" Oh, is mother sick again?" said little Ned with
falling countenance.

" Poor Neddie! he doesn't like mother to be ill.
We all have to be so quiet; and, then, there's
nowhere to be! It isn't like home when mother
isn't about."

" Mary is right," chimed in Charlie, the eldest of
the family; " if I were big enough, I should run away
and go to sea, mother's so often bad! But, father,
isn't it funny? Yesterday she was quite well, and
doing all sorts of horrid things, helping the maids to
clear out cupboards; and now, I daresay, she is too
ill to move or speak, and to-morrow, perhaps, she'll
be our jolly mother again, able to go shrimping with
us, or anything else."

" That's because your dear mother has no self,
Charlie, boy; no sooner does she feel a bit better than
she does more than she can for us all, and then she is
knocked up again. I wish we could teach her to be
selfish, for our sakes as well as hers, for to have her

with us is better than anything she can do for us; eh,
Charlie?"

"Indeed, yes! We'd take lots of care of her if
she'd let us. But her illness must be queer. You
know when we had scarlet fever, father? Well, for
weeks and weeks, after the fever was gone, I had no
more strength than a tom-tit; and you know I could
not go about and do things, however unselfish I was
(but I'm not, though). That's what is so queer. Do
you think Dr Prideau understands about mother?"

"Much better than you do, depend upon it, Charlie;
but I confess your mother's illness is puzzling to all
of us. There, children, off with you! I must write
a letter or two before I go out."

Mr Jumeau forgot to write his letters, and sat long,
with his head between his hands, pondering the nature
of his wife's ailments. What Charlie had put with a
boy's rude bluntness had already occurred to him
in a dim way. Mrs Jumeau's illness certainly did
not deprive her of bodily vigour; the attacks came
on suddenly, left her as suddenly, and left her apparently in perfect health and gay spirits. And this
was the more surprising because, while an "attack"
lasted, the extreme prostration, pallid countenance
and blue lips of the sufferer were painful to behold.
Besides, his wife was so absolutely truthful by nature,
so unselfish and devoted to her husband and family,
that it was as likely she should be guilty of flagrant
crime as that she should simulate illness. This sort
of thing had gone on for several years. Mr Jumeau
had spent his substance on many physicians, and
with little result. "No organic disease." "Overdone." "Give her rest, nourishing food, frequent
change of scene and thought; no excitement; Nature

will work the cure in time—*in time*, my good sir. We must be patient." This sort of thing he had heard again and again ; doctors did *not* differ, if that were any consolation.

He went up to have a last look at the sufferer. There she lay, stretched out with limbs composed, and a rigidity of muscle terribly like death. A tear fell on the cold cheek of his wife as Mr Jumeau kissed it, and he went out aching with a nameless dread, which, if put into words, would run—some day, and she will wake no more out of this death-like stillness.

And she? She felt the tear, heard the sigh, noted the dejected footfalls of her husband, and her weak pulse stirred with a movement of—was it joy? But the "attack" was not over; for hours she lay there rigid, speechless, with closed eyes, taking no notice of the gentle opening of the door now and then when one or another came to see how she was. Were not her family afraid to leave her alone? No ; we get used to anything, and the Jumeaus, servants and children, were well used to these "attacks" in the mistress of the house. Dr Prideau came, sent by her husband, and used even violent measures to restore her, but to no effect ; she was aware of these efforts, but was not aware that she resisted them effectually.

Business engagements were pressing, and it was late before Mr Jumeau, anxious as he was, was able to return to his wife. It was one of those lovely warm evenings we sometimes get late in May, when even London windows are opened to let in the breath of the spring. Nearly at the end of the street he heard familiar strains from *Parsifal,* played with the vigour Wagner demands. His wife? It could be

no one else. As he drew nearer, her exquisite touch
was unmistakable. The attack was over, then?
Strange to say, his delight was not unmixed. What
were these mysterious attacks, and how were they
brought on?

The evening was delightful. Mrs Jumeau was in
the gayest spirits: full of tenderness towards her
husband, of motherly thought for her children, now
fast asleep; ready to talk brightly on any subject
except the attack of the morning; any allusion to
this she would laugh off as a matter of too little consequence to be dwelt upon. The next morning she
was down bright and early, having made up her
mind to a *giro* with the children. They did not
go a-shrimping, according to Charlie's forecast, but
Kew was decided upon as "just the thing," and a
long day in the gardens failed to tire mother or
children.

"I must get to the bottom of this," thought Mr
Jumeau.

.   .   .   .   .   .

"Your question is embarrassing; if I say, Mrs
Jumeau is suffering from *hysteria*, you will most likely
get a wrong notion and discredit my words."

Mr Jumeau's countenance darkened. "I should
still be inclined to trust the evidence of my senses,
and believe that my wife is unfeignedly ill."

"Exactly as I expected: simulated ailments and
hysteria are hopelessly confounded; but no wonder;
hysteria is a misnomer, used in the vaguest way, not
even confined to women. Why, I knew a man, a
cleryman in the North, who suffered from 'clergyman's sore throat'; he was a popular evangelical
preacher, and there was no end to the sympathy his

case evoked; he couldn't preach, so his devoted
congregation sent him, now to the South of France,
now to Algiers, now to Madeira. After each delightful sojourn he returned, looking plump and well, but
unable to raise his voice above a hardly audible
whisper. This went on for three years or so. Then
his Bishop interfered; he must provide a curate in
permanent charge, with nearly the full emoluments
of the living. The following Sunday he preached,
nor did he again lose his voice. And this was an
earnest and honest man, who would rather any day
be at his work than wandering idly about the world.
Plainly, too, in the etymological sense of the word,
his complaint was not hysteria. But this is not an exceptional case: keep any man in his dressing-gown
for a week or two—a bad cold, say—and he will lay
himself out to be pitied and petted, will have half the
ailments under the sun, and be at death's door with
each. And this is your active man; a man of seden-
tary habits, notwithstanding his stronger frame, is
nearly as open as a woman to the advances of this
stealthy foe. Why, for what matter, I've seen it in a
dog! Did you never see a dog limp pathetically on
his three legs that he might be made much of for his
lameness, until his master's whistle calls him off at
a canter on all fours?"

"I get no nearer; what have these illustrations to
do with my wife?"

"Wait a bit, and I'll try to show you. The throat
would seem to be a common seat of the affection. I
knew a lady—nice woman she was, too—who went
about for years speaking in a painful whisper, whilst
everybody said, 'Poor Mrs Marjoribanks!' But one
evening she managed to set her bed-curtains alight,

and she rushed to the door, screaming, 'Ann! Ann! the house is on fire! Come at once!' The dear woman believed ever after, that 'something burst' in her throat, and described the sensation minutely; her friends believed, and her doctor did not contradict. By the way, no remedy has proved more often effectual than a house on fire, only you will see the difficulties. I knew of a case, however, where the 'house-afire' prescription was applied with great effect. It was in a London hospital for ladies; a most baffling case; patient had been for months unable to move a limb—was lifted in and out of bed like a log, fed as you would pour into a bottle. A clever young house-surgeon laid a plot with the nurses. In the middle of the night her room was filled with fumes, lurid light, etc. She tried to cry out, but the smoke was suffocating; she jumped out of bed and made for the door—more choking smoke—threw up the sash—fireman, rope-ladder—she scrambled down, and was safe. The whole was a hoax, but it cured her, and the nature of the cure was mercifully kept secret. Another example: A friend of mine determined to put a young woman under 'massage' in her own home; he got a trained operator, forbade any of her family to see her, and waited for results. The girl did not mend; 'Very odd! some reason for this,' he thought; and it came out that every night the mother had crept in to wish her child good-night; the tender visits were put a stop to, and the girl recovered."

"Your examples are interesting enough, but I fail to see how they bear; in each case, you have a person of weak or disordered intellect simulating a disease with no rational object in view. Now the beggars

who know how to manufacture sores on their persons
have the advantage—they do it for gain."

"I have told my tale badly; these were not persons
of weak or disordered intellect; some of them very
much otherwise; neither did they consciously simulate disease; not one believed it possible to make
the effort he or she was surprised into. The whole
question belongs to the mysterious borderland of
physical and psychological science—not pathological,
observe; the subject of disease and its treatment is
hardly for the lay mind."

"I am trying to understand."

"It is worth your while; if every man took the
pains to understand the little that is yet to be known
on this interesting subject he might secure his own
household, at any rate, from much misery and waste
of vital power; and not only his household, but perhaps
himself—for, as I have tried to show, this that is called
'hysteria' is not necessarily an affair of sex."

"Go on; I am not yet within appreciable distance
of anything bearing on my wife's case."

"Ah, the thing is a million-headed monster! hardly
to be recognised by the same features in any two
cases. To get at the *rationale* of it, we must take
up human nature by the roots. We talk glibly in
these days of what we get from our forefathers,
what comes to us through our environment, and consider that in these two we have the sum of human
nature. Not a bit of it; we have only accounted for
some peculiarities in the individual; independently of
these, we come equipped with stock for the business
of life of which too little account is taken. The
subject is wide, so I shall confine myself to an item
or two.

"We all come into the world—since we are beings of imperfect nature—subject to the uneasy stirrings of some few primary desires. Thus, the gutter child and the infant prince are alike open to the workings of the desire for esteem, the desire for society, for power, etc. One child has this, and another that, desire more active and uneasy. Women, through the very modesty and dependence of their nature, are greatly moved by the desire for esteem. They must be thought of, made much of, at any price. A man desires esteem, and he has meetings in the market-place, the chief-room at the feast; the *pétroleuse*, the city outcast, must have notoriety—the esteem of the bad—at any price, and we have a city in flames, and Whitechapel murders. Each falls back on his experience and considers what will bring him that esteem, a gnawing craving after which is one of his earliest immaterial cognitions. But the good woman has comparatively few outlets. The esteem that comes to her is all within the sphere of her affections. Esteem she must have; it is a necessity of her nature:

"'*Praise*, blame, love, kisses, tears, and smiles,'

are truly to her, 'human nature's daily food.'

"Now, experience comes to her aid. When she is ill, she is the centre of attraction, the object of attention, to all who are dear to her; she will be ill."

"You contradict yourself, man! don't you see? You are painting, not a good woman, but one who will premeditate and act a lie!"

"Not so fast! I am painting a good woman. Here comes in a condition which hardly any one takes into account. Mrs Jumeau will lie with stiffened limbs

and blue pale face for hours at a time. Is she simulating illness? you might as well say that a man
could simulate a gunshot wound. But the thing
people forget is, the intimate relation and co-operation
of body and mind; that the body lends itself *involuntarily* to carry out the conceptions of the thinking
brain. Mrs Jumeau does not *think* herself into pallor,
but every infinitesimal nerve fibre, which entwines
each equally infinitesimal capillary which brings colour
to the cheek, is intimately connected with the thinking brain, in obedience to whose mandates it relaxes
or contracts. Its relaxation brings colour and vigour
with the free flow of the blood; its contraction, pallor
and stagnation; and the feeling as well as the look
of being sealed in a death-like trance. The whole
mystery depends on this co-operation of thought and
substance of which few women are aware. The diag-
nosis is simply this, the sufferer has the craving for
outward tokens of the esteem which is essential to her
nature; she recalls how such tokens accompany her
seasons of illness, the sympathetic body perceives the
situation, and—she is ill; by and by, the tokens of
esteem cease to come with the attacks of illness, but
the habit has been set up, and she goes on having
'attacks' which bring real suffering to herself, and of
the slightest agency in which she is utterly unconscious."

Conviction slowly forced itself on Mr Jumeau; now
that his wife was shown entirely blameless, he could
concede the rest. More, he began to suspect something rotten in the State of Denmark, or women like
his wife would never have been compelled to make so
abnormal a vent for a craving proper to human
nature.

"I begin to see; what must I do?"

"In Mrs Jumeau's case, I may venture to recommend a course which would not answer with one in a thousand. Tell her all I have told you. Make her mistress of the situation.—I need not say, save her as much as you can from the distress of self-contempt. Trust her, she will come to the rescue, and devise means to save herself; and, all the time, she will want help from you, wise as well as tender. For the rest, those who have in less measure—

"'The reason firm, the temperate will'—

'massage,' and other devices for annulling the extraordinary physical sensibility to mental conditions, and, at the same time, excluding the patient from the possibility of the affectionate notice she craves, may do a great deal. But this mischief which, in one shape or other, blights the lives of too many of our best and most highly organised women, is one more instance of how lives are ruined by an education which is not only imperfect, but proceeds on wrong lines."

"How could education help in this?"

"Why, let them know the facts, possess them of even so slight an outline as we have had before us to-night, and the best women will take measures for self-preservation. Put them on their guard, that is all. It is not enough to give them accomplishments and all sorts of higher learning; these gratify the desire of esteem only in a very temporary way. But something more than a danger-signal is wanted. The woman, as well as the man, must have her share of the world's work, whose reward is the world's esteem. She must, even the cherished wife and mother of a family, be in touch with the world's needs, and must minister of the gifts she has; and that, because it is no dream that we are all brethren, and must therefore suffer from any seclusion from the *common* life."

    .   .   .   .   .   .

Mrs Jumeau's life was not "spoilt." It turned out as the doctor predicted; for days after his revelations she was ashamed to look her husband in the face; but then, she called up her forces, fought her own fight and came off victorious.

IX

"A HAPPY CHRISTMAS TO YOU!"

THE Christmas holidays! Boys and girls at school are counting off the days till the home-coming. Young men and maidens who have put away childish things do not reckon with date-stones, but consult their Bradshaws. The little ones at home are storing up surprises. The father says genially, "We shall soon have our young folk at home again." The mother? Nobody, not the youngest of the schoolgirls, is so glad as she. She thinks of setting out for church on Christmas Day with, let us hope, the whole of her scattered flock about her. Already she pictures to herself how each has altered and grown, and yet how every one is just as of old. She knows how Lucy will return prettier and more lovable than ever; Willie, more amusing; Harry, kinder; and, "how the elders will rejoice in baby May!"

And yet, there is a shade of anxiety in the mother's face as she plans for the holidays. The brunt of domestic difficulties falls, necessarily, upon her. It is not quite easy to arrange a household for a sudden incursion of new inmates whose stay is not measured by days. Servants must be considered, and may be tiresome. Amusements, interests, must be thought of, and then—— Does the mother stop short and avoid putting into shape the "and then," which belongs to the holiday weeks after Christmas Day is over?

"Let us have a happy Christmas, any way," she says, "we must leave the rest."

What is it? Pretty Lucy's face clouds into sullenness. Kind Harry is quick to take offence, and his outbursts spoil people's comfort. Willie, with all his nonsense, has fits of positive moroseness. Tom argues —is always in the right. Alice—is the child always quite straightforward? There is reason enough for the strain of anxiety that mingles with the mother's joy. It is not easy to keep eight or nine young people at their best for weeks together without their usual employments, when you consider that, wanting their elders' modicum of self-control, they may have their father's failings and their mother's failings, and ugly traits besides hardly to be accounted for. Is it a counsel of perfection that mothers should have "Quiet Days" of rest for body and mind, and for such spiritual refreshment as may be, to prepare them for the exhausting (however delightful) strain of the holidays?

Much arrears of work must fall to the heads of the house in the young folk's holidays. They will want to estimate, as they get opportunity, the new thought that is leavening their children's minds; to modify, however imperceptibly, the opinions the young people are forming. They must keep a clear line of demarcation between duties and pastimes, even in the holidays; and they must resume the work of character-training, relinquished to some extent while the children are away at school. But, after all, the holiday

problem is much easier than it looks, as many a
light-hearted mother knows.

There is a way of it, a certain " Open Sesame," which
mothers know, or, if they do not, all the worse for the
happiness of Holiday House. Occupation? Many
interests? Occupation, of course; we know what
befalls idle hands; but "interests" are only successful
in conjunction with the password; without it, the
more excitingly interesting the interests the more apt
are they to disturb the domestic atmosphere and make
one, sulky, and another, domineering, and a third,
selfish, and each, " naughty " in that particular way in
which " 'tis his nature to."

Every mother knows the secret, but some may have
forgotten the magic of it. Paradoxical as the statement may sound, there is no one thing of which it is
harder to convince young people than that their
parents love them. They do not talk about the matter,
but supposing they did, this would be the avowal of
nine children out of ten:

"Oh, of course, mother loves me in a way, but not
as she loves X."

" How ' in a way '? "

"You know what I mean. She *is* mother, so of
course she cares about things for me and all that."

" But how does she love X.? "

"Oh, I can't explain; she's fond of her, likes to
look at her, and touch her, and—now don't go and
think I'm saying things about mother. She's quite
fair and treats us all *just* alike; but who could help
liking X. best? I'm so horrid! Nobody cares for
me."

Put most of the children (including X.) of good
and loving parents into the Palace of Truth, children

of all ages, from six, say, to twenty, and this is the sort of thing you would get. Boys would, as a rule, credit "mother," and girls, "father," with the more love; but that is only by comparison; the one parent is only "nicer" than the other. As for appropriating or recognising the fulness of love lavished on them, they simply do not do it.

And why? Our little friend has told us; mother and father are quite fair, there is no fault to be found in them, but "I'm so horrid, nobody cares for me." There you have the secret of "naughtiness." There is nothing more pathetic than the sort of dual life of which the young are dimly conscious. On the one hand, there are premonitions of full and perfect being, the budding of those wings of which their thoughts are full, and for which their strong sense of justice demands credit. Mother and father ought to know how great and good and beautiful they are in possibility, in prospective. They must have the comprehension, appreciation, which, if they cannot get in the drawing-room, they will seek in the kitchen or the stable-yard. Alnaschar visions? If so, it is his parents, not young Alnaschar, who kick over the basket of eggs.

If the young folk are pugnacious about their "rights," and are over-ready with their "It's not fair!" "It's a shame!" it is because they reckon their claims by the great possible self, while, alas! they measure what they get by the actual self, of which they think small things. There is no word for it but "horrid"; bring them to book, and the scornful, or vain, or bumptious young persons we may know are alike in this—every one of them is "horrid" in his or her own eyes.

Now, if you know yourself to be horrid, you know that, of course, people do not love you; how can they? They are kind to you and all that, but that is because it's their business, or their nature, or their duty to be kind. It has really nothing to do with you personally. What you want is someone who will find *you* out, and be kind to you, and love you just for your own sake and nothing else So do we reason when we are young. It is the old story. The good that I would I do not, but the evil that I would not, that I do. Only we feel things more acutely when we are young, and take sides alternately with ourselves and against ourselves; small is the wonder that their elders find young people " difficult"; that is just what they find themselves.

"Fudge!" says the reader, who satisfies himself with the surface, and recalls the fun and frolic and gaiety of heart, the laughter and nonsense and bright looks of scores of young people he knows: of course they are gay, *because* they are young; but we should have many books about the sadness of youth if people in their "teens" might have the making of them. Glad and sad are not a whole octave apart.

How soon does this trouble of youth begin? That very delightful person, the Baby, is quite exempt. So, too, are the three, four, and five-year-old darlings of the nursery. They gather on your knee, and take possession of you, and make no doubt at all of your love or their deserts. But a child cannot always get out of the nursery before this doubt with two faces is upon him. I know a boy of four, a healthy intelligent child, full of glee and frolic and sense, who yet has many sad moments because one and another do not love him; and other very joyful, grateful moments because some little gift or attention assures him of love. His mother, with the delicate tact mothers have, perceives that the child needs to be continually reinstated in his own esteem. She calls him her "only boy," treats him half as her little lover, and so evens him with the two bright little sisters whom, somehow, and without any telling, poor Georgy feels to be sweeter in temper and more lovable than he. An exceedingly instructive little memorial of a child who died young came under my notice some time ago. His parents kept their children always in an atmosphere of love and gladness; and it was curious to notice that this boy, a merry, bright little fellow, was quite incapable of realising his parents' love. That they should love his sister was natural, but how *could* they love him?

The little ones in the nursery revel in love, but how is it with even the nursery elders? Are they not soon taught to give place to the little ones and look for small show of affection, because they are "big boys" and "big girls"? The rather sad aloofness and self-containedness of these little folk in some families is worth thinking about. Even the nursery is a microcosm, suffering from the world's ailment,— love-hunger, a sickness which drives little children and grown-up people into naughty thoughts and wicked ways.

I knew a girl whose parents devoted themselves entirely to training her; they surrounded her with care and sufficient tenderness; they did not make much of her openly, because they held old-fashioned notions about not fostering a child's self-importance and vanity. They were so successful in suppress-

ing the girl's self-esteem that it never occurred to her
that all their cares meant love until she was woman-
grown and could discern character, and, alas! had
her parents no more to give them back love for love.
The girl herself must have been unloving? In one
sense, all young beings are unloving; in another, they
are as vessels filled, brimming over, with love seeking
an outlet. This girl would watch her mother about
a room, walk behind her in the streets—adoringly.
Such intense worship of their parents is more common
in children than we imagine. A boy of five years
was asked what he thought the most beautiful thing
in the world. "Velvet," he replied, with dreamy
eyes, evidently thinking of his mother in a velvet
gown. His parents are the greatest and wisest, the
most powerful, and the best people within the narrow
range of the child's world. They are royal personages
—his kings and queens. Is it any wonder he
worships, even while he rebels?

But is it not more common, nowadays, for children
to caress and patronise their parents, and make all
too sure of their love? It may be; but only where
parents have lost that indescribable attribute—
dignity? authority?—which is their title to their
children's love and worship; and the affection which
is lavished too creaturely-wise on children fails to
meet the craving of their nature. What is it they
want, those young things so gaily happy with doll or
bat or racquet? They want to be reinstated; they
labour, some poor children almost from infancy, under
a sad sense of demerit. They find themselves so little
loveworthy, that no sign short of absolute telling
with lip and eye and touch will convince them they
are beloved.

But if one whom they trust and honour, one who *knows*, will, seeing how faulty they are, yet love them, regarding the hateful faults as alien things to be got rid of, and holding them, in spite of the faults, in close measureless love and confidence, why, then, the young lives expand like flowers in sunny weather; and, where parents know this secret of loving, there are no morose boys nor sullen girls.

Actions do not speak louder than words to a young heart; he must feel it in your touch, see it in your eye, hear it in your tones, or you will never convince child or boy that you love him, though you labour day and night for his good and his pleasure. Perhaps this is the special lesson of Christmas-tide for parents. The Son came—for what else we need not inquire now—to reinstate men by *compelling* them to believe that they—the poorest shrinking and ashamèd souls of them—that they live enfolded in infinite personal love, desiring with desire the response of love for love. And who, like the parent, can help forward this "wonderful redemption"? The boy who knows that his father and his mother love him with measureless patience in his faults, and love him out of them, is not slow to perceive, receive, and understand the dealings of the higher Love.

But why should good parents, more than the rest of us, be expected to exhibit so divine a love? Perhaps because they are better than most of us; anyway, that appears to be their vocation. And that it is possible to fulfil even so high a calling we all know, because we know good mothers and good fathers.

"Parents, love your children," is, probably, an unnecessary counsel to any who read this page; at any rate, it is a presuming one.   But let me say to reserved, undemonstrative parents who follow the example of righteous Abraham and *rule* their households,—Rule none the less, but let your children feel and see and be quite sure that you love them.

We do not suggest endearments in public, which the young folk cannot always abide.   But, dear mother, take your big schoolgirl in your arms just once in the holidays, and let her have a good talk, all to your two selves; it will be to her like a meal to a hungry man.   For the youths and maidens— remember, they would sell their souls for love; they do it too, and that is the reason of many of the ruined lives we sigh over.   Who will break down the partition between supply and demand in many a home where there are hungry hearts on either side of the wall?

Part II

Parents in Council

I

WHAT A SALVAGE!

" Now, let us address ourselves to the serious business
of the evening.   Here we are:

> "'Six precious (pairs), and all agog,
>   To dash through thick and thin!'

Imprimis—our desire is for reform!   Not reform by
Act of Parliament, if you please; but, will the world
believe?—we veritably desire to *be reformed!*   And
that, as a vicarious effort for the coming race.   Why,
to have conceived the notion entitles us to sit by for
our term of years and see how the others do it!"

"Don't be absurd, Ned, as if it were all a joke!
We're dreadfully in earnest, and can't bear to have
the time wasted.   A pretty President you are."

"Why, my dear, that's the joke; how can a man
preside over a few friends who have done him the
honour to dine at his table?"

"Mrs Clough is quite right.   It's 'Up boys, and at
it!' we want to be; so, my dear fellow, don't let any
graceful scruples on your part hinder work."

"Then, Henderson, as the most rabid of us all, you
must begin."

"I do not know that what I have to say should

come first in order; but to save time I'll begin. What I complain of, is, the crass ignorance of us—of myself, I mean. You know what a magnificent spectacle the heavens have offered these last few frosty nights. Well, one of our youngsters has, I think, some turn for astronomy. 'Look, father, what a great star! It's big enough to make the night light without the moon. It isn't always there; what's its name, and where does it go?' The boy was in the receptive 'How I wonder what you are' mood; anything and everything I could have told him would have been his—a possession for life.

"'That's not a star, it's a planet, Tom,' with a little twaddle about how planets are like our earth, more or less, was all I had for his hungry wonder. As for how one planet differs from another in glory, his sifting questions got nothing out of me; what nothing has, can nothing give. Again, he has, all of his own wit, singled out groups of stars and, like Hugh Miller, wasn't it?—pricked them into paper with a pin. 'Have they names? What is this, and this?' 'Those three stars are the belt of Orion'—the sum of my acquaintance with the constellations, if you will believe it! He bombarded me with questions all to the point. I tried bits of book knowledge which he did not want. It was a 'bowing' acquaintance, if no more, with the glorious objects before him that the child coveted, and he cornered me till his mother interfered with, 'That will do, Tom: don't tease father with your questions.' A trifling incident, perhaps, but do you know I didn't sleep a wink that night, or rather, I did sleep, and dreamt, and woke for good. I dreamt the child was crying for hunger and I had not a crust to give him. You know how vivid some dreams are. The moral flashed on me; the child had been crying to me with the hunger of the mind; he had asked for bread and got a stone. A thing like that stirs you. From that moment I had a new conception of a parent's vocation and of my unfitness for it. I determined that night to find some way to help ourselves and the thousands of parents in the same ignorant case."

"Well, but, Henderson, you don't mean to say that every parent should be an astronomer? Why, how can a man with other work tackle the study of a lifetime?"

"No, but I do think our veneration for science frightens us off open ground. Huxley somewhere draws a line between science and what he calls 'common information,' and this I take to mean an acquaintance with the facts about us, whether of Nature or of society. It's a shameful thing to be unable to answer such questions as Tom's. Every one should know something about such facts of Nature as a child is likely to come across. But how to get at this knowledge! Books? Well, I don't say but you may get to know *about* most things from books, but as for knowing the thing itself, let me be introduced by him that knew it before me!"

"I see what you mean; we want the help of the naturalist, an enthusiast who will not only teach but fire us with the desire to know."

"But don't you find, Morris, that even your enthusiast, if he's a man of science, is slow to recognise the neutral ground of common information?"

"That may be; but, as for getting what we want— pooh! it's a question of demand and supply. If you don't mind my talking about ourselves I should like just to tell you what we did last summer. Perhaps you may know that I dabble a little in geology—only dabble—but every tyro must have noticed how the features of a landscape depend on its geological formation, and not only the look of the landscape, but the occupations of the people. Well, it occurred to me that if, instead of the hideous 'resources'—save the word!—of a watering-place, what if we were to study the 'scape' of a single formation? The children would have that, at any rate, in visible presentation, and would hold a key to much besides.

"My wife and I love the South Downs, perhaps for auld sake's sake, so we put up at a farmhouse in one of the lovely 'Lavants' near Goodwood. Chalk and a blackboard were inseparably associated; and a *hill* of chalk was as surprising to the children as if all the trees were bread and cheese. Here was *wonder* to start with, wonder and desire to know. Truly, a man hath joy in the answer of his mouth! The delight, the deliciousness, of pouring out answers to their eager questions! and the illimitable receptivity of the children! This was the sort of thing—after scrawling on a flint with a fragment of chalk :—

"'What is that white line on the flint, Bob?'— 'Chalk, father,' with surprise at my dulness; and then the unfolding of the tale of wonder—thousands of lovely, infinitely small shells in that scrawl of chalk; each had, ages and ages ago, its little inmate—and so on. Wide eyes and open mouths, until sceptical Dick —'Well, but, father, how did they get here? How could they crawl or swim to the dry land when they were dead?' More wonders, and a snub for that small boy. 'Why, this hillside we are sitting on is a bit of that old sea-bottom!' And still the marvel grew, until, trust me, there is not a feature of the chalk that is not written down in *le journal intime* of each child's soul. They know the soft roll of the hills, the smooth dip of the valleys, the delights of travellers' joy, queer old yews, and black-berrying in the sudden 'bottoms' of the chalk. The endless singing of the lark—nothing but larks—the trailing of cloud-shadows over the hills, the blue skies of Sussex, blue as those of Naples—these things are theirs to have and to hold, and are all associated with the chalk; they have the sense of the earth-mother, of the connection of things, which makes for poetry.

"Then their mother has rather a happy way of getting pictures printed on the 'sensitive plate' of each. She hits on a view, of narrow range generally, and makes the children look at it well and then describe it with closed eyes. One never-to-be-forgotten view was seized in this way. 'First grass, the hill-slopes below us, with sheep feeding about: and then a great field of red poppies—there's corn, but we can't see it; then fields and fields of corn, quite yellow and ripe, reaching out a long way; next, the sea, very blue, and three rather little boats with white sails; a lark a long way up in the sky singing as loud as a band of music; and *such* a shining sun!' No doubt our little maid will have all that to her dying day; and isn't it a picture worth having?"

"Mr Morris's hint admits of endless expansion; why, you could cover the surface formations of England in the course of the summer holidays of a boy's school-life, and thus give him a key to the landscape, fauna, and flora of much of the earth's surface. It's admirable."

"What a salvage! The long holidays, which are

apt to hang on hand, would be more fully and use-
fully employed than schooldays, and in ways full of
out-of-door delights. I see how it would work.
Think of the dales of Yorkshire, where the vivid
green of the mountain limestone forms a distinct
line of junction with the dim tints of the heather on
the millstone grit of the moors, of the innumerable
rocky nests where the ferns of the limestone—hart's-
tongue, oak fern, beech fern, and the rest—grow
delicately green and perfect as if conserved under
glass. Think of the endless ferns and mosses and
the picturesque outlines of the slate, both in the Lake
Country and in Wales. What collections the children
might form, always having the geological formation
of the district as the leading idea."

"You are getting excited, Mrs Tremlow. For
my part, I cannot rise to the occasion. It is dull
to have 'delicious!' 'delightful!' 'lovely!' hailing
about one's ears, and to be out of it. Pray, do not
turn me out for the admission, but my own feeling
is strongly against this sort of dabbling in science.
In this bird's-eye view of geology, for instance, why
in the world did you begin with the chalk? At least
you might have started with, say, Cornwall."

"That is just one of the points where the line is
to be drawn; you specialists do one thing thoroughly
—begin at the beginning, if a beginning there be,
and go on to the end, if life is long enough. Now,
we contend that the specialist's work should be laid
on a wide basis of common information, which differs
from science in this amongst other things—you take
it as it occurs. A fact comes under your notice;
you want to know why it is, and what it is; but its
relations to other facts must settle themselves as

time goes on, and the other facts turn up. For instance, a child of mine should know the 'blackcap' by its rich note and black upstanding headgear, and take his chance of ever knowing even the name of the family to which his friend belongs."

"And surely, Mr Morris, you would teach history in the same way; while you are doing a county, or a 'formation'—isn't it?—you get fine opportunities for making history a real thing. For instance, supposing you are doing the—what is it?—of Dorsetshire; you come across Corfe Castle standing in a dip of the hills, like the trough between two waves, and how real you can make the story of the bleeding prince dragged over the downs at the heels of his horse."

"Yes, and speaking of the downs, do you happen to know, Mrs Tremlow, the glorious downs behind Lewes, and the Abbey and the Castle below, all concerned in the story of the great battle; and the ridge of Mount Harry across which De Montfort and his men marched while the royal party were holding orgies in the Abbey, and where, in the grey of the early morning, each man vowed his life to the cause of liberty, face downwards to the cool grass, and arms outstretched in the form of a cross? Once you have made a study on the spot of one of those historic sites, why, the place and the scene is a part of you. You couldn't forget it if you would."

"That is interesting, and it touches on a matter which I find very suggestive; have you noticed that in certain districts you come across, not only the spots associated with critical events, but monuments of the leading idea of centuries? Such as these are the ruined abbeys which still dominate every lovely dale in Yorkshire; the twelfth-century churches, four or five of which—in certain English counties—you come across in the course of a single day's tramp, and of which there is hardly a secluded out-of-the-way nook in some counties that has not its example to show; such, again, are the endless castles on the Welsh border, the Roman camps on the downs, each bearing witness to the dominant thought, during a long period, whether of war, or, of a time when men had some leisure from fighting."

"And not only so. Think of how the better half of English literature has a local colouring; think of the thousand spots round which there lingers an aroma of poetry and of character which seems to get into your brain somehow, and leave there an image of the man, *feeling* of his work, which you cannot arrive at elsewhere. The Quantocks, Grasmere, Haworth Moors, the Selborne 'Hanger,' the Lincolnshire levels—it is needless to multiply examples of spots where you may see the raw material of poetry, and compare it with the finished work."

"All this is an inspiring glimpse of the possible; but surely, gentlemen, you do not suppose that a family party, the children, say, from fifteen downwards, can get in touch with such wide interests in the course of a six weeks' holiday? I doubt if, even amongst ourselves, any but you, Mr Meredith, and Mr Clough, have this sort of grasp of historical and personal associations."

"We must leave that an open question, Mrs Henderson; but what I do contend for is, that children have illimitable capacity for all knowledge which reaches them in some sort through the vehicle of the senses: what they *see* and delight in you may pin endless facts, innumerable associations, upon, and children have capacity for them all : nor will they ever treat you to lack-lustre eye and vacant countenance. Believe me ''tis their nature to' hunger after know-ledge as a labouring man hungers for his dinner ; only, the *thing* must come in the first, the words which interpret it, in the second place."

"You mean that everything they see is to lead to a sort of object lesson ? "

"Indeed I do not ! Object lesson ! talkee, talkee, about a miserable cut-and-dried scrap, hardly to be recognised by one who knows the thing. I should not wonder if it were better for a child to go without information than to get it in this unnatural way. No, let him see the thing big and living before him, behaving according to its wont. Specimens are of infinite use to the scientist whose business it is to generalise, but are misleading to the child who has yet to learn his individuals. I don't doubt for a minute that an intelligent family out for a holiday might well cover all the ground we have sketched out, and more ; but who in the world is to teach them ? A child's third question about the fowls of the air or the flowers of the field would probably floor most of us."

"That's coming to the point. I wondered if we were meant to touch our subject again to-night. To skim over all creation in an easy, airy way is exciting, but, from an educational standpoint, it is comic to the father with a young swarm at home who care for none of these things."

"Of course they don't, Withers, if they have never been put in the way of it ; but try 'em, that's all. Now, listen to my idea ; I shall be too glad if any one strikes out a better, but we must come to a point, and pull up the next who wanders off on his own hobby. Each of us wishes to cover all, or more, or some of the ground suggested in our desultory talk. Difficulty, we can't teach because we don't know. We are in a corner with but one way out. *We must learn* what we should teach. How? Well, let us form ourselves into a college, or club, or what you like. Now, it's simply the A B C of many things we wish to learn. Once organised, we shall see our way to the next step. Even in the small party here to-night, some know something of geology, some are at home in the byways of history; what we cannot evolve from our midst we must get from outside, and either amateur recruits or professional folk must be pressed into service; recruits would be much the best, for they would learn as well as teach. Then, when we are organised, we may consider whether our desire is to exhaust a single district in the way suggested, or to follow some other plan. Only, please, if it be a district, let it be a wide one, so that our intercourse be confined to 'speaking' in passing, like ships at sea. Don't, for pity's sake, let it be a social thing, with tennis, talk, and tea !"

"Suppose we do enrol ourselves, how frequent do you think should be our meetings?"

"We'll leave that question; in the meantime, those in favour of Mr Morris's motion that we form ourselves into a society for the consideration of matters affecting the education of children—the parents' part of the work, that is—will signify the same in the usual way."

"Carried unanimously !"[1]

[1] Ancient history now; a forecast fulfilled in the formation of the Parents' National Educational Union.

II

WHERE SHALL WE GO THIS YEAR?

"Dost thou like fair lands?"

"Why should I not like fair lands? How? Is not that the fairest part of God's creation?"—*King Alfred* (*from his translation of Boetius*).

WHERE shall we go this year? is—the question of the day. We want to make the most of that delightful holiday month when we need do nothing but "enjoy ourselves." But, alas,

> "Pleasure is spread through the earth
> In stray gifts, to be claimed by whoever shall find";

and we are not always lucky. Pleasure may be spread in stray gifts, but the gifts lie in likely places, and the quest must be undertaken with circumspection. We crave "fair lands"; town dwellers, especially, sicken for "the green"; the sea, perhaps; but, any way, grass and trees. We look out for pure air and pretty country, and having secured these, we settle down and say, Let us be therewith content. For the first few days, all is delightful; we explore, we botanise, we find many interests; then, boredom sets in; and we secretly tick off the days that separate us from the labours and pleasures of our everyday lives.

Here is the whole secret of a successful holiday: the mind must be actively, unceasingly, and involuntarily engaged with fresh and ever-changing interests; and this is why, to take a holiday is by no means the easy thing it looks. The little child, indeed, is made happy day after day with spade and bucket, but that is because his unjaded imagination works without spur, and he is able to fill his sunny hours with glad interest, to make some ever new—

> "Little plan or chart,
> Some fragment of his dream of human life,
> Shaped by himself with newly-learned art."

But the child who has outgrown spade and bucket, and who is a little fagged with school work, needs, like his elders, engrossing interests which shall compel him to think new thoughts. Fresh air for the lungs, fresh scenes for the eye, are fully healing and helpful only when the mind, too, is taken into account, and the jaded brain is spoon-fed, as it were, with new ideas. This is why foreign travel is delightful; a delight which is, alas, commonly out of the question for the parents of growing children, much more so for the children themselves; and the question is, can we stay at home, and, with the minimum of expense, and the maximum of convenience, get all the stimulus of foreign travel?

Indeed we can; disclaimers should come from those, only, who have tried the plan; I *have* tried it, and know it to be easy, economical, and infinitely pleasant. Treat an English county as you would a foreign country; not a district, observe, but a county: we seldom realise how individual each county is, in its landscape and history, its weather and ways;—who, for example would confound the blue skies of Sussex with the blue skies of Cambridgeshire? "There is a delicateness in the air" of each, but it is not the same delicateness.   But, to be practical: we choose our county—almost any one will do, and the choice may well be influenced by the cost of taking a family far afield.   We get up, roughly, in advance, its history, geology, scenery, flora; and pleasant family evenings are spent over *Murray* and a map: but once on our travels, nothing will satisfy us but the literature indigenous to the spot, the lives of the people who have made their dwelling-place illustrious, the books these may have written, the scenes of English history here played out.   Having chosen our county, we fix upon some half-dozen centres, country towns, from which we can easily cover the interests of the whole county.   Lodgings for a family can be obtained easily in towns where visitors are few and far between; we want but little luggage, for only the simplest dread-nought garments are suitable for the sort of life we have in view.   It is easy to get from centre to centre; in an hour or two from leaving the last, the children are rejoicing in the investigation of new quarters.   Each centre will probably afford a dozen walks and excursions of extreme interest, while the cost of the little transits is more than saved, because the rates of lodging and living in unfrequented country towns are far less than in the ordinary watering-places.

But readers are not convinced; they still think it better to settle down quietly "in a place you know," than to wander like tramps about the country, where, "What is there to see after all?"   A single example is worth a peck of precepts, so let us glance at the possibilities of an English county, not a show county, either; but to know Hampshire is a liberal education in itself, and the recollection of its pleasant places and wonderfully interesting associations will stir

> " Sensations sweet,
> Felt in the blood, and felt along the heart,"

in many a dreary interval of life.

Are you an archæologist? You may examine half-a-dozen churches with fragments of the original Norman structure in the course of one day's walk, and get quite new ideas of what the Norman conquerors did in scattering centres of light through the land. Are you an ornithologist? You may study the graceful ways of the swallows, and the habits of many of the " feathered nation," in Gilbert White's own " sweet Selborne." Are you a botanist? Here are rare treasures for your herbarium; in and about the Great Wood of Alton alone you may find seventeen of the thirty-eight British species of orchis.[1] Do you care for history, for good and great men, for Miss Austen, for the *Christian Year*—does geology interest you? Here is a field " all dedicate " to each. Do you wish your children to enter fully upon the inheritance of culture and virtue which is theirs in right of their English birth? Bring them here, or to some other lovely and pleasant

---

[1] 1. *Orchis mascula* (early orchis); 2. *Orchis latifolia* (marsh orchis); 3. *Orchis maculata* (spotted orchis); 4. *Orchis morio* (green-winged orchis); 5. *Orchis pyramidalis* (pyramidal orchis); 6. *Orchis conopsea* (fragrant orchis) or *Gymnadenia*; 7. *Habenaria bifolia* (butterfly Habenaria or orchis); 8. *Habenaria chlorantha* (a variety or another species of No. 7); 9. *Ophrys apifera* (bee ophrys or orchis); 10. *Ophrys muscifera* (fly ophrys or orchis); 11. *Epipactis latifolia* (broad epipactis); 12. *Cephalanthera grandiflora* (large cephalanthera); 13. *Cephalanthera entifolia* (narrow cephalanthera); 14. *Neottia Nidus-anis* (bird's nest neottia); 15. *Listera ovata* (twayblade listera or twayblade); 16. *Spiranthes autumnalis* (lady's tresses).

county in the three kingdoms. A month spent thus in gathering the lore of a single county is more educative than five terms of vigorous school work.

A "county" is not to be commended for the babies who *must not be taught*, but children of six and upwards will take in without effort many nourishing ideas in the course of such a rambling holiday as I suggest.

One thing more : it is good, doubtless, to be cosmopolitan in our tastes, liberal and unprejudiced in our judgments ; but he who would love all the world must begin with the brother whom he has seen, and enlightened sympathy with other nations can coexist only with profound and instructed patriotism. In the noble character, patriotism is the warp with which every fine and delicate attribute is interwoven. The child who is not trained in patriotic feeling will not, as a man, live at the highest level possible to him ; and this noblest virtue is best instilled, not by vulgar vaunting of ourselves, but by the gradual introduction of the child to the lovely lives that have been lived, the great work that has been done, in quiet places in every county of Britain through the long period of our history.

III

THE A-B-C-DARIANS

"WE have listened to you, gentlemen, with great deference. We have profited much, and perceive a great field of work before us. I hope we may get a little outside help. I heard the other day of a young lady learned in mosses who is in the habit of taking the children she knows on 'mossing' expeditions. But what I wish to say is, education, like charity, begins at home, and you have chosen to lead us far afield at the very outset!"

"Truly, we did go off at a canter! But don't you think it is a matter for curtain discipline? If your son Tom had not 'wondered what you are' we might have begun quite at the beginning, if there be one; or, most likely, should have been till this moment wondering where to begin. We are grateful to you, Henderson, for starting us anywhere; and more so to Mrs Henderson for her axiom, Education begins at home."

"I daresay experienced people get to know all about it," said Mrs Clough; "but the mother of even two or three little ones has a sense of being at sea without rudder or compass. We know so little about children, or, indeed, about human beings at all!

Parents before our time had something to go upon; and the young mother could ask counsel of her elders on all matters from 'cinder tea' to the choice of a school. But now, science is abroad; many of the old wise saws turn out, not only mischievous, but ridiculous. We can't keep hold of the old, we can't get hold of the new, and there we are, like Mahomet's coffin."

"You have described our quandary exactly, Mrs Clough; and what you say accounts for many things. The older people complain that the children of these days are growing up lax, self-pleasing, disobedient, irreverent. Now, I think myself there is a great deal that's fine in our children. They are much more of *persons* than we were at their age; but that they do pretty much what is right in their own eyes, are neither obedient nor reverent, nor even respectful, is, I am afraid, a true bill. But don't you see how it is? We are afraid of them. We feel as a navvy might, turned in to dust the drawing-room ornaments! The mere touch of his clumsy great fingers may be the ruin of some precious thing. We parents, no doubt, get tenderness and insight from above to enable us for our delicate work; so I suppose it is our own fault that the children are beyond us."

"How do you mean, Mrs Meredith? And if you, mothers, don't know what to do with the children, who does? The enlightened father lays himself out for a snub if he sets up for an authority at home."

"Oh yes! you men make ludicrous blunders about children. But that's no help. A young mother gets a tender human creature into her keeping, full of possibilities. Her first concern is, not only to keep it in health, but, so to speak, to fill it with reserves of health to last a lifetime. At once her perplexities begin. I shall not even ask to be excused for venturing upon details; the affairs of a young human being are important enough to engage the attention of King, Lords, and Commons, did they but know it. Well, a mother I know wished her child to be clothed delicately, as befits a first-born. She sent to Ireland for a delicious baby trousseau of lace and cambric. You, gentlemen, don't understand. Hardly had the dear little garments gone through their first wash, when somebody tells her that 'oo' a' 'oo', is the only wear for babies and grown-ups. I doubt if to this day she knows why, but there was a *soupçon* of science in the suggestion, so the sweet cambrics were discarded and fine woollens took their place. By-and-by, when the child came to feed like other mortals, there was a hail of pseudo-science about her ears. 'Grape-sugar,' 'farinaceous foods,' 'saliva,' and what not; but this was less simple than the wool question. She could make nothing of it, so asked her doctor how to feed the child. Further complications arose: 'the child sees everything;' 'the child knows everything'; 'what you make him now he will be through life'; 'the period of infancy is the most important in his life.' My poor friend grew bewildered, with the result that, in her ignorant anxiety to do right, she is for ever changing the child's diet, nurse, sleeping hours, airing hours, according to the last lights of the most scientific of her acquaintances; and it's my belief the little one would be a deal better off brought up like its mother before it."

"Then you would walk in the old paths?"

"Not a bit of it! Only I want to see where I'm going. I think we live in an age of great opportunities. But my contention is, that you cannot bring up children on hearsay in these days; there is some principle involved in the most everyday matter, and we must go to school to learn the common laws of healthy living and well-being."

"Mrs Meredith is right: here is serious work sketched out for us, and of a kind as useful for ourselves as for our children. We *must* learn the first principles of human physiology."

"Would not it do to learn what is called Hygiene? I have a notion, that is physiology made easy; that is, you are just taught what to do, without going *fully* into the cause why."

"No, we must stick to physiology: I don't believe at all in learning *what* to do, unless founded upon a methodical, not scrappy, knowledge of *why* we do it. You see, all parts of the animal economy are so inter-dependent that you cannot touch this without affecting that. What we want to get at, is, the laws for the well-being of every part, for the due performance of every function."

"Why, man, you would have every one of us qualify to write M.D. to his name!"

"Not so; we shall not interfere with the doctors; we leave sickness to them; but the preservation of health, the increase in bodily vigour, must be our care. In this way; we acquaint ourselves fully with the structure of the skin, for example, with its functions, and the inter-dependence between these and the functions of certain internal organs. Now, secure vigorous action of the skin, and you gain exhilaration of spirits, absolute joy for the time, followed by a rise in the sense of general well-being, *i.e.*, happiness. You remember how a popular American poet sat on a gate in the sun after his bath, using his flesh-brushes by the hour, until he was the colour of a boiled lobster. He might have been more seemly employed, but his *joy* was greater than if daily telegrams had brought him word of new editions of his poems.   Well, if due action of the skin be a means to a joyous life, to health and a genial temper, what mother is there who would not secure these for her child?   But the thing is not so simple as it looks.   It is not merely a case of bath and flesh-brush: diet, clothes, sleep, bedroom, sun-shine, happy surroundings, exercise, bright talk, a thousand things must work together to bring about this 'happy-making' condition.   What is true of the skin is true all round, and we cannot go to work with a view to any single organ or function; all work together, and we must aim at a thorough grip of the subject.   Is it, then, decided 'without one if or but,' that we get ourselves instructed in the science of living?"

"The 'science of living'—yes, but that covers much beyond the range of physiology.   Think of the child's mind, his moral and religious potencies.   It seems to me that we already make too much of the body. Our young people are encouraged to sacrifice every-thing to physical training; and there is a sensuousness, well hit-off in George Eliot's 'Gwendoline,' in the importance given to every detail of the bath and the toilet.   One is weary of the endless magnification of the body and its belongings; and, what is more, I believe we are defeating our own ends.   'Groom' the skin, develop the muscles, by all means; but there is more to be thought of, and I doubt if to live to the flesh, even in these ways, is permissible."

"You are right.   But don't think for a moment that

physiology lends itself to the cult of muscle. Here
is a youth whose *biceps* are his better part: like most
of us, he gets what he aims at—some local renown as
an athlete. But what does he pay for the whistle?
His violent 'sports' do not materially increase the
measure of blood which sustains him: if the muscles
get more than their share, their gain implies loss elsewhere, to the brain, commonly, and, indeed, to all the
vital organs. By-and-by, the sports of youth over,
your brawny, broad-chested young fellow collapses;
is the victim of *ennui*, and liver, lungs, or stomach
send in their requisition for arrears of nourishment
fraudulently made away with."

"But, surely, Mr Meredith, you do not think lightly
of physical development? Why, I thought it one of
the first duties of parents to send their offspring into
the world as 'fine animals.'"

"So it is; but here, as elsewhere, there is a 'science
of the proportion of things,' and the young people
who go in violently and without moderation for
muscular feats are a delusion and a snare: in the end,
they do not prove 'fine animals'; they have little
staying power."

"But a child is more than an animal; we want
to know how mind and moral feelings are to be
developed?"

"Even in these matters, Mrs Tremlow, we should
find much help in the study of physiology—mental
physiology, if you like to call it so. I mean, the
habits a child grows up with appear to leave some
sort of register in his material brain, and, thus, to
become part of himself in even a physical sense.
Thus it rests with parents to ease the way of their
child by giving him the habits of the god life in

thought, feeling and action, and even in spiritual things. We cannot make a child 'good'; but, in this way, we can lay paths for the good life in the very substance of his brain. We cannot make him hear the voice of God; but, again, we can make paths where the Lord God may walk in the cool of the evening. We cannot make a child clever; but we can see that his brain is nourished with pure blood, his mind with fruitful ideas."

" I suppose all this would be encouraging if one were up to it. But I feel as if a great map of an unknown country were spread before me, where the few points one wants to make for are unmarked. How, for instance, are we to make a child obedient, kind, and true?"

"Your question, Mrs Tremlow, suggests further ground we must cover: a few set rules will be of little service; we must know a little, at anyrate, of the content of that which we call 'human nature.' We must add to our physiology, psychology, and, to psychology, moral science. Complex, yet most simple, manifold, yet one, human nature is not to be ticked off in a lecture or two as a subject we have exhausted; but there is no conceivable study which yields such splendid increase for our pains."

" And the spiritual life of the child? Does either of these 'ologies' embrace the higher life, or is it not susceptible of culture?"

" Ah, there we have new conditions—the impact of the Divine upon the human, which generates *life*, 'without which there is no living.' The life is there, imparted and sustained from above; but we have something to do here also. Spirit, like body, thrives upon daily bread and daily labour, and it is our part to set before the child those 'new thoughts of God, new hopes of Heaven,' which should be his spiritual diet; and to practise him in the spiritual labours of prayer, praise, and endeavour. How?—is another question for our Society to work out."

IV

"DIE NEUE ZEIT BEDARF DER NEUEN SCHULE"

A SCHOOLMASTER'S REVERIE

How hard it is to turn your thoughts on! Switzerland was a mistake, so far as that goes; but to have been alive in every pore for a month is something. This night train should help, though: here goes! let us face the situation. I, Michael St. John Harrowby, aged thirty-five, have got, more by good luck than merit, the Headmastership of the Wintonley Grammar School. One's first thought is, naturally, for wife and bairns, and Fanny was sadly pinched at Appledore. Dear girl! I hope the strain is at an end for her. She will enjoy mothering the boarders along with our own five.

But here am I on the old string which we have harped upon a thousand times since I got the post—the gain to ourselves and the children. There is nothing we have not canvassed, to the Butler schoolship for baby Tim, so why go over the ground again?

Oh, shade of Jack Horner, *enfant terrible*, does every man-jack of us eat his plum in his corner to the tune of "What a good boy am I"? Are effort and aspiration for those others who miss the plums? Well, I have my thoughts, if I could only get at them : cakes and ale are not everything.

. . . . . .

No, cakes and ale are not the whole, and now that a fair field offers, I wonder what I shall make of the thoughts that have been working in me for these last ten years! Three months ago I could have revolutionised the whole educational system—like Moses, who was plucky enough about the exodus till his time came. Give you a chance, though, and you feel that the other men have experience on their side, and that—what is, is best. But that is laziness, cowardice. Come, Michael, man! You know in your heart that this chance has come to you just because you have thought out a few things that should be of use. That is what the world wants, for somehow, people have grown too humble and teachable to think for themselves. These are wonderful times, beautiful times! We are all so open to conviction, so agog for the right and the true ; we may be gulled by false prophets, with their "lo, here!" and "lo, there!" but then, how ready we are to follow the lead of any with the least gift of insight!

In the matter of education, we are hovering round the truth: that education is not merely a preparation for life, but the work of the lifetime, is boldly announced. And, given thus much insight, is it conceivable that the education in question is no more than the cramming of a few text-books? Like religion, education is nothing or it is everything—a consuming fire in the bones. How is it that we do not see, through the hurry of eating and drinking, getting and having, that

our prime business here is to raise up a generation
better than ourselves?

.   .   .   .   .   .

" New schools for the new times" is the burden of
an old pamphlet I picked up at Offenbach, the outcome of a congress of the "*deutschen Freidenker-
bundes*" held a quarter of a century ago, which
indicates the date when Germany first began her
educational reform.   It is as well to know how we
stand with regard to certain burning questions, and
this pamphlet rather brings us to book.   " Knowledge
is power" is not an alarmingly new sentiment; that
the people have a right to the power which knowledge
gives, that the knowledge which avails is that which
qualifies a man for his life as a "social animal," we are
prepared to admit.   That the talent, the genius, which
smoulder to-day in the heated rooms of a thousand
factories, or are choked in a thousand damp cellar
dwellings, must be cherished by the schools of the
future to the infinite advantage of the whole common-
weal—that touches a burning question.   One is not
sure that cellars, any more than drawing-rooms, breed
geniuses by the thousand ; but that is not the point ;
the question concerns—"the pauper population," the
"criminal classes."   Shame on us that such phrases
are possible to our English speech ; we are glad and
willing to have the poor always with us to instruct us
in righteousness ; but what hope for us of health and
beauty as a nation with *this* cancer at our bowels?

Apart from these, the "unspeakable" residue, how
do we stand ?   That is, where there is work and bread,
how do the people fare for education, and what are
the chances for a working man's child blessed with
talent or genius ?   Tolerably good in the large towns ;

in ordinary cases, the possibilities of education are limited by the length of time the parents can afford to keep their child; indeed, the law steps in to constrain the parents and to fix a minimum standard of age and attainments without which the child is not free to labour; he must read, though not fluently; write, though not easily nor correctly; must be able to add and subtract, divide and multiply with some readiness. This is not much, but it is a setting of the gates ajar for the child of genius; and, supposing that his parents are able and willing to feed and clothe him during his adolescence, his prospects are good. He wins scholarships at the primary, which carry him through the secondary school, and there he may win scholarships which will cover his University career. I know of a dozen instances of University men who have worked their way up from very low estate—the sons of journeymen labourers, of mill "hands," of petty traders—and that, with honour and consideration too, for school and college alike bid for brains, seeing that their own status depends on the men they turn out. This state of things is a mere *pis aller*; we are told that they manage educational matters better elsewhere: but "reform" is in the air; our whole system is being overhauled; and, meantime, it is pleasant to know that education is *possible* to the son of the poor man who is born a genius, and is blessed with self-denying parents, and—one more qualification—who lives in a town.

What have we here? "Nothing," says Pädagoge Diesterweg, "has more attraction for man than truth. To find it he will wander into distant lands, over desert and mountain, will search the depths of the earth, will climb into the heavens; no effort is to him too great, no obstacle too fearful, no labour too hard;

his soul thirsts after truth." This is suggestive, and
the conclusion that, in the schools, the children should
be nourished upon truth, goes without saying. But
we come back to Pilate's world-famed question.

My pedagogue means something, however, "Moses,
Moses, *und immer* Moses," is the burden of a bitter cry.
He complains that, in the Fatherland, a sixth, and
sometimes more, of the time spent in school (in elementary schools) is devoted to religious instruction—
Bible-lesson and psalm, catechism and hymn; and
what time is left, is the cry, for literature, for
metaphysics, ethics, what not, the stores of wisdom
that should be laid open to poor as to rich ? But this
is a tale of the past, and we in England are well in
advance after all. Nowhere with us are two out of
twelve, much less sixteen out of twenty-four, school
hours devoted to religious instruction. Psalm, hymn,
and catechism have departed; the Bible lesson is
pared down to a shred ; and, in our zeal, we do not
see that we have deprived the people of the classics,
the metaphysics, the ethics—as well as the religion—
peculiarly their own. Instead, we have put into their
hands—"Readers"—scraps of science, of history, of
geography—saw-dust, that cannot take root downwards and bear fruit upwards in human soil.

.   .   .   .   .   .

But here is matter that concerns us more closely.
We learn for life, not for the schools: good and well;
nothing new in that. Here we have it :—*Wie ?—sagt
Prof. Dodel-Port in seiner neuesten Broschüre : Moses
oder Darwin.* Dodel-Port is plucky, or reckless, but
that is the situation. What think ye of Moses ? is the
crux. The worst of it is, a man may let his own
thoughts simmer, but the young will have something

definite, and you cannot hide anything from them. Say nothing, and they know what it means as well as if you proclaimed yourself from the house-top. Well, as a matter of fact, it is *not* " Moses or Darwin ? " with me. I receive both, not by way of compromise, but in faith, believing that each, though in differing degree, speaks a revealed word. But, how is one to put it to the boys? They *will* take sides, and they doubt your sincerity if you do not.

Loyalty shall be our key-note. In a home, children are under natural conditions, and each develops on his own lines. In a school, you must have an *enthusiasm*, must strike a note that vibrates in every breast to secure the common feeling without which there is no life. Loyalty will do—chivalrous loyalty to each other, to the school, to their homes, to those in authority : then, the highest enthusiasm, the loyalty of Christian service ; I hardly see how to work it yet, but when one is steadfastly purposed, ways arise. Supposing, then, the loyalty that does not permit itself to harbour dishonouring thoughts; suppose a passion of loyal service kindled in some breasts, and more or less affecting all—is criticism to be tabooed as disloyal? Are the boys to go into the world ignorant of the questions that are searching many hearts, to be staggered by the first shock of evidence and opinion running counter to the old thoughts? No ; but how I wish I could do the boys the like inestimable service that a great teacher has done for me and many another! It is difficult to put into words, but, some-how, one is landed on the other side of the contro-versies of the day: they are of immense interest, but are not vital. It is just, to compare lesser things with great, as the husband of a famous woman might listen to discussions about his wife's works or published letters. Are they hers or are they not? Do they disclose facts of her life or fancies? Are the opinions put into the mouths of her best characters truly her own? It is most interesting to hear what the world says, but, for him, he *knows* where the world guesses; besides, these things are not vital; the vital thing is herself and their mutual relations. So, but infinitely more so, of our apprehension of the Highest, and our cognisance of the supreme relationship. Reveal to the eyes of youth the vision of the infinite Loveliness, lay bare the heart of youth to the drawings of the irresistible Tenderness, let the young know, of their own intimate knowledge, that,

"The thoughts of God are broader than the measures of man's mind,
And the heart of the Eternal is most wonderfully kind,"

and all other knowledge and relationships and facts of life will settle themselves. Thus, only, is it possible to live joyfully, purposefully, diligently. Without this—madness! or, the foolish playing of a foolish mummer's part in the presence of the " eternal verities." But, boys religiously brought up turn out indifferent or ill? Exactly so, when they have had the outward and visible signs without the inward part or thing signified; of all sawdust, this is the driest. No soul, once laid open to the touch of the divine tenderness, can go away and forget. Go away, a wilful soul may, but come back, it needs must. Well, it is something to see one's work; but, how to do it? At any rate, seeing these things, a man must go softly all his days and wait for light.

.   .   .   .   .   .

In this connection we must face the attitude of
public opinion with regard to the Sacred Books.
"Yea, hath God said?" is the question of the hour,
and probably will be the question of the hour so long
as the world endures. We who teach must hold
unalterable convictions in this regard, unalterable and
therefore our grounds must be deep, broad, and high,
covering and underlying every point of attack. We
must know with absolute certainty that here is
revelation—its claim to be so resting upon internal
evidence alone, the quality of that which is revealed.
Let us ask what is the subject of revelation. The
history of the people called Jews? The history of
the beginning, and predictions of the end of all
things? We are told to-day that upon the one as
upon the other the light is thrown "through storied
windows richly dight"; that the apple and the garden
bear no more direct, material interpretation than the
"tree which bears twelve manner of fruits, whose
leaves are for the healing of the nations"; that,
"without a parable spake he not unto them" applies
more or less to what we call the history of the Bible.
Perhaps the marvellous and inspired quality of the
Scriptures is more brought out by attacks upon their
historic truth then in any other way. Whether men
choose to regard the story of the Fall as a record, a
poem, a fable, a parable, a vision, its inherent teaching
is the same. We have here the story of the decline
and fall and hope to rise again of every soul of man.

The history of the Jews, again, what is it more, say
the enlightened, than a collection of the myths of the
heroic age of a nation—when the gods walked with
men : myths that have their parallels, often curiously
close, in the sacred legends of nations to which we do

not allow divine inspiration? Here, again, the history
justifies itself by its truth to human experience. The
sun stands still, even now, for the finishing of our
righteous acts; the Jordan parts before us in our
extremities. Here we have, whether by way of
historic fact or luminous fable, parables of our lives to
be spiritually discerned, and, more, here we have an
unfailing key to the interpretation of our times : this
is by inspiration of God.

.   .   .   .   .   .

The "carnage," the "wholesale slaughterings,"
ascribed to Almighty God, wrought directly by His
hand, or according to His will, are brought forward as
irreconcilable with our conceptions of the All-good.
These things happen to-day, and we have not the
courage to ascribe them to God. Few amongst us are
able to stand up and say, " Though He slay me *and my
fellows*, yet will I trust in Him." We dare not say,
" Here is the finger of God"; so we describe these
events by a string of epithets, all of more or less pagan
origin. Fortune, the stars, the fates, work us mischief.
We suffer from misfortunes, mischances, casualties,
catastrophes, disasters, fatalities—more reassuring,
doubtless, and more scientific than the creed of the
Old Testament ! Is it true, then, that flood and
famine, and slaughter in battle, are the will and the
work of the good God? The Old Testament asserts
as much, and the New has a tender word about a
sparrow falling to the ground, which goes to prove
that these things are, at any rate, permitted. Perhaps,
life and death are less momentous than we suppose ;
death, conceivably, is no way final whether as regards
opportunity or existence ; what if it even open a
chance to " try again "? We cannot know ; revelation

is silent; and as for science, when science has a definite utterance to make about the facts of life under her eyes, we shall be willing to hear what she says about these other mysteries. At any rate, in that Heart where every pain found its pity, there was none for the three who tasted death—only for the grief that mourned them. As for all the anguish of life, the miseries of the mind distressed, the writhings of the suffering body, who shall find his pain intolerable when he thinks upon the Cross?

.   .   .   .   .   .

We schoolmasters must face the situation; we must shirk nothing, take nothing for granted; we must fortify the boys against attack, and arm them for a chivalrous defence. As for definite tactics, suppose we concede for the moment, and for argument's sake, all that is attacked, and then see where we are. The earthworks thrown up from time to time are sadly torn up, but the fortress is intact. Panic gives way to confidence; come who may, we are ready, and not only so, we take up the offensive; our position is proof against all sallies; it is the enemy who are exposed. This seems to me important. Defensive warfare is never carried on with the enthusiasm of conviction which warms him who attacks. As a matter of fact, we are prepared to yield no iota of the Sacred Scriptures, while of the obscurities of the Old Testament, as of the Apocalypse, we say only—

> "Lord, I believe what herein I do read,
> But, alas, I do not understand."

But religious training, and the Bible? It is so hard to know what to teach when everything is an "open question." Courage. Nothing is lost yet, and the future is for us. We yield, not the Scriptures, but one or other of the old canons of interpretation, as Science shows it to be untenable; but we look her in the eyes and interrogate her sharply; and, above all, we are intolerant of the assumption of infallibility in a teacher who is ever (and this is her glory) smearing out with wet finger some lesson of yesterday, because it is not the truth of to-day. Are we not on the verge of a new criticism, not historical, and not natural, but *personal*? Is not physiology hurrying up with the announcement that to every man it is permitted to mould and modify his own brain? That, not heredity, and not environment, but education is the final and the formative power? That *character* is the man, and education is the maker of character, howsoever much she owe her material to the other two?

. . . . . .

And how should this affect our study of Holy Writ? By concentrating criticism upon the personages of the Bible rather than upon the recorded events. First upon the authors—known or unknown: the instruction in righteousness is not less or more, whether Moses or another, Isaiah or another, wrote the words. Is it in human nature, is it in the nature of *authors*, for a man to suppress himself as do the authors here? Where do the little affectations and vanities of the man of letters crop up? Where are the turgid utterances, the egotistical, the bombastic? Even Plutarch, prince of biographers, cannot refrain himself: he gives you his opinion of his man, and illustrates it by delightful anecdotes; but, to set the man himself before you for judgment without a yea or a nay—not Plutarch or another has been able for this, least of all the biographers of to-day. Where, in the stories of Abraham, Isaac, or Jacob, of prophet, priest, or king, have we moral disquisitions? Is not rather the principle made plain all along the line that right and wrong are self-evidenced, calling for neither praise nor blame; unadorned straightforward narrative is enough when every man carries the judge in his bosom. And then the persons—how the springs of human action are laid bare in them, how they rise from out the sacred page, not a gallery of Hebrew portraits, but a procession of the living, more manifest than the people with whom you sit at table every day! Whence is this, if not by the inspiration of God? And how majestical do some of them take shape before us! How feeble are patriotism, enthusiasm, altruism, all the fine words of to-day, to express the law-giver of Israel, the prophet, the poet, the leader of men, a man of like passions with ourselves, too, but greater than we. "*Moses, Moses, und immer Moses!*" Truly this one character is enough to stimulate us to the bringing up of godly and manly youth. In what two or three wonderful touches have we set before us the education that made him; and, all the time, no praises, never a story told for his exaltation, no more ever than the flow of lucid narrative showing only events in their course. Here is essential truth; here is a twofold inspiration; first, to produce the man Moses; next, to portray him. Ah, but, consider the "evolution of history"? Truly, if man is to be measured by the heaped-up praises of his biographers, every year we produce many, not only greater than Moses, but greater that Christ; for when does biography issue from the press so free of laudations as are the four evangels? Oh, "the sweet reasonable-

ness of Christianity," the most sober sanity of that
great company elected to hand on to us the counsels
of God !

.   .   .   .   .   .

Do I incline with lingering fondness rather to the
things of the past than to the eager stir of the present,
the promise of the future? Not so; I appreciate to
the full the joy of living in days characterised by child-
like frankness, openness to conviction, readiness to try
all things and choose that which is good. We have
our faults—grave and depressing enough—but we are
ready for better things, ready, indeed, for any great
crusade, if some modern Luther or Savonarola should
arise and tell us the thing to do. To 'endeavour
ourselves' to the daily effort of education, to live and
act, think and speak before the children, so that they
shall be hourly the better for all that *we are*, is harder,
no doubt, than to make one enormous sacrifice. But
even for this we shall be enabled in these inspiring
days, when it seems to some of us that the people are
being made *willing* in the day of His power. The
outlook is very cheering: we begin to see that education is the elected handmaid of religion, and get
stimulating glimpses of the stature of the perfect man,
possible to redeemed humanity.

.   .   .   .   .   .

But the past offers us its accumulated treasures of
wisdom and experience—

> " And (we) could wish (our) days to be
> Bound each to each by natural piety."

Few things could be more disastrous (as, alas, few are
more imminent) than a sudden break with the traditions of the past; wherefore, let us gently knit the

bonds that bind us to the generation all too rapidly dying out. Without a thought of disloyalty towards our own most earnest days, perhaps some of us feel that the cultivated men and women of the middle decades of the last century had more breadth and sweetness—any way, more delightful humour—than we perceive in our contemporaries. It is well that we gather up, with tender reverence, such fragments of their insight and experience as come in our way; for we would fain, each, be as an householder, bringing forth out of his treasures things new and old.

V

A HUNDRED YEARS AFTER

(At the Cloughs' dinner-table, Sept. 10, 1990.)

" It's a capital idea! the thing ought to be com-
memorated. At any rate, we can give a little dinner
in honour of it. Whom shall we have?"

" Dr and Mrs Oldcastle, and Harry's form-master,
young Mr Hilyard, and his wife, will represent school-
work; *we* shall stand for parents in general; and, with
Dr and Mrs Brenton for our medical advisers, and
the Dean and Mrs Priestly to witness for things
spiritual, we shall be quite a ' representative gathering.'
Will my list do?"

" Famously! It couldn't be better. We all know
the subject and each other, and I shouldn't wonder if
we have some good things said."

Mr Clough was a City merchant, as had been his
fathers before him for four or five generations; he was
reputed wealthy, and was a rich man, but one who
held his wealth as a public trust, reserving for personal
uses only what should keep his family in refined and
comfortable living. Not that there was much virtue
in this, for he, and others like him, held in aversion
luxurious living, and whatever savoured of the "bar-
barous opulence" of earlier days. Dr Oldcastle was

the head-master of an old-established foundation
school; for the remaining guests, they have been
sufficiently introduced by Mrs Clough.

During the dinner there was the usual gay talk,
and some light handling of graver subjects, until the
ladies retired, with a view to the discussion of certain
practical matters among themselves. Then—

"I wonder, gentlemen, has it occurred to you why
my wife and I have been so pertinacious in trying to
get you here to-night?"

Every one's countenance showed that he was struck
by an interesting, if vague, recollection.

"A little circumstance connected with this room,
and a certain date that I fear I may have mentioned
more than once or twice?"

"Oh, to be sure," said the Dean; "haven't I said a
dozen times to my wife, 'There's but one thing that
Clough plumes himself on—that the "Fathers' and
Mothers' Club" was born in his dining-room!'"

"But why to-night more than any other night?"

"Why, to-night is the hundredth anniversary of
that great event!" A good-humoured smile passed
round. "Yes, gentlemen, I know I'm house-proud,
and give you leave to laugh. But would not you
cherish an old-fashioned house in a by-street, when
it's the one thing that links you to history?"

"But, my dear fellow, why in the world should this
Club with the stuttering initials (how I hate initials!)
be glorified? It does not get in my way, as a head-
master, it's true; but, mind you, a man can't play up
to his Busby in the face of it! There was a man for
his calling! How he'd walk over your 'F. M. C.'s.'
Fumble! aye, that's the word. I knew 'F. M. C.'
reminded me of something."

" I'm slow to see how our Club links us with history, certainly," murmured Dr Brenton reflectively.

" Why, in this way : if the Club did not initiate, it certainly marked a stage in the progress of the great educational revolution in which we have been moving for the last hundred years. Wait for two or three centuries, and you will find this revolution of ours written down as the epoch of the 'Children's *Magna Charta.*'"

" Sorry to disoblige you, but I'm afraid none of us sees his way to more than a century of waiting, though it be to verify the statements of his best friend. But go on, old fellow, I'm with you! Make the 'revolution' plain sailing for us."

" Thanks, Hilyard ; your sanction emboldens me. But which am I to 'go on' with, the word or the thing ?"

" A distinction *with* a difference. If I say 'the thing,' off we go to the Dark Ages themselves ; and shall come out to find the ladies cloaked and hooded in the hall ! "

" A thing endurable to us elder Benedicts."

" Now, Doctor! As if you weren't tied to Mrs Oldcastle's apron-string every minute you're not in school. Fanny and I follow you for encouragement when we feel our bond growing slack."

" To order, gentlemen, to order ! or we shall get neither word nor thing. We shall all want to put in a word anent 'my wife and I.'"

" Brenton's right. Seer, take up thy parable, and go ahead ! "

" Who would contemn a behest of the Church ?" (with a bow which threatened a candle-shade, deftly saved by Hilyard). " I go ahead ; I'm not to talk about the thing, but the name. Why I call this, which has been working itself out in the last hundred years or more, an educational *revolution.* In the first place, what was called 'Education' a century since and what we call Education are essentially different things."

"Come, come! Isn't that rather strong? We go in for the classics and mathematics; and so did the schools of a hundred, or, for the matter of that, five hundred years ago. It is true we have to work much more with modern languages, natural science, and other subjects of which we can give but a smattering, to the confusion alike of boys and masters. Give me a classical education, or, in default, a mathematical; it's training! And, for my part, I vote for the pre-Revolutionists, if that's what you choose to call them";— said Dr Oldcastle, with a subdued snort, which epitomised much that was not civil to the reform party.

"How much clearing of the decks must take place for even a friendly discussion! Tell us, gentlemen both, what you mean by education?"

"Mean by education, Doctor? I should not have thought our united wisdoms need be called on to answer that! A boy is educated when he knows what every gentleman should know, and when he is trained to take his place in the world."

"Dr Oldcastle's definition suits me as well as another. Putting aside the polite acquirements, the question turns on the training—how much it includes, and how it is to be given."

"There you have it, Clough," put in Dr Brenton; "and my contention is, that you owe the incalulable advance in *character* which has taken place in the

period we are considering entirely to us, doctors.
Wasn't it we who found out for you that you were
all blundering in the dark ; that you hadn't even set
your feet on the scientific basis of education; that
all your doings were tentative? About a hundred
years ago, men spent a third of a lifetime on mathematics. Cambridge made men Senior Wranglers in
those days, and, perhaps, the distinction was worth the
work. But the world said, in that weighty way in
which the world likes to talk : 'Mathematics afford a
mental discipline, a fortifying of character, which no
other study gives.' Now I'm not denying the worth
of mathematics as a factor in education ; but look at
your mathematician ; do you find him more to the
fore, more his own master, than other men? Often
enough, he is irritable, obstinate, all the more wrong-
headed the more he's in the right. But now *we*
(observe the *we*—royalty itself couldn't make more of
it) find you fumbling about blindly, snatching up now
this tool, now that, natural science, languages, or what
not, in order to work upon material you knew nothing
about, was it mind, or morals, or what? To effect
issues you had not determined on—intellectual power?
Force of character? In the slough we found you—
parent, schoolmaster, parson—all whose business is,
more or less, the bringing up of the young ; and what
have we done for you? Why, we've discovered to
you the nature of the material you have to work upon,
the laws according to which it must be wrought. We
have even put it into your hands as clay in the hands
of a potter, and we've shown you what is the one
possible achievement before you; that is, *the elevation
of character*. Education which fails to effect this,
effects nothing. There, that's what *we*'ve done.

Every man to his trade, say I; and there's nothing like leather!"

"Well, but, but,—all this is very fine talk; but what demonstration can you give? And where in the world have I been while all this was going on? Pshaw! You delude yourselves, my dear friends. This airy talk makes flighty brains; but do you suppose I've been a schoolmaster these forty years while all this has been taking place, and yet know nothing of it?"

"That comes of fumbling over our 'F. M. C.', instead of holding us up with both hands. But, honour bright, Dr Oldcastle, do you see in these days any change in the manner of boy that comes to your hands fresh from his home?"

"Yes, yes! a thousand times, yes!"

"If Mr Hilyard's courtesy had permitted me to answer for myself, I, also, should have said 'yes.' I see a most remarkable change, upon which society is to be congratulated. But what would you have? Civilisation and education must of necessity produce results, appreciable even within a single lifetime."

"Don't you think, Doctor, you might have made a trilogy of it, and promoted Christianity?" interposed the ever suave and gentle tones of the Dean. "I, myself, feel, with Dr Brenton, 'every man for his master,' and would fain lay every advance at the feet of mine."

"I must beg the Dean to look over a little assumed pugnacity. That we all agree with him, he may rest assured; and for this reason; every other avenue towards perfection leads you, after weeks or months or years of delightful going, to a blank wall. You see nothing beyond; all that remains is to retrace your steps, and retrogression is always bitter. You try through Christ, and find yourself in the way of endless progress cheered by perennial hope. But the talk is growing serious. We of the Club take to ourselves some of the credit of the advances Dr Oldcastle perceives, and as testimony from an alien is very valuable, perhaps he would not mind telling us in detail what differences he discerns between the young boys of to-day and their kind of forty years ago ?"

"Let me consider a moment; your question is not easy to answer in a breath. . . . Well, in the first place, they are more apt to learn: I conceive that there has been an extraordinary advance in intelligence during the last half-century. The work we would grind over for hours in my day, these youngsters have at their finger-ends in half an hour, and are on the alert for more. I do believe they have a real appetite for knowledge—a weakness of which not more than one or two in a hundred were guilty when I was a boy."

"Will you let me, as a parent, give you our explanation of these facts? For, with deference to Dr Brenton, who justly claims so much for his craft, I think we parents deserve a pat, too. You may bring a horse to the well, but you can't make him drink. The advance, I think, is not in intelligence, but in power of attention. This, the 'Fathers' and Mothers' Club' and its agencies recognise as the practical power of man ; that which makes all the difference between the able and successful man and the poor lag-last. Attention is the power and habit of concentrating every faculty on the thing in hand. Now this habit of attention, parents, mothers especially, are taught to encourage and cultivate in their children from early infancy. What you regard with full attention, if only for a minute, you know, and remember always. Think of the few scenes and conversations we, each, have so vividly fixed that we cannot possibly forget them. Why? Because at the moment our attention was powerfully excited. You reap some benefit from this early training directly the boy goes to school. The psychologists—not your craft, this time, Doctor—tell us that enormous curiosity, a ravenous appetite for knowledge, is as natural to children as bread-and-milk hunger. Put the two together; the boy has an eager desire to know—has the power of fixing his whole mind on the new thoughts set before him, and it's as easy as A B C; of course he learns with magical quickness. The field has been ploughed by the parents, and you have only to sow your seed."

"H'm! it sounds rational; I must think it over. Anyway, the results are pleasant enough. Four hours a day instead of six or seven—and much more work done, mind you—is good for both masters and boys. Then, most of them have resources and are on nobody's hands. You'd be astonished to hear how much these fellows know, and each has his speciality. One little chap has butterflies, for instance. Ah, that reminds me! Don't tell, or I might be invited to resign ; but I don't to this day know the difference between a moth and a butterfly. It's the sort of thing one ought to know, so I set up a classification of my own, no doubt correct, because it was mine! Well, this befell me. 'What have you there?' I asked a little chap, who had evidently netted a prize. 'A moth, sir, the——,' scientific name, pat. 'A moth, boy! That beautiful creature is no moth. Moths live in houses.' You should have seen the fellow suppress his grin! I couldn't ask, so don't know now, but make a point of not meeting that little chap's eye. A friend of mine, a Fellow of his College, was worse. 'I say, Oldcastle, the poets make a mighty pother about the song of the lark. Now, do tell me—do you know it when you hear it?' But as for the boys that enter now, there's not the natural object that they don't both recognise and know all about. Their collections are of scientific worth—at least, so that fellow Hilyard thinks, so we are going in for a museum of local natural history!"

"Why, Dr Oldcastle, you're like the man in the play, who talked prose all his life, and at last found it out! You're our warmest friend, though you decline the connection. This, again, is the work of mothers working out our scheme of thought. We make a great point of giving play to the intelligent curiosity of the children about all that lives and grows within their ken. For instance, I should think most of 'our' mothers would feel disgraced if her child of six were not able to recognise any ordinary British tree from a twig with *leaf-buds* only. It's Nature's lore, and the children take to it like ducks to the water; the first six or seven years of their lives are spent out of doors—in possible weather—learning this sort of thing, instead of pottering over picture-books and A B C. But do fill the witness-box a minute longer. All this is delightful; an outsider who speaks with authority is worth a score of partisans."

"I bow my thanks, Clough, for the handsome things you are good enough to say. Of course my impartial witness would be quite as valuable if it told on the other side. Why, Hilyard, you're nowhere! It is I am the man of the day. But no; he's the go-ahead fellow, and I'm the drag; yet a drag has its uses."

"Granted, if you go down hill. But out of thine own mouth art thou convicted, most learned Master! What hast thou talked all this night but progress? But one thing more: tell us, do you find these Admirable Crichtons of yours the least in the world priggish? Or are they namby-pamby youths, who do as they're bid, and haven't much taste for unlawful adventure?"

"Taste for adventure! Why, little fellows of nine come, able to swim, row, ride, do everything man or boy needs do, and how are fellows of that sort to be kept out of adventures? But they do as they're bid, I grant you, and the way they do it shows fifty times the spirit of the fellows who shirked. Mind, I'm speaking of the boys who have been *brought up* at home, not of those who have 'growed.' But don't run away with the notion that the best of them are perfect; we must be *at it* all the time, or the ground gained is gone from under our feet."

"Look, look! do look at Brenton: something will happen if he doesn't get an innings."

"Gentlemen, you must, you really must, hear me on this matter! You must let me show Dr Oldcastle the 'reason why' of what he observes."

"Hear, hear! Let's have it, Doctor. Don't spare a word."

"Well, to begin at the beginning (no! not with Adam, nor even with the Dark Ages); some five-and-twenty years or so before Clough's EVENT, men of science began to grope for a clue to the understanding of this queer riddle of human nature. That action (including speech) depends on thought, and that action—repeated action—forms character, had long ago been got at by inductive processes. Now,

those meddling scientific fellows were not content
with, It is, because it is! they must needs go
poking round with their everlasting—'Why?' This
particular 'Why' proved a most hard nut to crack;
indeed, it is only within living memory that their
guesses at truth have become entirely demon-
strable; but, as early as I said, they had thus much
ground under their feet—analogy and probability
were altogether on their side, and it was impossible
to prove, or even to show a fair case for, the contrary
view. These scientists perceived that they were undermining the methods, the aims, the very idea of
education as popularly held. They indicated new
lines, suggested new principles. But their discoveries
were to be like that corn of wheat—first they must
fall into the ground and die. Years passed before
educationalists woke up to what had been done. At
last it dawned upon them that it was now possible
to formulate a *science of education*; to propose laws
which should work out definite ends with proximate,
if not mathematical, certainty. The days of casual
bringing-up were numbered. A basis, and that a
physical basis, was found. The principle which under-
lies the possibility of all education was discovered to
them, as it is to us to-day. They were taught that
the human frame, brain as well as muscle, *grows to the
uses it is earliest put to.* In a hundred years, we have
advanced no further in principle, but we have applied
the principle in many directions. It is, indeed, hardly
possible to get beyond the ground covered by this
so simple-sounding axiom: that is, it is hardly within
our power to overstate the possibilities of education.
Anything may be made of a child by those who first
get him into their hands. No doubt, propagandism

becomes the immediate duty of any who have perceived a saving principle for the race. And efforts were made in many directions to bring before parents of all classes the notion that the formation of habits is among the chief aims of education. Our host's EVENT is one of these efforts, and the Parents' Club spread like wildfire; every one was ready for it, because people were beginning to feel the wretched uncertainty of the casual method. How is it, they asked, that, bring up two boys in the same way, and one turns out a villain, the other, a credit to his family? Now, Education as we understand it, deals entirely with individuals; not with children, but with the child; the faulty habit is supplanted, observe the word, the desirable habit produced, within a definite period, say one month or six, and then the parents' easy work is to keep the child upon the lines of habit thus produced."

"Now, stop a minute, Doctor, stop a minute! I'm afraid I'm about' to lose my easily won laurels. You, who are a classical scholar, must know how familiar to the mind both of Roman and Greek was this doctrine of habit. Again, a poet of our own, an eighteenth-century man—wasn't it Dryden?—expresses capitally the time-out-of-mind English feeling on this subject—

> "'Children, like tender osiers, take the bow,
> And, as they first are fashion'd, always grow;
> For what we learn in youth, to that alone
> In age we are by second nature prone.'"

"Most happy; but don't you see, Dr Oldcastle, I began by admitting that people have always had a notion that they must bring up their children in good habits, and suppress faulty ones. But now, they have something more than a notion; they have scientific certainty. And, instead of dawdling through the whole period of childhood with spasmodic efforts to get a boy to tie his shoe-strings fast, they take it in hand once and for all, until the habit is ingrained in the stuff of the child's character. Now, don't you see that this is a very different thing from the desultory way in which a child was allowed to try off and on for a habit all his days, and never got it?"

"I admit there's a difference; it tallies, too, with what I notice in the young boys who enter with us. You mean that their mothers have definitely set themselves for one month or six, say, to form a habit—now obedience, now truthfulness, now attention, and so on—and that is why the boys come to me with *character*, not mere disposition?"

"Yes, that's what I mean; and it's on these lines we have been advancing for a whole century. In another direction, too, education has been going forward; but, here, we have only analogy to guide us, not yet certainty. It cannot be predicted as yet, whether we are simple or complex beings, whether in each of us is bound up one life or several. It is not impossible, for instance, that, just as our physical life is sustained because multitudinous organisms come to life, feed, grow, multiply, and die, perpetually in our substance, so, perhaps, what we may call our immaterial life is sustained by multitudinous lives such as our philosophy has never dreamed of. An idea, for instance, what is it? We don't know yet; but this we know, that every idea we get is quick within us as a living thing, that it feeds, grows, multiplies, and then, behold it is no more! There are bodies natural and there are bodies spiritual. Perhaps this sort of thing is too immature to be pressed into service ; but of other parts of us to which names and ideas of something like personality are attached—conscience, will, our spiritual being— this it is quite safe to assert: they thrive upon their appropriate meat and work, they perish of inanition and idleness. This, too, we take into our scheme of education, and with great results."

The Dean took the word :—

" I, for one, must heartily thank Dr Brenton for his most suggestive lecture. No, don't look 'castigated,' Doctor; it is a lecture for weight and worth, but of commendable brevity. Speaking for the 'cloth,' I should like to say how much we owe to this educa-tional revolution. A century ago, our Church was supposed to show some signs of decadence; to-day she is *quick* to her remotest extremities. And why? simply because she has gone with the times in following up the advances of educational thought. She, with the rest of you, perceives that the world has ever one great thing to do—to bring up the young in advance of the generation before them ; that the sole valuable inheritance the present has to leave behind is — exalted national character. Wherefore, she has laboured assiduously on the two lines Dr Brenton emphasises to-night—'that Habit is *ten* natures'; and, that the spiritual life must flourish or decay as it is duly nourished and exercised, or allowed to lie idle and unfed. Therefore is every clergyman instructed, above all, to minister to the young of his parish—of all classes. The growing soul cannot thrive upon husks—therefore must the truth be divested of the husks of the past, and clothed upon with the living thought of the present. The young soul must be taught its work, the spiritual exercises of prayer and praise, the bodily exercise of service; and as no man can teach what he does not know, the minister to the young must be qualified and ever active in these. Seeing these and kindred truths, our clergy are raising up about them a body of ardent young spirits to whom self-devotion is a law ; labour in spiritual uplands a necessity. And for much of this progress, I say, we are indebted to the labours of the Educationists, whom we therefore gladly hold up with both hands."

" This is very gratifying hearing ; we have all along been very sensible of the cordiality and helpfulness of the clergy, who so commonly throw in their lot with us. But that we should be doing them some service all the time—this is news indeed. May I imitate Mr Dean, and say a word professionally? We doctors have reaped where we sowed—and abundantly. In the old days, families had each ' their doctor,' who was called in now and then to do battle with disease which had already made head-way. But now, people are beginning to see that low vitality, poor physique, and even organic disease —hereditary or other—are very commonly the results of faulty education, or bringing up, if that is the better way of putting it. What is the consequence? Why, the doctor is retained, like husband or wife, for sickness and health; he is the medical adviser by the year, or usually by the lifetime. He thrives, not on sickness, but upon health. Drops in on his clients unawares, finds one girl doubled up over a book, another standing on one foot, notes the hectic flush and bright eye of this child, the tendency to drowsiness in that—

the flabby arms and quick intelligence of the little town-bred family, the stolid dulness of the farmer's boy—for rich and poor come in course to him. He does not wait for disease to be set up, but averts the *tendency*; and though he has found no elixir of life, nor means of averting death—this, he may almost venture to promise his clients, that so long as they live, they shall live with eye not waxed dim, nor natural force abated. And all this, because he knows that the body, too, must have its education, its careful regulation, and that bone and muscle and vital organs alike grow to the *habits* you set up in them."

Mr Hilyard had been using his pencil for the last few minutes, and was evidently preparing to show on what lines the schools, too, had been advancing during this age of many revolutions, when—"It's eleven o'clock, and the ladies!" brought the discussion to an end.

Part III

Concerning Youths and Maidens

I

CONCERNING THE SCHOOLBOY AND SCHOOLGIRL

THE RELATIONS BETWEEN SCHOOL LIFE AND HOME LIFE—SCHOOL DISCIPLINE AND HOME TRAINING

SCHOOL, A NEW EXPERIENCE

WHEN the child goes to school a new life begins for him; not only so, but no change that may come to him afterwards will be in the same sense a new life. And for this reason: socially speaking, two lives are possible to us—private and public life; we live as members of a family, and as members of a commonwealth. Hitherto, the child has lived in the family; his duties have all been pretty plain, and his affection pretty fairly bestowed. Of course he loves and obeys his parents, more or less, and is fond of his brothers and sisters—there is no choice for him; and the law of the family and the love of the family follow him when he is allowed to mix with the outside world. "Mother says" is his law, "Father told me" his supreme authority. But when he goes to school, all that is changed: though he is still loving and dutiful towards those at home, other things have come in, and the child looks upon the world from a new standpoint. Parents may think, when they send their children to school, that the masters or mistresses and the studies are the points to be considered; that the children go to learn, *i.e.* to learn out of books, and that the heads of the school are, for the time being, in the place of parents to the children.

How far this may be true depends on another factor, sometimes left out of count, namely, the " All the boys " and " All the girls " of schoolboy and schoolgirl phrase. The wise parent, in selecting a school for his child, is not satisfied to examine the syllabus and to know that the masters bear a high character; he sends out feelers to test the direction of *public opinion* in the school: if public opinion set with a strong current towards order, effort, virtue, that is the school for him ; his boy, he is assured, once entered there, will be carried along towards the right. No doubt there will be a few turbulent spirits in every considerable school, and lawlessness is contagious, but the thing to find out is, how far the lead of the scapegraces is followed by the rest.

But the direction of " public opinion," it is said, rests with the master. Not altogether: he will do his best to get it on his side ; but he may be, like Arnold and Thring, years before he succeeds, and that, though he may have everything in his own character to fit him for the office of schoolmaster. We know how little to be depended upon is public opinion in the world; far more, in the little world of school, it veers with every shifting of the wind, just because boys and girls are less reasonable, more emotional, than men and women. Yet, little as it is to be depended upon, this *vox populi* within the school governs the school, and the masters are nowhere except as they get it on their side. Now, this fact shows the real constitution and government of the school : the family is a limited *monarchy*, with sovereign parents ; the school is a *republic*, with an elected president. Of course the master may hold his post in spite of the boys, but his authority and influence, the real matters in question, he only holds so far as they go with him ; that is, so far as they *elect* him to administer their affairs.

Now, we see why it is that the child finds himself in a new and very stimulating element when he goes to school. For the first time, he has to find his footing amongst his equals. At home, he has seldom had more than one equal, and that his friend—the brother or sister next him in age. Here, he has a whole class of his fellows, some stronger, some weaker than himself, working with him, shoulder to shoulder, running neck and neck with him in lessons and games. It is very exciting and delightful. The new boy catches the tone of the school : if the boys work, he works ; if they dawdle, he dawdles,—unless he have been exceptionally well brought up. Happily, it is not too much to say that, as a rule, schoolboys and schoolgirls do work, in these days. School opinion is on the side of order and effort ; and this, for several reasons. It is not that the young people are better or more diligent than young people used to be, but more powerful incentives are put before them ; in fact, the motives to work are stronger than the motives to idle.

EXAMINATIONS

The Universities' Local Examinations, and those of other public examining bodies, have effected a great change in the feeling of middle-class schools, both public and private, in this respect: it is possible for almost any boy or girl to get a distinction worth having, and enough care to make the effort to carry the rest along. *Work* is the order of the day: the desire of distinction, a strong spirit of emulation, stimulated by marks and prizes, do the work of government, and the teachers have little difficulty, except with the few rebellious spirits who decline to go the way of the others.

This looks so well on the face of it, that we ask, Is there nothing to set on the other side? But thus much, at least, must be allowed by both utilitarian and moralist—that the habit of work, the power of work, rapidity in work, the set of the will to a given task, are "the making" of man and woman; that the boy who has done the definite work necessary to pass a given examination is, *other things being equal*, worth twenty per cent. more than he who has not been able to pull his forces together. But these "other things" must be looked into. Is the boy who prepares for a public examination—we are not speaking of prizes open only to a few, such as scholarships at the Universities, but of examinations where success is open to all who are up to a certain reasonable standard—is the boy who goes in for one of these in any respect at a disadvantage compared with him who does not?

Here comes in for consideration the question of "overpressure," a possibility—too serious to be passed over without investigation—which parents naturally dread more for their girls than their boys. In the first place, work, regular disciplinary exercise, is so entirely wholesome for the brain, that girls, even more than boys, should be the better for definite work with a given object. It cannot be too strongly put, that, as a matter of health, growing girls cannot afford to be idle, *mentally* ; it is just as pernicious that they should dawdle through their lessons as that they should lounge through the day. There is no more effectual check to the tendency to hysteria and other nervous maladies common to growing girls than the habit of steady brain-work. But then, it must be work under conditions : fit quantities at fit times, with abundant leisure for exercise and recreation.

Now, the question is, Is it possible to prepare for an examination, say, the Universities' Local Examination, Junior or Senior, under these conditions? For a girl of average intelligence, who has been fairly well taught up to her thirteenth year, it certainly is. It is not the steady work during the year that produces the symptoms of "brain-fag," but a few weeks of *cram* at the end, the struggle to go over the work of the year in a month or so, the excessive strain on the attention, the prolonged hours of study at the expense of play. This is, indeed, *overpressure*, and does harm. But it is unnecessary, because, as a matter of fact, it is useless ; a name, or a date, a lucky shot or two, is all that comes of this senseless " grind." It is seldom that this kind of thing is done at the instance of teachers—the pupils invent the necessity for themselves and go to work blindly ; and, therefore, parents can the more easily put it down, especially in day schools. It rests with them to say that their children shall go in for any examination, public or private, only on condition that little extra time be spent in study previous to the examination. Again, it is possible to reduce or increase the time appropriated to given subjects—language or science, say, according to the power of the pupil. And with these two precautions, there is no reason why the preparation for a public examination should do more than give the pupil a year's definite and wholesome work.

The next point to be considered is the quality of the work. There is no doubt that definite work, on a well-considered programme, with a given object in view, is a clear gain, leading to definiteness of purpose and concentration of effort and attention, the qualities that go to make a successful man. But what is to be said for the style of teaching, the method of study, encouraged by the system of school-work organised with a view to public examinations? and with what is it to be compared? And, in the first place, is it not assuming too much to suppose that these examinations do tell very greatly on the general work of middle-class schools? The *Times*, some years ago, spoke within the mark in saying that the universities had entirely revolutionised the system of education in secondary schools by their "Local Examinations." It is not as if the regulations of the examining bodies affected only the few candidates; the whole of the first division of the school is worked upon the syllabus adopted; the second, the third, down to the lowest division, is worked towards that syllabus: that is, every pupil in the school gets the sort of teaching that is supposed to tell when his time comes to be examined; and so soon as the work of the school begins to take hold of the child, he is making efforts towards this grand result.

Nor did the *Times* say too much in praise of the impulse these examinations have given to secondary education, nor of the practical sterling value of the work obtained. It is a rare thing, now, to meet with a school of any standing which does not do thorough work, commonly tested by the fact that it sends in candidates for some examination. One hears of schools which obtain telling results by a system of cram, of no educative worth at all; but, as a whole, middle-class schools have reached a fair average level —few are much better or much worse than the rest. It used not to be so; a school was a place of real education or of miserable sham, according to the character of its head; but now, a scheme of work is prescribed; any man can see it carried out by assistants, if not by himself, and then his school is as good as another. In a word, the standing of a school no longer depends altogether upon force of character and organising power in its principal.

This levelling tendency of our school routine has its disadvantages; it is not easy to produce individuality in either school or pupil under the present conditions. Individuality, character, culture, public examinations—and a system of school-work based on such examinations—must necessarily strike at the head of these. For what is it possible to examine upon, when the same examination is held simultaneously all over the empire—what the pupil *thinks*, or what he *knows*, what he has seen set down in black and white? The latter, plainly, for it would be unfair to allow examiner or examinee any latitude of opinion in a matter that concerns so many. Therefore, facts,

examinable matter, is the mental *pabulum* of the
school life. If the master be given to discursive
teaching, he pulls himself up, and sticks to facts ; it
is only upon matters of fact that it is possible to
examine, and, therefore, it is upon his power of receiving, retaining, classifying, and reproducing facts
that the pupil's success depends. There is no doubt
that this fact-lore is an invaluable possession. But
it is not culture ; it does not, necessarily, produce a
cultivated mind, the habits of reading and reflection :—

> " A primrose by the river's brim
> A yellow primrose is to him,
> And it is nothing more "—

he, being the boy brought up with a view to successful
examinations, and who has not found for himself a
way to get out of the groove of his work.

Again, the routine of school-work becomes, at the
same time, so mechanical and so incessant, there is
so much hurry to get over the ground, so little leisure,
so little opportunity for the master to bring himself *en
rapport* with his pupil, to feel, as it were, the moulding
of the boy's character under his fingers, that there
is no space for the more delicate moral training, the
refining touch, which a man of superior parts should
bestow upon his pupil. The work, the routine itself,
affords bracing moral training. Diligence, exactness,
persistence, steady concentrated effort, are not to be
despised ; but something more is wanted, not easy to
define, to be got only in sympathetic intercourse with
our betters, morally and mentally, and this something
is being pushed out in the press of work.

What is to be said then ? Give up examinations,
and let teachers and taught dawdle on in the old

vague way? By no means: too much would be lost. Let the children go to schools as they now are, but withdraw them from examination? No; for the training which schools offer now all hinges more or less upon the examinations; and if you do not get that, you get nothing in its place. But the thing is, to look the matter in the face: take the good the schools provide, and be thankful; take count of what they do *not* provide, and see that any culture or moral training which the schools fail to offer is to be had in the home.[1]

THE PLAYGROUND

This parental duty is the more to be insisted on, because school life is so exigent that the modern schoolboy or girl is nearly as much given up by parents as was the Spartan child of whom the State took possession. The boys and girls away at school are treated very much as visitors while at home, made much of at first, and then, before the long holidays are over, found slightly in the way; but it is not often that the parents take them under training as they do the young children who have not yet left the parent wing. The day school should offer the advantage of keeping the children constantly under home influence; but does it do so? As a matter of fact, are not the children so much occupied with school tasks, and their leisure so taken up with school companions and school interests, that the parents gradually lose hold

---

[1] There is no doubt a more excellent way; Lord Selborne found it out for the examination of naval cadets; and for many years the *Parents' Union* has practised a manner of education lending itself to examinations which test intelligence and not successful " cram." But this subject has been taken up fully in another volume of this Series.

of them? Then, the young people set up a code of their own: "Oh, nobody does so!" "Nobody thinks so!" "All the boys" or, "All the girls" say so-and-so, is supposed to settle most matters of discussion. And the worst of it is, many parents, with the diffidence of good people, are ready to believe that their children get something better at school than they have power to give; that, in fact, all proper and suitable training is given there, and they just make a merit of not interfering.

This absorption in school life is the more complete because the young people are, for the time, conscious of no want which the school does not supply. *Work* and *play*, given these in due proportion and of the fitting kind, and life is delightful: and nowhere in the world are work and play so well balanced as in the school—the boys' school, at any rate; it is less easy to make provision for the play of girls. Parents prize the discipline of the playground almost as much as that of the schoolroom; and rightly so—not only for the unequalled physical training that the games afford; but for the "pluck," the "endurance, foresight, strength, and skill," the obedience to law, the deference to authority, the readiness to give place to the best man, the self-reliance, the faithfulness to each other, even in a bad cause, cultivated by means of the school games—with their laws, their captains, their contests, their rivalries. And what finer training could the boys have for a world in which pluck and temper win the prizes?

One is half inclined to regret that the games of the girls, even when they adopt the very games of the boys, can hardly be taken in such terrible earnest, and, therefore, do not exercise the same discipline; but up to the present time, at any rate, life does not offer such rough after-usage to girls as to boys, and, therefore, the same training to hardihood is not called for. The influence which these organisations for play have on the characters of boys is not to be measured. Athletic and, at the same time, thoughtful young masters perceive that, if they are to influence boys, it must be as they are able to make a good figure in the playground, and thereby show that they are in sympathy with the prime interests of a boy's life. So of friendships, comradeships; it is in the playground the boy finds his ideal of manly excellence, the example he sets himself to follow.

SCHOOL GOVERNMENT

The playground does invaluable work, and has much to do with the making of what is best and most characteristic in Englishmen ; but, indeed, the training of the playground, as that of the schoolroom, is incomplete. The fact is, that the discipline of schoolroom and playground alike is largely carried on by stimulating and balancing, one against another, those desires which are common to us all as human beings —the desires of power, of society, of esteem, of knowledge, of mere animal activity, of excelling the rest, of work, or action, even avarice—the desire of wealth. Here is a formidable list ; and it is quite possible, by playing upon and adjusting these natural desires, to govern a human being so that he may make a respectable figure in the world, while yet he has little sense of duty, feeble affections, and dispositions left to run wild, wanting the culture which should train mere *disposition* into *character.*   Now, this way of governing a person through his desires is the easiest in the world.   The nurse knows it very well; his desire, of praise, or play, or lollipops, leaves something always in her hands wherewith to reward the child's good behaviour.   When attempts are made to stimulate people *en masse*, it is through their desires.   They want work or play or power, money or land, and whoever plays upon any one of these desires gets the popular ear. Because this government through the desires is the easiest kind of government it is the most common, in the school as elsewhere; prizes, praise, place, success, distinction, whether in games or examinations, these are enough to keep a school going with such vigour, such *éclat*, that nobody is conscious of the want of other springs of action.

All these desires are right in themselves, within certain limits, and we may believe they were implanted in us as spurs to progress ; the man who has no desire of wealth, no ambition, does not help himself and the world forward as does he who has these desires. Again, in the school the desires are, on the whole, well regulated, one brought into play against another, and the result is, such sturdy qualities, sterling virtues, as "make a man" of the boy brought under school discipline.   The weak place is, that boys and girls are treated too much "in the rough," without regard to the particular tendencies in each which require repression, or direction, or encouragement.   The vain girl is made vainer, the diffident is snubbed: there is no time to hand a crutch to the lame, to pick up the stumbling. All must keep the pace or drop out of the race. It is astonishing how crude may be the character, how unformed the principles, how undeveloped the affections towards country, kindred, or kind, after a successful school career ; the reason being, that the principle of government through the desires has left these things out of count. Nor is this the whole ; the successful schoolboy too often develops into a person, devoid of intelligent curiosity, who hates reading, and shirks the labour of thought. I should like, here, to say a word about that most distressful evil which exceedingly depresses the thoughtful Heads of many of our great schools, and is, to parents, a terrorising, ambushed peril. As to what parents may do to prepare their boys for the risks to be encountered, I will say no word. Every one knows what may be done, and it is possible that too much has been said already.

We are apt to forget that every manner of offence is conceived in thought before it is produced in act ; that, in fact, the offence is committed potentially once it is so conceived. Therefore, there is possible danger in all teaching which tends to occupy the mind with sexual matters: we may, in our blind zeal, befoul, for the young, the beauty of flowers, besmirch the innocence of birds. If we teach with a certain object in view, we are very likely to be the unwilling suggesters of evil, because young people are always aware of the *arrière pensée*. The teacher who deals with scientific facts, *quâ* science, and caring for nothing else, does no harm ; while the virtuous man, with a moral end in view, unconsciously suggests the very evil he would fight most strenuously. The boys are aware that he is aware, and that is enough. I believe that safety lies in an unsuspected quarter. The unoccupied mind offers harbourage, as we know, to the seven devils, and intellectual emptiness, inanition, is probably the provocative cause of much that we deplore. Perhaps few schoolboys give a thought to their studies beyond the mere grind necessary to get them over; and yet boys are by nature consumed with intelligent curiosity. Give them entrancing studies which shall occupy their thoughts, and afford subjects for talk, as we all talk about the book we are reading, and there is no longer a vacuum for unclean imaginings to fill.

There are schools and schools; schools where mental discipline of the highest kind is combined with conscientious development of the character of the individual boy, and with such spiritual insight and teaching as help him into the better life; but such schools are not to be found in every street, and parents would do well not to take it for granted that it is one of these their boy attends : better, to take the school for what it is worth, thankful for the training it does afford; to look its deficiencies in the face, and take pains to supply by means of *home* training what the school fails to give.

GIRLS' SCHOOLS

Girls are, on the whole, worse off than boys as regards what they get out of school life. There is an element of generosity, of free and friendly "give and take" in boys' games, which is wanting to the girls. Beautiful and lasting girl friendships are formed in most schools, but girls do not always do each other good; perhaps because they are more delicate, nervous, and, consequently, irritable by organisation than the boys, they often enough contrive to get the worst and not the best out of each other. They have not the common bond which boys find in their games, and their alliances rest upon talk, which too often turns into gossip, possibly into sentimental and unwholesome gossip. A girl of fine, pure, noble character is like salt which seasons a whole school, and such girls are, happily, plentiful enough; but it is well parents should bear the other possibility in mind, that their daughter may be thrown amongst girls, not vicious, but with nothing in them, who will bring her down to their commonplace level.

Because girls, constitutionally sensitive, are open to the small envyings, jealousies, "cliquishness," which hinder them from getting all the good they should of each other's society, they are more dependent on the character of their head, and on their opportunities of getting in touch with her. If she be a woman of clear and vigorous mind, high principles, and elevated character, it is astonishing how all that is lovely in the feminine character is drawn towards her as by a magnet, and the girls about her mould themselves, each according to her own nature, and yet each after the type of the mistress, the "sympathy of numbers" spurring them on towards virtue, and each—

"Emulously rapid in the race."

Given, to adapt words used in describing Dr Lant Carpenter as a schoolmaster, a woman with a power of "commanding the reverence and reconstituting the wills" of her pupils, of "great and varied intellectual power, with profound sense of right pervading the whole life and conversation, with the insight derived from a thorough and affectionate sympathy with (girl) nature," and she will "daily achieve triumphs which most teachers would believe impossible"; above all, this will be true if she succeed in putting into the hands of her pupils the key to the spiritual life. Such a woman gets all that is beautiful in girl-nature on her side—its enthusiasm, humility, deference, devotion: love works wonders, and the parents see their daughter growing under their eyes into the perfect woman they long to see their child become.

But schoolmistresses, as schoolmasters, of this type are rare; and, indeed, it is as well they are, for if the parents' highest functions are to be fulfilled by outsiders, what is left for father and mother to do? Parents will, no doubt, take care to place their daughters under generally estimable women, and having done that, they will estimate the training the school affords at its value, and endeavour to supplement it at home. How great the value of school discipline is to girls, they can appreciate who have had experience of the vagueness, inaccuracy, want of application, desultoriness, want of conscience about their work, dawdling habits—of young women brought up at home under the care of governesses. Of course there are exceptions, governesses and governesses, and the girl trained under a woman who delights in knowledge for its own sake, will probably surpass the schoolgirl in range of non-personal interests, delight in life, and power of initiative. Girls often fare well when their fathers have a hand in their education. The home-taught girl may, in happy circumstances, excel in intellectual keenness and moral refinement; but for habits of work, power of work, conscientious endeavour in her work, the faithful schoolgirl is, as a rule, far before the girl who has not undergone school discipline, but has been taught by a commonplace untrained governess.

HOME TRAINING—PHYSICAL

It is not necessary to discuss here the respective merits of large and small schools, of day and boarding schools. We may assume at once that the discipline of the school is so valuable, that the boy or girl who grows up without it is at a disadvantage through life; while, at the same time, the training of the school is so far defective that, left to itself, it turns out very imperfect, inadequate human beings. The point for our consideration is, that the duty of the parents to *educate* their child is by no means at an end when he enters upon school life; because it rests with them to supplement what is weak or wanting in the training of the school.

Now, as hitherto, education has a fourfold bearing —on the body, the mind, the moral, and the religious nature of the pupil. As far as physical education goes, the parent who has boys at school may sit at his ease; they are as fish in the water, in the native element of that well-regulated animal activity which should train them up towards a vigorous, capable, and alert manhood.

The schoolboy is so well off in the matter of physical training, that the rest of the world may envy him. But the schoolgirl is less fortunate; her chief dependence is upon gymnastics, dancing, and calisthenics; and some of the severer kinds of gymnastics cannot be attempted without risk by girls in their "teens." Little provision is made in their case, as in that of the boys, for thorough abandonment to games as part of the business of life. If they have tennis-courts, only a few can play at a time; if they have playgrounds, the games are haphazard affairs, and the girls are not encouraged to a healthful exercise of their lungs. Day schools can seldom undertake to make full provision for the physical development of girls, and, therefore, that duty falls back upon the parents. Skipping-rope, shuttle-cock, rounders, cricket, tennis, archery, hockey, cannot be too much encouraged. Long country walks with an object, say, the getting of botanical specimens, should be promoted on at least two days a week. Every day, two or three hours in the open air should be secured, and when that is not possible, on account of the weather, the evening should end with a carpet dance, or with good romping games.

Where is the time to come from? That is a question requiring serious consideration on the part of mothers, on whose good management it must depend if their children are to grow up with that sense of leisure which should be a prerogative of youth. For it is very true that the time of the girls is too fully occupied, and it is only by careful mapping out that enough *growing-time* can be secured for them. Say, their waking-day is fourteen hours long, from seven in the morning till nine at night: something like five hours will be spent in the schoolroom—goings and comings count for open-air exercise, though not of the best; from an hour to an hour and a half will be required for home work, "preparation"; an hour, at least, for "practice" on the piano; two hours for meals, an hour for dressing, etc.; now, three hours and a half is all that is left upon the closest calculation; and two hours and a half of this should be given up without stint to the girls' physical culture and amusement.

The younger children, who have fewer or no home

tasks, and take less time for practising, will have the more for play.   But, if the schoolgirl is to get two or three hours intact, she will owe it to her mother's firmness as much as to her good management.   In the first place, that the school tasks be done, and done well, *in the assigned time*, should be a most fixed law. The young people will maintain that it is impossible, but let the mother insist; she will thereby cultivate the habit of *attention*, the very key to success in every pursuit, as well as secure for her children's enjoyment the time they would dissipate if left to themselves. It seldom happens that home work is given which should occupy more than an hour to an hour and a half, and a longer time is spent in the habit of mental dawdling—a real wasting of brain substance.   It is a mistake to suppose that efforts in this direction run counter to the intention of the teachers; on the contrary, the greatest impediment they meet with is that mental inertness in the children, who will rather dawdle for an hour over a task than brace the attention for five minutes' steady effort.   There is promise that a certain strain will, by-and-by, be taken off home life by the removal of home work or evening ' preparation ' from the school curriculum.   Teachers will gradually discover that if they let their pupils work from fitting books in the three or four school hours, more ground will be covered in less time, and the occasion for home tasks (or evening work in schools) will disappear.

Firmness on the mother's part in enforcing prompt-ness in the taking off and putting on of outdoor clothes, etc., and punctuality at meals, and in not allowing one occupation to overlap another, secures many a half-hour of pleasant leisure for the young people, and has the double advantage of also making them feel themselves under a firm *home rule*.

HOME TRAINING—INTELLECTUAL

The intellectual training of the young people must be left, in the main, to the school authorities. It is useless to remark further upon the subjects or the methods of study; the schoolmaster settles all that, and he, as we have seen, is greatly influenced by the lines laid down by certain examining bodies. Even where the teaching of the school is not satisfactory, there is little to be done: there is neither time nor opportunity for any other direct mental training; and to attempt it, or to criticise unfavourably the working of the school, has a bad effect on the pupil—he learns to undervalue what his school has to give him, but gets nothing else. But though parents can, and should, do nothing counter to the teachers, they may do much by playing into their hands.

It is important that parents should, so far as possible, keep up with their children, should know where they are and how they are getting on in their studies, should look into their books, give an eye to their written work, be ready with an opinion, a hint, a word of encouragement. They may feel and show hearty interest in the *matter* of their children's studies, and when the subject is less dry than the declension of a Latin noun, may throw side-lights upon it by making it matter of table-talk. And this, for a double reason,—both as holding up the hands of the schoolmaster, and as strengthening their own. Parents do not always consider how far a word of interest from them goes to convert the dead words of a lesson into a living idea, never to be lost; and there is no excuse left for getting rusty in these days of many books. The schoolmaster reaps the benefit of such efforts—his task is lightened; he has to teach boys capable of responding; but of more consequence is it that the parents themselves keep their place as heads of the family. They keep the respect of their children; for once a boy begins to look down on the intellectual *status* of his parents, the entire honour and deference he owes them are at an end. Any pains taken to keep ahead should be repaid by the glow of honest pride the young people feel at every proof of intellectual power in their parents.

HOME TRAINING—MORAL

(a) *Honour towards Parents.*—This brings us to the consideration of that education in *morals* which the young people must get at home, or not at all. The chief of their duties, that which should be kept always before the young, is the duty they owe to their parents: from this stem, all their other duties, to kindred, commonwealth, and neighbours, branch out; and more, they only perceive their obligations to Almighty God in proportion as they know what they owe to their human parents.

Now, parents do not always think wisely on this subject. There is a feeling abroad, that the behaviour of a child to his parent is a matter between those two alone; that if the parent choose to absolve his child from any close confidence, from obedience, respectful demeanour,—that is his business: he has as much right to do so as the slave-owner has to manumit his slaves. At the same time, two other notions prevail,—that the kindest and best thing parents can do by their children is to give them "a good time," as the Americans put it; and, that the children of these days are so much in advance of anything that went before them, that it is rather absurd to keep them in subordination to parents not half so clever as themselves. The outcome of these three popular fallacies is, that many parents give up the *government* of their children at a very early age—so soon, that is, as the school steps in to take possession: lax discipline, imperfect confidence, free and easy manners, the habit of doing that which is right in their own eyes, are permitted to grow up.

That school boys and girls should be thus thrown upon their own government is a blow to the interests of society, and a great loss to themselves—the loss of that careful moral training which it is the bounden duty of their parents to afford, throughout school life, at any rate, and through the two or three years that follow it. The problem is, how to maintain due parental dignity, to repress anything like a "hail, fellow, well met!" style of address, and yet to keep up the flow of affectionate intimacy, confidence, and friendly playfulness. Now, here is the secret of home government—put the child into the attitude of a receiver, the parent into that of an imparter, not merely of physical care and comfort, but of a careful and regular training for the responsibilities of life, and the rest comes easy. The difficulty is, that many parents find it hard to maintain this superiority to their children as the latter advance in age and set up other standards than those of home. They possibly feel themselves less clever, less worthy, than some others with whom their children come in contact; they are too honest to assume a dignity to which they doubt their right, so they step down from the rostrum, and stand on the same level as their children, willing to owe to affection and good-nature the consideration which is their lawful due.

Very likely such parents are not less, but more worthy than the persons they give place to; but that is not the question; they are invested with an *official* dignity; it is in virtue of their *office*, not of personal character, that they are and must remain superior to their children, until these become of an age to be parents in their turn. And parents are invested with this dignity, that they may be in a position to instruct their children in the art of living. Now, office in itself adds dignity, irrespective of personal character; so much so, that the judge, the bishop, who does not sustain his post with becoming dignity has nothing to show for himself. So of the parent; if he forego the respectful demeanour of his children, he might as well have disgraced himself before their eyes; for in the one case as in the other, he loses that power to instruct them in the art and science of living, which is his very *raison d'être* in the Divine economy.

If parents put it to themselves that their relation to their children is not an accident, but is a real *office* which they have been appointed to fill, they would find it easier to assume the dignity of persons called upon to represent a greater than themselves. The parent who feels that he has a Power behind him,—that he is, strictly, no more than the agent of Almighty God, appointed to bring the children under the Divine government, does not behave with levity and weakness; and holds his due position in the family as a trust which he has no right to give up.

And now, given the parents in their due position as heads of the family, and all the duties and affections which belong to the family flow out from that one principle as light from a sun. The parents are able to show continual tenderness and friendliness towards their children, without partiality and without weak indulgence. They expect, and therefore get, faithful and ready obedience. Their children trust them entirely, and therefore bestow confidence, and look for counsel; and, of course, treat their parents with due honour and respect. There is a spurious dignity which sometimes brings the parental character into discredit; a selfish and arbitrary parent requires much from, and gives little to, his children, treating them *de haut en bas*; and the children rebel, setting up their claims in opposition to those of their parents. But cases of this kind do not touch the point. Few children resist the authority of a parent who consistently and lovingly acts as the agent of a higher Authority. He is all the more a sovereign because he is recognised as a *deputy* sovereign.

But there are times when the "relations are strained"; and of these, the moment when the child feels himself consciously a member of the school republic is one of the most trying. Now, all the tact of the parents is called into play. Now, more than ever, is it necessary that the child should be aware of the home authority, just that he may know how he stands, and how much he is free to give to the school. "Oh, mither, mither! why gar ye no' *mak'* me do it?" was the cry of a poor ne'er-do-weel Scotch laddie who had fallen into disgrace through neglect of his work; and that is just what every schoolboy or schoolgirl has a right to say who does not feel the pressure of a firm hand at home during the period of school life. They have a right to turn round and reproach their parents for almost any failure in probity or power in after-life. But no mere assertion of authority will do: it is the old story of the sun and the wind and the traveller's cloak. It is in the force of all-mighty gentleness that parents are supreme; not feebleness, not inertness—there is no strength in these; but purposeful, determined *gentleness*, which carries its point, only "for it is right." "The servant of God must not strive," was not written for bishops and pastors alone, but is the secret of strength for every "bishop," or overlooker, of a household.

(*b*) *Gratitude towards Parents.*—The parent will find that, for the sake of his child, tasks of some delicacy fall to him, which would be almost impossible as between man and man, and even in the relations of parent and child require tact and discrimination. For instance, he must foster *gratitude* in his child. There is nothing left to be said for the ungrateful person; even amongst the ancients, ingratitude was held heinous; and yet, what in the world is more natural than to take benefits as matters of course, our own due, and the duty of those who bestow them? We think so highly of our own deservings, are so unready to put ourselves in the place of another and see at what cost he is kind, that, certainly, gratitude is not to be held a wild fruit native to the soil of the human heart. Now, no one can ever owe so much to any living soul as to devoted parents; and if the man is to experience the holy emotion of gratitude, it is as these same parents cultivate in him the delightful sense of their love and their never-failing kindness.

It is a pity, but so it is; the children are so obtuse

that they think no more of their parents' kindness as a personal matter than they do of sunshine or flowers, or any other pleasant thing in life. A mother sits up till midnight darning stockings for her boys; she says nothing about it, and the boys put their stockings on, scarcely knowing whether they are in holes or not. But "how hateful to be always reminding the children of such things, with a 'There now, see how I've had to work for you! I hope the time will come when you will do as much for me.'" Hateful, indeed, and most mischievous; that sort of thing not only irritates the hearer, but cancels the debt. But gentle rallying on "those great holes which kept mother up till midnight," with a " Never mind, my boy; you know, work for you is pleasure to your mother," sinks deep; and the boy is not worth his salt who, after that, does not *mean* to buy his mother silks and satins, gold and jewels, "when I'm a man!" If ever it is necessary to pinch, to do without things for the children's sake, let them know it; but do not reproach them with it; do not treat it as a hardship, but as a pleasure, for their sakes. That is, it is lawful for parents to bring their good deeds before their children as a child offers a flower to his mother, as a show of love, but not as a demand for service. For gratitude is nothing else but a movement of love, and only love kindles love.

(c) *Kindness and Courtesy.*—So of the other manifestations of love—kindness, courtesy, friendliness; these the parents must get from their children, not upon demand, but as love constrains them. Make occasions for services, efforts, offerings: let the children feel that their *kindness* is a power in the lives of their parents. I know of a girl upon whom it dawned for the first time, when she was far in her "teens," that she had any power to gratify her mother.   Do not let the little common courtesies and attentions of daily life slip,—the placing of a chair, the standing aside or falling behind at proper times, the attentive eye at table, the attentive ear and ready response to question or direction.   Let the young people feel that the omission of these things causes pain to loving hearts, that the doing of them is as cheering as the sunshine ; and if they forget sometimes, it will only be that they forget, not that they are unwilling, or look upon the amenities of life as " all bosh !"

Again, let there be a continuous flow of friendliness, graciousness, the pleasantness of eye and lip, between parent and child.   Let the boy perceive that a bright eye-to-eye " Good-morning, mother," is gladness to her, and that a cold greeting with averted face is like a cloud between his mother and the sun.   Parents are inclined to drop these things because they are unwilling to take even their own children by the throat, with a " Pay me that thou owest "; but that is not the way to look at the matter; it is not a personal question at all.   Wordsworth has a deeply suggestive little poem illustrating what I mean :—

> " There is a change—and I am poor ;
>   Your love hath been, nor long ago,
> A fountain at my fond heart's door,
>   Whose only business was to flow ;
> And flow it did ; not taking heed
> Of its own bounty, or my need.
>
> " What happy moments did I count !
>   Blest was I then, all bliss above !
> Now, for this consecrated fount
>   Of murmuring, sparkling, living love,
> What have I—shall I dare to tell ?
> A comfortless and hidden WELL.

> "A well of love—it may be deep ;
>   I trust it is—and never dry ;
> What matter? if the waters sleep
>   In silence and obscurity.
> Such change, and at the very door
> Of my fond heart, hath made me poor."

There is in the heart of every child a fountain of love,

> "Whose only business is to flow" ;

and this it is the part of the parents to keep un-
sealed, unchoked, and flowing forth perennially in the
appointed channels of kindness, friendliness, courtesy,
gratitude, obedience, service. Keep the fountain
flowing, and it will gladden not only the parents,
towards whom is the first rush of the current, but all
about them and beyond them—the family, the household, friends, kindred, schoolfellows, neighbours, the
needy, the world, so far as it can reach. But let the
spring be choked in its rise, in its natural outlet towards parents, and the chances are, it is lost, a mere
buried well of love. How is the fountain to be kept
aflow? Partly by this method of the poet's "*Complaint.*" Let son and daughter perceive the gladness
which every outgoing of their love produces—the
cloud that falls on the parent's heart when the love of
the child is restrained. Natural reticence and pride
incline us to take the "bounty" of the children's love
for granted, and to make no sign of the pain caused
by their thoughtless omissions. But these barriers of
reserve should be broken down for the sake of the
children, and they should be permitted to see, so far
as possible, what is in the hearts of their parents
towards them. And this, because no education tells
so much, Godward or manward, as this education of
the power of loving.

Another point to be borne in mind is, that love grows, not by what it gets, but by what it gives. Therefore, the young people must not get out of the habit of rendering services of love.   There is danger of confounding mere affection, a more or less animal emotion, showing itself in coaxing and fondling, in "Mother, darling," "Father, dear," and—no more, with love, which, however affectionate it be in word and gesture, does not rest in these, but must exhibit itself in service.   The little children are demonstrative, ready to give and take caresses, "loving" in their ways; but the boys and girls have, partly out of *gaucherie*, partly from a growing instinct of reticence, changed all that. They want at this awkward stage of life a great deal of tact and tenderness at the hands of their parents, and the channels of service, friendliness, and obedience must be kept visibly open for the love which will no longer flow in endearments.

THE AWKWARD AGE

Indeed, this, of the growing boy or girl, is not only an awkward, but a critical stage of life.   For the first time, the young people are greatly occupied with the notion of their own *rights*: their *duties* are nowhere. Not what they owe, but what is due to them, it is, that oppresses their minds.   "It's a shame," "It's not fair," "It's too bad," are muttered in secret, when no one ventures to murmur aloud,—and this, with aggravating unreasonableness, and a "one-sidedness" which grown-up people can hardly understand.   But this tiresome behaviour does not arise from any moral twist in the young people; they really have more right than reason on their side: their claims might often be yielded, if there were none but themselves to consider. What they want, is, to have their eyes opened that they may see the rights of others as clearly as their own; and their reason cultivated, that they may have power to weigh the one against the other. This aggressiveness is not mere naughtiness. They must be met on their own ground. Care must be taken not to offend their exaggerated sense of justice as to all that affects themselves. They must get the immunities they can fairly claim; and their parents must be at the trouble to convince them, with good humour, when they are clearly in the wrong.

In the meantime, the state of feeling must be dealt with which would lead a boy to say, "I shan't," if he dared. He must be reached through his affections; the very feelings which make him offensive when centred upon himself, are beautiful and virtuous when they flow in the channels of justice and benevolence towards others. And this is a change not only possible, but easy and pleasant for parents to bring about. The feelings are there already; the strong sense of justice; and the love, which has become exaggerated self-love only because the attention has been allowed to fix upon self and its claims to the exclusion of others. It rests with the parent to turn the attention from self to other people, and the affections will flow in that direction to which the attention is turned.

For instance, let the young people feel that the happiness of home is a trust which every member of it has in charge; that the child who sits down to table with a sullen face destroys for the time the happiness of his whole family, just as a hand's-breadth held close to the eyes will shut out the whole light of the sun. What is it that makes the happiness of

every day—great treats, great successes, great delights ?
No, but constant friendly looks and tones in those
about us, their interest and help in our pursuits, their
service and pity when we are in difficulty and trouble.
No home can be happy if a single member of it allow
himself in ugly tempers and bad behaviour.   By
degrees, great sensitiveness to the moral atmosphere
of the home will be acquired; the happiness of a single
day will come to be regarded as a costly vase which
any clumsy touch may overthrow.   Now, the attention
is taken off self and its claims, and fixed upon brother
and sister, father and mother, servants and neighbours ;
so slight a thing as a friendly look can add to the
happiness of every one of these.

Affection flows naturally towards those to whom
we can give happiness. A boy who feels himself of
little account in his family will give all his heart to
his dog; he is necessary to Puck's happiness, at any
rate; and, as for the dog,—"I think it is wrong to let
children have dogs. It spoils them for mankind,"
said the late Lord Lytton. Let the boy have his dog,
but let him know to how many others even a pleasant
word from him gives happiness for the moment.
Benevolence, the delight in giving happiness, is a
stream which swells as it flows. The boy who finds
he really can make a difference to his home is on the
look-out for chances. A hint as to what father or
sister would like is not thrown away. Considerate
obliging behaviour is no hardship to him when he is
not "bothered" into it, but produces it of his own free
will. Like begets like. The kindliness he shows is
returned to him, and, by him, returned again, full
measure, pressed down, and running over. He looks,
not on his own things, but on the things of others.

His love of justice shows in the demand for " fair play "
for others now ; he will not hear others spoken ill of in
their absence, will not assign unworthy motives, or
accuse another easily of unworthy conduct ; he is just
to the conduct, the character, the reputation of others.
He puts himself involuntarily in the place of the other,
and judges as he would be judged.

> " Teach me to feel another's woe,
>   To hide the faults I see ;
> That mercy I to others show,
>   That mercy show to me,"

is his unformed, unconscious prayer.

His benevolence, again, his kindness, will reach, not
only to the distresses of others, but will show itself in
forbearance towards tiresome tempers, in magnanim-
ity in the forgiveness of injuries.   His habits of kind
and friendly behaviour will, by degrees, develop into
principles of action ; until at last his character is
established, and he comes to be known as a just and
virtuous man.   Towards this great result the parents
can do little more than keep the channels open, and
direct the streams ; they draw the attention of their
son to the needs and claims of others, and point out to
him from time to time the ways in which he holds the
happiness of others in his hands.   It is needless to
say how a selfish or worldly maxim thrown in—" Take
care of yourself," " Look after your own interests,"
" Give tit for tat,"—may obstruct the channel or choke
the spring.   Does, then, the whole of moral training
resolve itself into the culture of the affections ?   Even
so ; it is no new thing to us to learn that—

> " As every rainbow hue is light,
>   So every grace is love,"

HOME TRAINING—RELIGIOUS

With regard to the training of the young in the religious life, I am chiefly anxious to call the reader's attention to the power and beauty of a holy youth. We are content, in this matter, with too low a standard for the children as for ourselves, looking for less than that which many a beautiful child attains in his degree —a life, "holy, harmless, undefiled, separate from sinners":—

> "Who aimeth at a star,
> Shoots higher, far,
> Than he who means a tree."

For the few practical hints I shall venture to offer, they are in this, as in other matters of education, only what thoughtful mothers already carry out.

In the first place, "every word of God" is the food of the spiritual life; and these words come to us most freely in the moments we set apart in which to re-collect ourselves, read, say our prayers. Such moments in the lives of young people are apt to be furtive and hurried; it is well to secure for them the necessary leisure—a quiet twenty minutes, say—and that, early in the evening; for the fag end of the day is not the best time for its most serious affairs. I have known happy results where it is the habit of the young people to retire for a little while, when their wits are fresh, and before the work or play of the evening has begun.

Again, the Christian life should be a *progressive* life. The boy should not be allowed to feel himself like a door on its hinges, always swinging over the same ground. New and definite aims, thoughts, subjects of prayer should be set before him week by week, that "something attempted, something done," may give him courage; and that, suppose he is harassed by failure, he may try in a new direction with new hope. Even those who do not belong to the Church of England would find her Sunday Collects, Epistles, and Gospels helpful, as giving the young people something definite to think about, week by week. We can hardly hope in this life to grow up to all there is in those weekly portions, but the youngest Christian finds enough to go on with, and has the reposing sense of being led, step by step, in his heavenward progress. I am not suggesting this as a substitute for wider reading of the Bible, only as a definite thought, purpose, and prayer for every week as it comes, in addition to whatever other prayers general or special needs may call for. The bringing of the thought of the collect and its accompanying scriptures home will afford occasion for a few earnest words, week by week, not to be readily forgotten. And this in itself is a gain, for we all experience some difficulty in speaking of the best things to the people we live amongst, especially to the young people.

Only one point more—a word as to the manner of keeping Sunday in the family. Do not let the young people feel themselves straitened by narrow views: give them freely the broad principle that what is right on Saturday is right on Sunday—right, but not in all things convenient; the Sunday has pursuits of its own; and we are no more willing to give up any part of it to the grind of the common business or the common pleasures of life, than the schoolboy is to give up a holiday to the grind of school-work. Even for selfish reasons of health and comfort we cannot afford to give up the repose to body, mind, and spirit which we owe to the change of thought and occupations the day brings.

Having made the principle of Sunday-keeping plain, make the practice pleasant. Let it be a joyous day—everybody in his best temper and gentlest manners. Put anxious cares aside on Sunday, for the children's sake; and if there be no "vain deluding mirth," let there be gaiety of heart and talk.

Let the day be full of its own special interests and amusements. An hour's reading aloud, from Sunday to Sunday, of a work of real power and interest, might add to the interest of Sunday afternoon; and this family reading should supply a pleasant *intellectual* stimulus.

A little poetry may well be got in: there is time to digest it on Sunday; not only George Herbert, Vaughan, Keble, and the like, but any poet who feeds the heart with wise thoughts, and does not too much disturb the peace of the day with the stir of life and passion. The point in the Sunday readings and occupations, is, to keep the heart at peace and the mind alive and receptive, open to any holy impression which may come from above, it may be in the fields or by the fireside. It is not that we are to be seeking, making efforts all day long, in church and out of it. We may rest altogether, in body and spirit; on condition that we do not become *engrossed*, that we keep ourselves open to the influences which fall in unexpected ways. This thought determines the choice of the Sunday story-book. Any pure, thoughtful study of character, earnest picture of life, will do to carry our thoughts upward, though the Divine Name be not mentioned; but tales full of affairs and society, or tales of passion, are hardly to be chosen.

It is inadvisable to put twaddling "goody-goody"

story-books into the hands of the young people: a revulsion of taste will come, and then, the weakness of this sort of literature will be laid to the charge of religion. Music in the family is the greatest help towards making Sunday pleasant; but here, again, it is, perhaps, well to avoid music which carries associations of passion and unrest. There can, however, be little difficulty in making a suitable choice, when it is hardly too much to say that the greatest works of the greatest masters are consecrated to the service of religion.

"The liberal soul deviseth liberal things" is a safe rule once the principle is recognised, the purpose and meaning of the Sunday rest. I venture to enter so fully into this subject because the question of Sunday observances is one which comes up to be settled between the parents and every growing-up family.

HOME CULTURE—BOOKS

Although any attempt at intellectual training must be abandoned by the parents when once their children have gone to school, intellectual *culture* is a different matter, and this the young people must get at home, or nowhere. By this sort of culture I mean, not so much the getting of knowledge, nor even getting the power to learn, but the cultivation of the power to appreciate, to enjoy, whatever is just, true, and beautiful in thought and expression. For instance, one man reads—

> ". . . He lay along,
> Under an oak, whose antique root peeps out
> Upon the brook that brawls along this wood;
> To which place a poor sequester'd stag,
> That from the hunter's aim had ta'en a hurt,
> Did come to languish;"—

and gets no more out of it than the four facts of the reclining man, the oak, the brook, and the wounded stag.   Another reads, and gets these and something over—a delicious mental image, and a sense of exquisite pleasure in the *putting* of the thought, the mere ordering of the words.   Now, the second has, other things being equal, a hundredfold the means of happiness which the first enjoys ; he has a sixth sense, a new inlet of pleasure, which adds enjoyment to every hour of his life.   If people are to live in order to get rich, rather than to enjoy satisfaction in the living, they can do very well without intellectual culture ; but if we are to make the most of life as the days go on, then it is a duty to put this power of getting enjoyment into the hands of the young.

They must be educated up to it.   Some children, by right of descent, take to books as ducks to the water ; but delight in a fine thought, well set, does not come by nature.   Moreover, it is not the sort of thing that the training of the schools commonly aims at ; to turn out men and women with enough exact knowledge for the occasions of life, and with wits on the alert for chances of promotion, that is what most schools pretend to, and, indeed, do, accomplish.   The contention of scholars is, that a classical education does more, turns out men with intellects cultivated *and* trained, who are awake to every refinement of thought, and yet ready for action.   But the press and hurry of our times and the clamour for *useful* knowledge are driving classical culture out of the field ; and parents will have to make up their minds, not only that they must supplement the moral training of the school, but must supply the intellectual culture, without which knowledge may be power, but is not pleasure, nor the means of pleasure.

The habit of casual reading, about which Sir John Lubbock says such wise and pleasant words, is a form of mild intellectual dissipation which does more harm than we realise. Many who would not read even a brilliant novel of a certain type, sit down to read twaddle without scruple. Nothing is too scrappy, nothing is too weak to "pass the time!" The "Scraps" literature of railway bookstalls is symptomatic. We do not all read scraps, under whatever piquant title, but the locust-swarm of this class of literature points to the small reading power amongst us. The mischief begins in the nursery. No sooner can a child read at all than hosts of friendly people show their interest in him by a present of a "pretty book." A "pretty book" is not necessarily a picture-book, but one in which the page is nicely broken up in talk or short paragraphs. Pretty books for the schoolroom age follow those for the nursery, and, nursery and schoolroom outgrown, we are ready for "Mudie's" lightest novels; the succession of "pretty books" never fails us; we have no time for works of any intellectual fibre, and we have no more assimilating power than has the schoolgirl who feeds upon cheese-cakes. Scott is dry as dust, even Kingsley is "stiff." We remain, though in another sense than that of the cottage dame, "poor readers" all our days. Very likely these strictures do not touch a single reader of this page, and I am like a parson of the three-decker age inveighing against the ways of the thieves and drunkards who were *not* in the pews. But the mischief is catching, and the children of even reading parents are not safe.

Guard the nursery; let nothing in that has not the true literary flavour; let the children grow up on a few books read over and over, and let them have none, the reading of which does not cost an appreciable mental effort. This is no hardship. Activity, effort, whether of body or mind, is joyous to a child. We older people who went out of our *Robinson Crusoe* into our Scott did not find the strong meat too much for us. I wonder does any little girl in these days of many books experience the keen joy of the girl of eleven I can recall, crouching by the fireside, clasping her knees, and listening, as she has never listened since, to the reading of *Anne of Geierstein*? Somehow, the story has never been re-read; but to this day, no sense impressions are more vivid than those of the masked faces, the sinking floor, the weird trial, the cold bright Alpine village—and no moral impression stronger than that made by the deferential behaviour of "Philip" to his father. Perhaps the impression made later by the *Heir of Redclyffe* ranks next in intensity. But we must adapt ourselves to new conditions; "books for the young" used to be few and dull; now, they are many and delightful.

In connection with this subject let me add a word about story-telling. Here are some of the points which make a story worth studying to tell to the nestling listeners in many a sweet "Children's Hour"; —graceful and artistic details; moral impulse of a high order, conveyed with a strong and delicate touch; sweet human affection; a tender, fanciful link between the children and the Nature-world; humour, pathos, righteous satire, and last, but not least, the fact that the story does not turn on children, and does not foster that self-consciousness, the dawn of which in the child is, perhaps, the individual " Fall of Man." But children will not take in all this? No; but let it be a canon that no story, nor part of a story, is ever to be explained. You have sown the seed; leave it to germinate.

Every father and mother should have a *repertoire* of stories—a dozen will do, beautiful stories beautifully told; children cannot stand variations. " You left out the rustle of the lady's gown, mother!" expresses reasonable irritation; the child cannot endure a suggestion that the story he lives in is no more than the " baseless fabric of a vision." Away with books, and " reading to "—for the first five or six years of life. The endless succession of story-books, scenes, shifting like a panorama before the child's vision, is a mental and moral dissipation; he gets nothing to grow upon, or is allowed no leisure to digest what he gets. It is contrary to nature, too. " Tell us about the little boy who saved Haarlem!" How often do the children who know it ask for that most hero-making of all tales! And here is another advantage of the story told over the story read. Lightly come, lightly go, is the rule for the latter. But if you have to make a study of your story, if you mean to appropriate it as bread of life for your children, why, you select with the caution of the merchantman seeking goodly pearls. Again, in the story read, the parent is no more than the middle-man; but the story told is *food* as directly and deliberately given as milk from the mother's breast. Wise parents, whose children sit with big eyes pondering the oft-told tale, could tell us about this. But it must be borne in mind that the story told is as milk to the child at the breast. By-and-by comes the time when children must read, must learn, and digest for themselves. By the way, before a child begins school work may be the time to give a little care to a subject of some importance.

·   ·   ·   ·   ·   ·

We are in a bad way for epithets: there are hardly more than a dozen current amongst us; and of these one person has seldom more than one or two in everyday use. A cup of tea, a dress, a picture, a book, a person,—is "nice," "perfect," "delicious," "delightful," "jolly," according to the speaker; not at all according to the thing spoken of. Adverbs help a little; a thing may be "nice," "how nice!" or "too awfully nice!" but the help is rather in the way of force than of variety. J. finds all agreeable things "too awfully nice!" while B. finds the same things only "nice." As a rule, things and persons have each one distinctive quality; to see what that is in a flash, and to express it in the fittest word, is a proof of genius, or of the highest culture. "That abysmal question, the condition of East London":—if one had not known that the speaker was a man of just perceptions and wide range of thought, intimately conversant with the questions of the day, that one phrase of a short conversation would have conveyed all that and more. The fitness of this use of "abysmal" stamped the speaker. Little children often surprise and amuse their elders by the fitness and elegance of their phraseology. We have only to foster this power of theirs, to put good words in their way, to treat the perpetual use of "jolly" or "delicious" as rather idiotic, and we are not only fitting our children to shine in society, but doing something to conserve the treasures of the beautiful mother-tongue of our inheritance. It might be worth while to hunt up good strong Saxon epithets for everyday use from the writers of the sixteenth and seventeenth centuries. Milton alone affords a treasure-trove. In the hymn beginning,

> "Let us with a gladsome mind,"

there are half-a-dozen adjectives used with original force ; perhaps half-a-dozen *peculiar to that hymn*, in their use if not in their form. We cannot go about talking of the " golden-tressèd sun " ; that is too good for us ; but to get "gladsome" into our common speech is worth an effort. " Happy-making," again, in the wonderful *Ode to Time*,—could we have a fitter word for our best occasions ?

LETTER-WRITING

Is it true that the charming art of letter-writing has gone out with the introduction of the halfpenny post-card ? " There is a great deal to be said on both sides " would, doubtless, be Sir Roger de Coverley's decision ; anyway, if we do not write letters, the useful little post-card is not to blame. But, do we not ? Have we not all correspondents whose epistles are delightful in their rippling, sparkling flow of talk, with just the little touches of tenderness and confidence which make a letter a personal thing ? Do we not know what it is to open an envelope with the certainty that we shall take pure delight in every line of its enclosure ? Because we love the writer ? Not necessarily. The morning's post may bring you an epistle from an unknown correspondent which shall captivate you, fill you with a sense of well-being for a whole day; and this, not because of the contents, but simply because the gracious courtesy of it puts you on good terms with yourself and the world. One man may refuse a favour and another grant it; and the way in which the refusal is couched may give you more pleasure than the concession.

Possibly, sincere deference is the ingredient which gives flavour to a gracious letter; and if we do not write epistles as charming as those of our grandfathers and grandmothers, is it because we do not think enough of one another to make a spontaneous out-pouring worth while? The children of parents living in India usually write and receive interesting letters, and this, because children and parents are glad to make the most of the only means of knowing each other. Perhaps no opportunity of writing detailed, animated letters to children should be omitted. Let them grow up with the idea that it is worth while to write good letters. That schoolboy whose corre-spondence for a term was comprised in two post-cards, "All right:" "Which train?" is not a good model, except as brevity is the soul of wit!

READING ALOUD

There is little opportunity to give intellectual culture to the boy taken up with his school and its interests; the more reason, therefore, to make the most of that little; for when the boy leaves school, he is in a measure set; his thoughts will not readily run in new channels. The business of the parent is to keep open right-of-way to the pleasant places provided for the jaded brain. Few things help more in this than a family habit of reading aloud. Even a dry book is readable when everybody listens, while a work of power and interest becomes delightful when eye meets eye at the telling bits. To read *The Newcomes* to yourself is like sitting down to a solitary feast of strawberries and cream ; every page has that in it which demands to be shared.

There are few stronger family bonds than this habit of devoting an occasional hour to reading aloud, on winter evenings, at any rate. The practice is pleasant at the time, and pleasant in the retrospect, it gives occasion for much bright talk, merry and wise, and quickens family affection by means of intellectual sympathy. Indeed, the wonder is that any family should neglect such a simple means of pure enjoyment, and of moral, as well as intellectual culture. But this, of reading aloud, is not a practice to be taken up and laid down at pleasure. Let the habit drop, and it is difficult to take it up again, because every one has in the meantime struck a vein of intellectual entertainment for himself—trashy stuff, it may be,—which makes him an unwilling listener to the family " book." No ; let an hour's reading aloud be a part of the winter evening at home — on one or two evenings a week, at any rate—and everybody will look forward to it as a hungry boy looks for his dinner.

If reading is to be pleasant to the listeners, the reading itself must be distinct, easy, and sympathetic. And here is something more which parents must do for their children themselves, for nobody else will get them into the habit of reading for the pleasure of other people from the moment when they can read fluently at all. After indistinct and careless enunciation, perhaps the two most trying faults in a reader are, the slowness which does not see what is coming next, and stumbles over the new clause, and the habit of gasping, like a fish out of water, several times in the course of a sentence.

The last fault is easy of cure: "Never breathe through the lips, but always through the nostrils, in reading," is a safe rule: if the lips be closed in the act of taking breath, enough air is inhaled to inflate the lungs, and supply "breath" to the reader: if an undue supply is taken in by mouth and nostrils both, the inconvenience is caused which relieves itself in gasps.

The stumbling reader spoils his book from sheer want of attention. He should train himself to look on, to be always a line in advance, so that he may be ready for what is coming. Faults in enunciation should be dealt with one by one. For instance, one week the reader takes pains to secure the "d" in "and"; the other letters will take care of themselves, and the less they are heard the better. Indeed, if the final consonants are secured, *d*, *t*, and *ng* especially, the reading will be distinct and finished.

Another advantage of the family *lecture* is, that it enables parents to detect and correct provincialisms; and, however anxious we may be, on historical grounds, to preserve *dialect*, few people desire to preserve it in the persons of their own children. For the rest, practice makes perfect. Let everybody take his night or his week for reading, with the certainty that the pleasure of the whole family depends on his reading well.

THE BOOK FOR THE EVENING LECTURE

To attempt a list of books suitable for the family lecture would be as hopeless as it is unnecessary; but it is possible to discuss the principles on which the selection should be made.   In the first place, to get information is *not* the object of the family reading, but to make the young people acquainted with the flavour of, to give them a *taste* for a real "*book*"—that is, roughly speaking, a work of so much literary merit, that it should be read and valued for the sake of that alone, whatever its subject-matter.

This rule makes a clean sweep of the literature to be found in nine houses out of ten—twaddling story-books, funny or "good"; worthless novels; second-rate writing, whether in works of history or of general literature; compendiums, abstracts, short sketches of great lives, useful information in whatever form.   None of these should be admitted to the evening lecture, and, indeed, the less they are *read* at all, the better. A good encyclopædia is an invaluable storehouse of facts, and should be made use of to elucidate every difficulty that occurs in general reading; and information got in this way, at the moment it is wanted, is remembered ; but it is a mistake to read for information only.

Next, the book must be as interesting, amusing, or pathetic, as may be, but not too profound; the young people have been grinding all day, and now they want relaxation.   One is sorry for girls and boys who do not hear the Waverley Novels read at home ; nothing afterwards can make up for the delight of growing up in the company of Peveril of the Peak, Meg Merrilees,

Jonathan Oldbuck, the Master of Ravenswood, Caleb Balderstone, and the rest; and every page is a training in righteous living and gentlemanlike feeling. But novels are not the only resource; well-written books of travel are always charming; and, better than anything, good biographies of interesting people; not any of the single-volume series of "Eminent" persons, but a big two-volume book that gives you time to become at home with your man.

Important historical works had better be reserved for the holiday, but historical and literary essays by *men of letters* afford very delightful reading. There is no hurry. The evening reading is not task work. It is not important that many books should be read; but it is important that only good books should be read; and read with such ease and pleasant leisure, that they become to the hearers so much mental property for life.

The introduction to a great author should be made a matter of some ceremony. I do not know whether a first introduction to Ruskin, for instance, is the cause of such real emotion now as it was to intelligent young people of my generation; but the *Crown of Wild Olive* still, probably, marks a literary epoch for most young readers.

One other point: it is hopeless and unnecessary to attempt to keep up with current literature. Hereafter, it may be necessary to make some struggle to keep abreast of the new books as they pour from the press; but let some of the leisure of youth be spent upon "standard" authors, that have lived through, at least, twenty years of praise and blame.

POETRY AS A MEANS OF CULTURE

Poetry takes first rank as a means of intellectual culture. Goethe tells us that we ought to see a good picture, hear good music, and read some good poetry every day; and, certainly, a little poetry should form part of the evening *lecture.* "Collections" of poems are to be eschewed; but some one poet should have at least a year to himself, that he may have time to do what is in him towards cultivating the seeing eye, the hearing ear, the generous heart.

Scott, of course, here as before, opens the ball, if only for the chivalry, the youthful enthusiasm of his verse. Then, there is always a stirring story in the poem, which is a recommendation to the young reader. Cowper, who does not tell many stories, is read with pleasure by boys and girls almost as soon as they begin to care for Scott; the careful, truthful word-painting of *The Task*, unobscured by poetic fancies, appears to suit the matter-of-fact young mind. It is pleasant, too, to know poetry which there are frequent opportunities of verifying :—

> "Now from the roost, or from the neighb'ring pale,
> Come trooping, at the housewife's well-known call,
> The feather'd tribes domestic :"—

who that has ever been in the country has not seen that? Goldsmith, and some others, take their places beside Cowper, to be read or not, as occasion offers. It is doubtful if Milton, sublime as he is, is so serviceable for the culture of the "unlearned and ignorant" as are some less distinguished poets; he gets out of reach, into regions of scholarship and fancy, where these fail to follow. Nevertheless, Milton must be duly read; the effort to follow his "high themes" is culture in itself. Also, "Christopher North" is right; good music and fine poetry need not be understood to be enjoyed:—

> "Together both, ere the high lawns appeared
> Under the opening eyelids of the morn,
> We drove a-field, and both together heard
> What time the gray-fly winds her sultry horn,
> Battening our flocks with the fresh dews of night,
> Oft till the star, that rose at evening bright,
> Toward heaven's descent had sloped his westering wheel:"—

the youth who carries about with him such melodious cadences will not readily be taken with tinsel. The *epithets* of *Lycidas* alone are an education of the poetic sense.

Many of us will feel that Wordsworth is the poet to read, and grow thereby. He, almost more than any other English poet of the last century, has proved himself a power, and a power for good, making for whatever is true, pure, simple, teachable; for what is *supersensuous*, at any rate, if not spiritual.

The adventures of Una and her tardy, finally victorious knight offer great food for the imagination, lofty teaching, and fine culture of the poetic sense It is a misfortune to grow up without having read and dreamt over the *Faerie Queene*.

There is no space to glance at even the few poets each of whom should have his share in the work of cultivating the mind. After the ploughing and harrowing, the *seed* will be appropriated by a process of natural selection; this poet will draw disciples here, that, elsewhere; but it is the part of parents to bring the minds of their children under the influence of the highest, purest poetic thought we have. As for

Coleridge, Keats, Shelley, and others of the "lords of language," it may be well to let them wait this same process of selection.

And Shakespeare?   He, indeed, is not to be classed, and timed, and treated as one amongst others,—he, who might well be the daily bread of the intellectual life; Shakespeare is not to be studied in a year; he is to be read continuously throughout life, from ten years old and onwards.   But a child of ten cannot understand Shakespeare.   No; but can a man of fifty?   Is not our great poet rather an ample feast of which every one takes according to his needs, and leaves what he has no stomach for?   A little girl of nine said to me the other day that she had only read one play of Shakespeare's through, and that was *A Midsummer Night's Dream.*   She did not understand the play, of course, but she must have found enough to amuse and interest her.   How would it be to have a monthly reading of Shakespeare—a play, to be read in character, and continued for two or three evenings until it is finished?   The Shakespeare evening would come to be looked on as a family *festa*; and the plays, read again and again, year after year, would yield more at each reading, and would leave behind in the end rich deposits of wisdom.

It is unnecessary to say a word about the great later poets, Browning, Tennyson, and whoever else stands out from the crowd; each will secure his own following of young disciples from amongst those who have had the poetic taste developed ; and to develop this appreciative power, rather than to direct its use, is the business of the parents.

So much for the evening readings, which will in themselves carry on the intellectual culture we have in view: given, the right book, family sympathy in the reading of it, and easy talk about it, and the rest will take care of itself.

The evening readings should be entertaining, and not of a kind to demand severe mental effort; but the long holidays are too long for mere intellectual dawdling. Every Christmas and summer vacation should be marked by the family reading of some great work of literary renown, whether of history, or purely of *belles lettres.* The daily reading and discussion of one such work will give meaning and coherence to the history "grind" of the school, will keep up a state of mental activity, and will add zest to the general play and leisure of the holidays.

Yet be it confessed, that in the matter of reading, this sort of spoon-feeding is not the best thing, after all. Far better would it be that the young people should seek out their own pastures, the parents doing no more than keep a judicious eye upon their rovings. But the fact is, young people are so taken up with living, that, as a rule, they do *not* read nowadays; and it is possible that a course of spoon-meat may help them over an era of feeble digestive power, and put them in the way of finding their proper intellectual nourishment.

TABLE-TALK

The character of the family reading will affect that of the talk; but considering how little parents see of young people once entered on their school career, it is worth while to say a few words of the table-talk which affords parents their best opportunity of influencing the opinions of the young. Every one is agreed that animated table-talk is a condition of health. No one excuses the churlish temper which allows a member of a family to sit down absorbed in his own reflections, and with hardly a word for his neighbours. But conversation at table is something more than a means of amusement and refreshment. The career of many a young person has turned upon some chance remark made at the home table. Do but watch the eagerness with which the young catch up every remark made by their elders on public affairs, books, men, and you will see they are really trying to construct a chart to steer by; they want to know what to do, it is true, but they also want to know what to *think* about everything.

Parents sometimes forget that it is their duty to give their children grounds for sound opinions upon many questions which concern us as human beings and as citizens; and then they are scandalised when the young folk air audacious views picked up from some advanced light of their own age and standing. But they *will* have views; the right to have and to hold an opinion is one of those points on which the youth makes a stand.

A few parents are unjust in this matter. It is not only the right, but the duty of the growing intelligence to consider the facts that come before it, and to form conclusions; and the assumption that parents have a right to think *for* their children, and pass on their own views unmodified upon literature and art, manners and morals, is exceedingly trying to the young; the headstrong resent it openly, the easy-going avoid discussion, and take their own way. But, it is said, the young are in no condition to form sound opinions; they have neither the knowledge nor the experience which should guide them. That is true, and they know it, and hang on the lips of their elders for what may help them to adjust their views of life. Here is the opportunity of parents: the young people will not take ready-made opinions, therefore suppress yours; put the facts before them in the fairest, fullest light, and leave them to their own conclusions. The more you withhold your opinions, the more anxious they are to get at them. People are, for them, sharply divided into good and bad; actions are vicious or virtuous; events come as blessings or misfortunes. They have not arrived at the "years that bring the philosophic mind"; they are inclined to be severe, and have no notion of a middle view.

Now, this period in the life of a boy or girl, when he or she feels the necessity of having an opinion upon every subject under the sun, is a critical one—a turning-point, for better or worse, in the lives of many young people, and for this reason; they *will* find somewhere the confidant who is to mould their opinions for them. Many a mother can put her finger on the moment when her boy or girl came under the influence of So-and-so, and took to giddy or godless courses. The culture of judgment in the crude mind of the youth is one of the most delicate tasks inposed on the parent. He must not be arbitrary, as we have seen. He must not be negligent. He must not be didactic; the young cannot stand preaching. He should be liberal, gentle, just, inclined to take large kindly views, to praise rather than to blame, but uncompromising on questions of principle, quick to put his finger on the blot, ready to forgive, but not to excuse; and, at the same time, ready to allow virtues to the man who exhibits one vice.

This last is important; the young, with their sharp

demarcations, when they find themselves in his company, discover that the devil is not so black as he was painted, and, forthwith, conclude that he is a very good fellow, and that the bad things said of him are mere slanders. This is the natural history of half the ruinous companionships young people form. If, on the contrary, they come forth armed with this sort of opinion, —"So-and-so is a forward girl; she is really honest and good-natured, but her lawlessness makes her an undesirable companion,"—the case is altered; the girl has had fair play; and no further drawings are felt towards her companionship.

Allowing that it rests with the parents to give their children grounds for sound opinions on men and movements, books and events, when are they to get opportunity for this sort of culture? Whenever they fall into talk with, or in the presence of, their children; but especially at table—other opportunities come by chance, but this is to be relied on. I was once spending an evening in company with a wise and learned man, and had much delightful talk until he unfortunately said, "I jotted down so-and-so as a subject of conversation"; that spoiled it. But, indeed, it is very well worth while for parents to lay themselves out for conversation with their children, and to store up from day to day a few subjects of general interest, only they must not reveal the "jotting down." If the parents come to table with preoccupied minds, the young people either remain silent, or get the talk into their own hands; in which case, it is either the "shop" of school and playground, or the

"Who danced with whom, and who is like to wed,"

of a more advanced age.

This is the opportunity to keep the young people informed upon the topics of the day,—who has made a weighty speech; who has written a book, what its merits and defects; what wars and rumours of wars are there; who has painted a good picture, and what are the characteristics of his style. The *Times* newspaper and a good weekly or monthly review will furnish material for talk every day in the week. The father who opens the talk need not be afraid he will have to sustain a monologue; indeed, he had better avoid prosing; and nothing is more delightful than the eager way the children toss the ball to and fro. They want to know the inns and outs of everything, recollect something which illustrates the point, and inevitably corner the thing talked about for investigation—is it " right," or " wrong," " good," or " bad "; while the parents display their tact in leading their children to form just opinions without laying down the law for them. The boys and girls are engaged with the past, both in their school-work and their home reading, and any effort to bring them abreast of the times is gratifying to them; and it has a vivifying effect on their studies.

ÆSTHETIC CULTURE

In venturing to discuss the means of æsthetic culture, I feel that to formulate canons of taste is the same sort of thing as to draw up rules of conscience; that is, to attempt to do for other people what every one must do for himself. It may be vicious to have a flower pattern on our carpet, and correct to have such a pattern on our curtains; but if so, the perception of the fact must be the result of growth under culture. If it come to us as an edict of fashion that we adorn our rooms with bulrushes and peacocks' feathers; that we use geometrical forms in decorative art, rather than natural forms conventionally treated; that we affect sage-green and terra-cotta,—however good may be the effect of room or person, there is little taste displayed in either. For *taste* is the very flower, the most delicate expression of individuality, in a person who has grown up amidst objects lovely and befitting, and has been exercised in the habit of discrimination. Here we get a hint as to what may and what may not be done by way of cultivating the æsthetic sense in young people. So far as possible, let their surroundings be brought together on a principle of natural selection, not at haphazard, and not in obedience to fashion. Bear in mind, and let them often hear discussed and see applied, the three or four general principles which fit all occasions of building, decorating, furnishing, dressing: the thing must be *fit* for its purpose, must harmonise with both the persons and the things about it; and, these points considered, must be as lovely as may be in form, texture, and colour; one point more —it is better to have too little than too much. The child who is accustomed to see a vase banished, a chintz chosen, on some such principles as these, involuntarily exercises discriminating power; feels the jar of inharmonious colouring, rejects a bedroom water-jug all angles for one with flowing curves, and knows what he is about. It may not be possible to surround him with objects of art, nor is it necessary; but, certainly, he need not live amongst ugly and discordant objects; for a blank is always better than the wrong thing.[1]

[1] "Nothing can be a work of art which is not useful, that is to say, which does not minister to the body when well under the command of

It is a pity that, in pictures and music, we are inclined to form "collections," just as in poetry.   Let us eschew collections.   Every painter, every composer, worth the name, has a few master ideas, which he works out, not in a single piece, but here a little and there a little, in a series of studies.   If we accept the work of the artist as a mere external decoration, why, a little of one and a little of another does very well; but if we accept the man as a teacher, who is to have a refining, elevating effect upon our coarser nature, we must study his lessons in sequence, so far as we have opportunity.   A house with one or two engravings from Turner in one room, from Millet in another, from Corot's pictures in a third, would be a real school of art for the child; he would have some little opportunity of studying, line by line, three masters at least, of comparing their styles, getting their characteristics by heart, perceiving what they mean to say by their pictures, and how they express their meaning.   And here is a sound foundation for art-education, which should perhaps, for most of us, consist rather in drawing out the power to appreciate than the power to produce.   At the same time, give the young people one or two good water-colour sketches to grow upon, to show them what to see in landscape.

It is not, however, always possible to choose pictures according to any such plan; but in default of more, it is something to get so thoroughly acquainted with even a good engraving of any one picture, that the image of it retained by the brain is almost as distinct as the

the mind, or which does not amuse, soothe, or elevate the mind in a healthy state.   What tons upon tons of unutterable rubbish, pretending to be works of art in some degree, would this maxim clear out of our London houses."—WILLIAM MORRIS.

picture itself. All that the parents can do is to secure
that the picture be *looked at*; the refining influence,
the art-culture, goes on independently of effort from
without. The important thing is, not to vitiate the
boy's taste; better to have a single work of art in the
house upon which his ideas form themselves, than to
have every wall covered with daubs. That the young
people must commonly wait for opportunities afforded
by picture-galleries to learn how the brush can catch
the very spirit and meaning of nature, is not so great
a loss as it would seem at first sight. The study of
landscape should, perhaps, prepare them for that of
pictures: no one can appreciate the moist solid freshness of the newly ploughed earth in Rosa Bonheur's
pictures who has not himself been struck by the look
of the clods just turned up by the plough. But, on
the other hand, what is to be said to this, from *Fra
Lippo Lippi*?—

> "Don't you mark, we're made so that we love
> First when we see them painted, things we have passed
> Perhaps a hundred times, nor cared to see :
> And so they are better painted—better to us,
> Which is the same thing. Art was given for that—
> God uses us to help each other so,
> Lending our minds out. Have you noticed now
> Your cullion's hanging face? A bit of chalk,
> And, trust me, but you should though. How much more
> If I drew higher things with the same truth !
> That were to take the prior's pulpit-place—
> Interpret God to all of you !"

Pictures or landscape, all the parents can do is to
put their children in the way of seeing, and, by a
suggestive word, get them to look. The eye is trained
by seeing, but also by instruction ; and I need hardly
call attention to Mr Ruskin's *Modern Painters*, as

the book which makes art-education possible to outsiders.

If culture flows in through the eye, how much more through the ear, the organ of that blessed sixth sense, which appears to be distributed amongst us with partial favour. A great deal of time and a good deal of money is commonly spent to secure to the young people the power of performing indifferently upon an instrument; nor is even an indifferent performance to be despised: but it is not always borne in mind that to listen with discriminating delight is as educative and as "happy-making" as to produce; and that this power might, probably, be developed in everybody, if only as much pains were spent in the cultivation of the musical sense as upon that of musical facility. Let the young people hear good music as often as possible, and that *under instruction*. It is a pity we like our music, as our pictures and our poetry, mixed, so that there are few opportunities of going through, as a listener, a course of the works of a single composer. But this is to be aimed at for the young people; let them study occasionally the works of a single great master until they have received some of his teaching, and know his style.

II

CONCERNING THE YOUNG MAIDENS AT HOME

YOUNG MAIDENHOOD—THE FORMATION OF CHARACTER AND OPINIONS

"For life in general there is but one decree. Youth is a blunder."—DISRAELI.

THE idea of staying at home "for good" is delightful to the schoolgirl, and her parents look forward with equal pleasure to having their daughter about them in her bright fresh youth. If the young girl be docile and gentle, and ready to fall into the relation of pupil-friend to her parents, and if they be wise and kind enough to put themselves in the place of their daughter, and realise how much teaching and counsel she still requires of them, the relation is a very sweet one. If, on the other hand, the parents are content to let their young daughter shake down into her place with the notion that all they have to do now is to give her a fair share of whatever "home" offers, the relation is found embarrassing, both by the girl and her parents. Her maiden sweetness notwithstanding, the parents are disappointed to find their daughter so little formed. She is not an interesting companion at present, poor

child! Her talk is full of "oh," "well," "you know."
She has many unreasoning enthusiasms and aversions,
and these are her opinions, such as they are. She has
brought some little knowledge out of the schoolroom,
but this appears to do little towards giving her sound-
ness of judgment.

Her affections are as lawless as her opinions: all
the emotional sentiment in her is bestowed on some
outsider, girl or woman friend, most likely, while the
people who have claims on her are overlooked royally.
So of her moral sense: duties she acknowledges, and
will move heaven and earth to fulfil them—overstrained
loyalty to a friend, excessive religious observances, perhaps; while she is comically blind to duty as her elders
see it; does not scruple about disobedience, evasions,
even deliberate fibs. She could do great things in a
great cause, so she thinks, but the trivial round, the
common task, afford her occasions of stumbling. She
likes to talk about herself—what she feels, thinks, pur-
poses, and her talk is pathetic, as showing how far she
is in the dark as to the nature of the *self* about which
her thoughts are playing curiously. And this is a
thoroughly nice girl, a girl who will make something
of herself at last, even if left to her own devices, but
whom a little friendly help may save from much
blundering and sadness.

There are girls of another pattern, who have no
enthusiasms—other than a new "frock" excites; who
do not "gush," have no exaggerated notions of duty
or affection, but look upon the world as a place
wherein they are *to have* and *to get*, but not, save
under compulsion, *to do*, *to bear*, and *to give*: these
three, which make up the ideal of a noble life, have
no part in their thoughts. Girls of this sort are

easier to get on with than the others, because they have marked out a line for themselves, and know what they are about; but there is no principle of growth in such natures. Then, there are maidens so sweet, that, like the lilies of the field, they seem in need of no human culture. But the average nice girl, who leaves school with her education "finished," so she thinks, and is yet in a crude, unformed state, what is to be done with her?

The very insufficiency of her young daughter appeals as strongly to the mother as does the helplessness of her infant. The schools have not finished, but begun the education of the girl, and now she has come home to be taught how to make the best of herself, and *how she is to succeed in life,*—for that is the problem before her. The girl who has been brought up at home, under her mother's eye, is, in this respect, in very much the same case as the school-girl; she, too, has yet to learn *to live.* Rich or poor, married or single, she may be, but it is not upon these that the success of a woman's life depends. Many a rich woman, whose children run over her, whose husband slights her, knows sorrowfully that she has made a failure of life; while many a poor woman is a queen in her own house, or is "made much of" in a house that is not hers. The woman who has herself well in hand, who thinks her own thoughts, reserves her judgments, considers her speech, controls her actions—she is the woman who succeeds in life, with a success to be measured by her powers of heart, brain, and soul.

CULTURE OF CHARACTER

(*a*) *By Instruction.*—A woman's success in life depends on what force of *character* is in her; and character is to be got, like any other power, by dint of precept and practice: therefore, show the girl what she is, what she is not, how she is to become what she is not, and give her free scope to act and think for herself. What she is, is an exceedingly interesting study to the young girl, and open discussion on this subject helps her out of foolish and morbid feeling. She is full of vague self-consciousness, watching curiously the thoughts and emotions within her—an extraordinary spectacle to her inexperienced mind, leading her to the secret conviction that she is some great one, or, at any rate, is peculiar, different from the people about her. Hence arises much *mauvaise honte*, shyness, awkwardness; she feels herself the ugly duckling, unappreciated by the waddling ducks about her. She is clumsy enough at present, and is ready to own it; but wait a bit, until the full-grown swan appear, and *then* they will see!

Now, this stage of self-consciousness and ignorant much-doubting self-exaltation, this "awkward age," as people call it, is common to all thoughtful girls who have the wit to perceive that there is more in *them* than meets the eye, but have not begun to concern themselves about what may or may not be in other people. It is a moral complaint, in which the girl requires treatment and tender nursing—only of a moral kind—as truly as she did when she had measles. If left to herself, she may become captious, morbid, hysterical; the years in which the foundations of sound character should be laid are wasted; and many a peevish, jealous, exacting woman owes the shipwreck of her life to the fact that nobody in her youth taught her to think reasonably of herself and of other people. It is only a few who founder; many girls are graciously saved: but this does not make it the less imperative on the mother to see her child safely through the troublous days of her early youth.

The best physic for the girl is a course of moral and mental science; not necessarily a profound course, but just enough to let her see where she is; that her noble dream of doing something great or good by-and-by—for which achievement she is ready to claim credit beforehand—is shared, in one form or other, by every human being; because the desire of power, the desire of goodness, are common to us all; that the generous impulse, which makes her stand up for her absent friend, and say fierce things in her behalf, is no cause for elation and a sense of superior virtue, for it is but a movement of those affections of benevolence and justice which are implanted in every human breast.

By the time the girl has discovered how much of her is common to all the world, she will be prepared to look with less admiring wonder at her secret self, and with more respect upon other people. For it is not that she has been guilty of foolish pride; she has simply been filled with honest and puzzled wonder at the fine things she has discovered in human nature as seen in herself. All her fault has been the pardonable mistake of thinking herself an exceptional person; for how is it possible that the people about her should

have so much in them and so little come of it? Let
her know that she is quite right about herself—that
she has within her the possibilities she dreams of, and
more; but that so have others, and that upon what
she makes of herself, not upon what is in her, judgment
will be passed.

It is true that a life of stirring action and great
responsibility is the readiest means of developing
character—better or worse: but not one woman in
a thousand leads such a life; and then, not until she
has reached maturity. Put into the hands of the girl
the means of doing for herself what only exceptional
circumstances will do for her; teach her, that is, the
principles and methods of *self*-culture, seeing that you
cannot undertake to provide for her the culture of
circumstances. To point out these principles and
methods in detail would be to go over the ground I
have attempted to cover in a former volume.[1] By
the time the girl has some insight into the nature of
those appetites, affections, emotions, desires, which
are the springs of human action; into the extraordinary power of habit, which, though acquired by
us, and not born in us, has more compelling force
than any or all of the inborn principles of action;
into the imperious character of the will, which rules
the man, and yet is to be ruled and trained by the
man; into the functions of conscience, and into the
conditions of the spiritual life,—by the time she has
some practical, if only fragmentary, notions on these
great subjects, she may be led to consider her own
nature and disposition with profit. So far from encouraging the habit of morbid introspection, such a
practical dealing with herself is the very best cure for

[1] *Ourselves, our Souls and Bodies*, Kegan Paul, London.

it. She no longer compares herself with herself, and judges herself by herself; but, knowing what are the endowments and what the risks proper to human nature, she is able to think soberly of, and to deal prudently with, herself, and is in a position to value the counsels of her parents.

(*b*) *By Training in Practical Affairs.*—These counsels come to her aid in the small practical affairs of life, as telling her, not what she must do, but the principles on which she should act. Thus: she goes to the draper's; looks at this stuff, at that, at the other; now she will have this, now the other; no, neither will do; and at last she turns to her mother in despair and says, "You choose." That will not do; that is, by so much, a failure in life. Her mother takes her to task. Before she goes "shopping," she must use her reason, and that rapidly, to lay down the principles on which she is to choose her dress,—it is to be pretty, becoming, suitable for the occasions on which it is to be worn, in harmony with what else is worn with it. Now, she goes to the shop; is able to describe definitely what she wants; to say "No" instantly to the wrong thing, "Yes" to the right; judgment is prompt to decide upon the grounds already laid down by reason; and what is more, the *will* steps in to make the decision final, not allowing so much as a twinge of after-regret for that "sweet thing" which she did *not* buy. For the sake of cultivating decision of character, even a leap in the dark, like that of Sydney Smith's little maid, Bunch, when she chose, quick as thought, between venison and wild duck, having never tasted either, is to be preferred to the endless dilly-dallying, deliberation, taking of advice here and there, in which

the lives of some women are passed—to the trial of
their friends.

Again, she is given to dawdling : a letter, some slight
household task, " lasts out " ; an hour is spent on what
should be done in fifteen minutes.   Want of attention
is, probably, the failing her mother comes down upon.
Many a mother of energetic character brings up for
herself a dawdling daughter, for this reason—the mother
is so " managing," so ready to settle the employments
and amusements of everybody about her, that the girl's
only chance of getting a few minutes at her own dis-
posal is to dawdle ; and this leads to small deceptions,
furtive readings of story-books, any of the subterfuges
of the weak in dealing with the strong.

The mother's task in dealing with her growing
daughter is one of extreme delicacy.   It is only as her
daughter's ally and confidante she can be of use to her
now.   She will keep herself in the background, de-
clining to take the task of self-direction out of her
daughter's hands.   She will watch for opportunities to
give word or look of encouragement to every growing
grace.   She will deal with failings with a gentle hand,
remembering that even failures in veracity or integrity,
distressing as they are, arise usually from the very
moral weakness which she is setting herself to
strengthen.

On discovering such fault, the mother will not cover
her daughter with shame ; the distress she feels she
will show, but so that the girl perceives her mother is
sharing her sorrow, and sorrowing for her sake.   What
is the root of the error ?   No due sense of the sanctity
of truth, an undue fear of consequences, chiefly of loss
of esteem.   The girl is betrayed into a deliberate lie ;
she has *not*, she says, written such and such a letter,

said such and such words, you knowing all the time that she *has* done this thing. Deal gently with her: she is no longer a child to be punished or "disgraced" at her parents' pleasure; it is before her own conscience she must stand or fall now. But do not let her alone with the hopeless sense that there is no more to be done for her. Remember that conscience and intellect are still immature, that will is feeble. Give her simple sincere teaching in the nature of truth. Let her know what truth is—the simple statement of facts as they are; that all our spoken words deal with facts, and that, therefore, the obligation of truth is laid upon them all; we should never open our lips without speaking the truth. That even a jest which *misleads another* is a lie; that perfect truthfulness, in thought, speech, and act, is an obligation laid upon us by God. That the duty is binding, not only with regard to our friends, but towards every one with whom we hold speech.

The Christian mother will add deeper teaching about the Truth from Whom all truth proceeds. She will caution her daughter as to the need of self-recollected-ness in speech. She says she is "quite well, thank you," when she has a headache; that she "will be done in a minute," when the minute means half an hour; these departures from fact slip out without thought—therefore, think first, and speak after. But such trifles surely do not matter? if so, who may cast a stone? Most of us might mend our ways in this matter; but every guard she can place upon herself is of real value to the girl with an inadequate sense of truth, as a means of training herself in the truthful *habits* which go to form a truthful *character*. Then, train her by trusting her. Believe her always; give her opportunities to condemn herself in speaking the truth, and her courage will answer the demand upon it.

A bare enumeration of the duties which truthfulness comprehends, of the vices which are different forms of lying, is helpful and instructive. The heart rises and resolves upon the mere hearing that *veracity* is that truthfulness in common talk which is careful to state the least important fact as it is ; that *simplicity* tells its tale without regard to self, without any thought of showing self to advantage in the telling; that *sincerity* tells the whole truth purely, however much it might be to the speaker's advantage to keep any part back ; that *frankness* is the habit of speaking of our own affairs openly and freely—a duty we owe to the people we live amongst ; that *fidelity*, the keeping of our trusts, in great things and small, belongs to the truthful character.

LIBERTY AND RESPONSIBILITY

"With household motions light and free,
    And steps of virgin liberty,"

says Wordsworth of the girl who was to become that "perfect woman."   Now, it sometimes happens that the mothers who take most pains to make their daughters deft and capable in "household motions," forget the "steps of virgin liberty."   If the girl is to become a free woman with the courage of her opinions, she must grow up to the habit of liberty—not license, but liberty, for the use of which she is open to be called to account. Let her distribute her time as she likes, but count her tale of bricks; let her choose books for her own reading, but know what she chooses; let her choose her own companions, but put before her the principles on which to choose, and the home duties which should prevent their having too much of her time. Let her have the spending of money,—first, a small allowance out of which certain necessary expenses must come, as well as spendings for her pleasure, and a reserve for gifts and alms; and as soon as she can be trusted with it, an allowance large enough to dress herself out of,— that she may learn prudence by doing without necessaries when she wastes on fancies. One reason why she should have the spending of her own allowance is, that she may learn early the delight and the cost of giving, and may grow up in the habit of appropriating a fixed part of her little income to the help of the needy.

The care of her own health is another responsibility which should be made over to the young maiden. She cannot learn too soon that good health is not only a blessing, but a *duty*; that we may all take means to secure more or less vigorous health, and that we are criminal in so far as we fail to make use of these means. Any little book on the laws of health will put her in possession of the few simple principles of hygiene: the daily bath, attended with much friction of the skin; regular and sufficient exercise in the open air; the vigorous use of all the limbs; exercise of moderation in diet and in sleep; the free admission of fresh air to the bedroom; the due airing of the underclothing taken off at night; the necessity for active habits, for regular and hard, but not excessive brain-work; the resolute repression of ugly tempers and unbecoming thoughts,—all of these are conditions of a sound mind in a sound body.

And for keeping ourselves in this delightful state of

existence we are all more or less responsible.   The girl
who eats too much, or eats what does not suit her,
and is laid up with a bilious attack ; the girl who sits
for hours poring over a novel, to the damage of her
eyes, her brain, and her general nervous system, is
guilty of a lesser fault of the nature of suicide.   We
are all apt, especially in youth, to overlook our account-
ability in the matter of health, and to think we may do
what we like with our own ; but, indeed, no offences
are more inevitably and severely punished by the action
of natural law than the neglect of the common principles
of hygiene.

  " Thine own friend and thy father's friend forsake
not."   The responsibility of keeping up courteous and
kindly relations, by letter, call, or little attentions, with
near and distant neighbours and friends is wholesome
for the young people, and is a training in that general
kindliness of spirit in which the ardour of their particular affections sometimes causes them to fail.

CONDUCT

  The *conduct* of a well-brought-up girl—that is, her
behaviour in various circumstances—will, on the
whole, take care of itself.   But in this, as in greater
matters,

> " More harm is wrought through want of thought,
>   Than e'er through want of heart ";

and the mother will find opportunities to bring before
her daughter the necessity for circumspection, reticence, self-control, the duty of consideration for
others.   Conduct at home is regulated by such plain
principles of duty, that I need do no more than say

a word as to the proprieties of life which should be kept up in the home circle as in any other society: behaviour which would be unbecoming in any drawing-room, is unbecoming in that of home.

In the street, the concert-room, the shop, in whatever public places she frequents, the young maiden has a distinct *rôle*, and must give a little study to her part. It will not do for her to go through the world with open mouth, wide-gazing eyes, head turned to this side and that, heedless tongue, like a child at a fair. But should not the girl behave *naturally* in public as in private? Alas! the fact is, that none of us, not even the little children, can afford to behave quite naturally, except in so far as use has become second nature to us in the acquired art of conducting ourselves becomingly. *Noblesse oblige:* maidenly dignity requires the modest eye, the quiet, retiring mien, subdued tones, reticence in regard to emotions of wonder, pleasure, interest, the expression of which might make the young girl a spectacle in the public streets—that is, might cause a passer-by to look at her a second time. For, excepting the children, there is nothing so interesting to be seen in public places as the young maidens approaching womanhood. They cannot fail to attract attention, but they owe it to themselves not to lay themselves open to this attention.

One claim, however, the public, in the shape of the casual passer-by, certainly has; he has a right to a gentle, not repellent, if retiring, expression of countenance, and to courtesy, even deference, of tone and manner in any chance encounter; and this, even more if he be in the garb of a working man than if in that of a gentleman. It is worth while to bear in mind the "Madam, respect the burden," with which Napoleon Bonaparte moved out of the path of a charcoal-carrier. This propriety of behaviour is mincing affectation if it be no more than a manner put on with the girl's out-of-door garments: it must be the outcome of what her mother has brought her up to think that she owes to herself and to other people; and from few but a mother can a girl acquire this mark of a gentlewoman.

How to conduct herself in society is a question of enormous interest to the maiden making her *début*. The subject is so large as to have called forth a literature of its own; but the principle lies in a nutshell. In society, as in the streets and public places, the girl whose mother has caused her to comprehend the respect due to herself, and the respect due to other people, will not make any grave *faux pas*. She goes into a room persuaded that she has claims upon the respect and consideration of the persons she may meet there; and she moves with ease, talks with quiet confidence, possesses herself in repose of manner. She is persuaded that her rights in this respect are not a matter of successful rivalry, but that each person in the room has equal claims upon her courtesy, and upon that of every other; and that her entertainers for the time being are entitled to peculiar deference. She will preserve self-possession and self-respect in intercourse with those who are socially her superiors, and will behave with deference to her inferiors. So of her intercourse with gentlemen: due self-respect and due respect for them will cause her to conduct herself with the simplicity,

courtesy, and ease which she shows in her intercourse with women. In fact, these two principles
will carry her with dignity and grace through all
social occasions and in all social relations.

And how is the mother to enhance her daughter's
self-respect? Is she to tell her, never so indirectly,
that she is clever, pretty, charming, that no one can
fail to admire her? If she do, her daughter may, not
impossibly, become a forward young woman. No;
she must put forward none but common claims. Because she is a woman, because she is a lady, because
she is a guest, a fellow guest, because she is a stranger,
or because she is a friend—these, and such as these,
are incontestable claims upon the courteous attention
of every person she meets in society. One quietly
confident in such claims as these seldom experiences
a rebuff. Whatever she may receive or give, over and
above, on the score of *personal* merit, settles itself;
but the thing to be established in a girl's mind is a
due sense of the claims she has and of the claims she
must yield.

PLEASURE AND DUTY

We now come to consider a perplexing question
which comes up for settlement upon the close of a
girl's school career. Two rival claimants upon her
time and interest are in the field—pleasure and duty;
the question is, what is to be allowed to each, and
how far may they clash. Kind-hearted parents, who
find that their daughter is continually wanted for
picnic or tennis, ball or concert, for morning lounge
or evening party, withdraw the claims of duty, and
leave the field to giddy pleasure. They say, " Poor

child, she will never have a second youth." "Every dog must have its day." "We have been young ourselves; let her have a 'good time' and 'enjoy herself while she can.'" "If we hold her back from taking her pleasure, she will only crave for it the more; let her have a surfeit—she will settle down the more readily to a quiet life afterwards," and so on.

But before they launch their daughter—

"Youth at the prow, and Pleasure at the helm,"

it behoves parents to look into the matter. In the first place, the result, the gain of the girl's whole education hitherto is at stake. She might as well have been allowed to play ever since she was born as to play uninterruptedly now. For the gain of her education is not the amount of geography, science, and French that she knows; she will forget these soon enough unless well-trodden tracks be kept up to the brain-growth marking these acquirements. But the solid gain education has brought her lies in the powers and habits of attention, persistent effort, intellectual and moral endeavour, it has educed. Now, habits which are allowed to fall into disuse are all the same as though they had never been formed; powers not exercised grow feeble and are lost. The ground which has been gained in half-a-dozen years may be lost in a single one. And here we have the reason why many girls who have received what is called a good education read nothing weightier than a feeble or trashy novel, are not intelligent companions, and show little power of moral effort.

As for settling down by-and-by, that is not the question: if she is to recover the ground lost, she must begin all over again, and at an age when it

is far more difficult to acquire habits and develop
powers than in childhood. Again, the taste for parties
of pleasure, for what may be called organised amusement, is an ever-growing taste, and dislodges the *habit*
of taking pleasure in the evening reading, the fireside
games with the children, the home music, the chat
with friendly neighbours, the thousand delights that
home should afford. For

> " Pleasure is spread through the earth
> In stray gifts, to be claimed by whoever shall find ";

and not the least evil of incessant party-going and
pleasure-seeking is, that it blinds people to the nature
and conditions of pleasure; pure and true pleasure
is of impromptu occurrence, a *stray* gift, to be *found*
not sought; it is just a thing to happen upon by the
way.

What, then, of those parents who take the opposite
line,—ordain that their daughters shall stay at home
and help their mothers? *They* did not run after
pleasure, and neither shall their girls; they had home
duties to attend to when they were young, and so
shall their daughters, " for no good comes of gadding
about."

Well, to turn the tables, it is well these should remember that you cannot put an old head on young
shoulders; that young things will frolic, whether they
be kittens or lambs or maidens; that what becomes
deliberate pleasure-seeking in older people, comes to
the girls as—

> "Stray gifts to be claimed by whoever shall find ";

that parties of pleasure are delightful just because
they give the girls opportunities of meeting their kind,

other young people, in whom they rejoice, "as 'tis their nature to." Prospero was not sufficient for Miranda. Birds of a feather flock together, and, the young to the young.

The thing then is, to draw the line wisely. Either extreme is mischievous. The girl must have definite duties on which pleasure schemes are rarely allowed to encroach—a rule, for going out once, twice, a week? —some evenings reserved for home pleasures, the mornings for regular occupations and duties, and, so far as the unfortunate habits of society allow, evening amusements avoided which spoil the following morning. But to suggest rules on this subject would be presumptuous; every mother ordains for her own daughters, remembering how—

> "All work and no play makes Jack a dull boy;
> All play and no work makes Jack a mere toy."

OPINIONS

Let us turn to a question too often overlooked in the bringing up of girls. A girl may have opinions upon questions of figure and style, fashion and furniture, but who cares what she thinks about public men and questions, books and events? All the same, what she thinks is of consequence to the world; even if she is not to be the mother of future fathers and mothers, she will make her mark somehow.

The young maiden should have a general and a special preparation towards the forming of just opinions. For the first, she should be made to use her common-sense upon the questions that occur. "What do you think of so-and-so?" says the parent, making a little wholesome fun if her thinkings be foolish. But the special preparation requires more thought. What are the subjects upon which thinking persons generally must have opinions? It is upon these the girl should be qualified to judge.

In the first place, her success in life will depend greatly upon the relations with other people into which she lets herself be drawn. She must have some knowledge of character, human motives; and, therefore, as much as for the sake of her own development, every girl ought, as I have said, to go through some easy course of moral philosophy. We know how easily a girl is carried away by plausible ways of putting things, until she may find herself bound to a worthless friend or unworthy lover. And what is the poor girl to do if she have nothing to oppose to—"Oh, everybody thinks so now!" "That's a mere old-world grandmother's notion of propriety"; "A man's first duty is to look after himself, and it stands to reason that if everybody does that, nobody need trouble himself about other people"?

Again, women should know something of the principles of political economy. How many ladies are ready to decide off-hand that "it would be good for trade if an earthquake shook down all the houses in London"; that, "if all the landowners in England excused their tenants paying rent, bread would be cheaper"; or, that "the wealth of England would have been increased if the country had contained gold-mines, instead of our iron and coal"; in fact, to fall into any one of the little traps which Mrs Fawcett sets for the unwary in her *Political Economy for Beginners*,—which is, by the way, as interesting as it is instructive, and the girl who studies it with thoughtful attention will be in a position to form sensible opinions on some of those questions of the day which come up to be dealt with, not as matters of opinion, but as causes, powerful to set class against class. It would be for the welfare of the country if educated women had just ideas on subjects of this nature, not only that they should share the interests of husband and brothers, but in order that they should see, and keep before the men of their families, the *other side* of questions which the press of affairs would incline the latter to look at from a personal standpoint.

Possibly, a mission is devolving upon educated women. A mediator is wanted between labour and capital, not only to persuade the master to endure in gentleness, but to open the eyes of the men to the difficulties and responsibilities of the masters ; and this mediator, the lady, with her tact, sympathy, and quick intuitions, is fitted to become, if she will take pains to get the necessary knowledge. Not that she need step out of her proper sphere to meddle with public matters ; only that she should qualify herself to speak an *understanding* and kindly word on these subjects to the wife, if not to the husband, in her cottage visitings. A single sentence, showing a mastery of the subject in question, spoken in one cottage may go far to turn the tide of feeling in a whole community of work-people.

Women have been clamorous for their rights, and men have, on the whole, been generous and gentle in meeting their demands. So much has been granted, that we have no right to claim immunities which belong to the seclusion of the harem. We are not free to say, " Oh, these things are beyond me ; I leave such questions to the gentlemen." It is not impossible that, in the course of Providence, women have of late been brought so much to the front, that they may be in a condition to play the part of mediators in these times of dangerous alienation between class and class. That we are in the early stages of a revolution, is patent to thinking persons; and whether this revolution is to be bloodless, unmarked by the horrors which have attended others we know of, rests, more than they realise, with the women of Britain. It is time for them, at any rate, to away with the frivolous temper which "cares for none of these things."

Nor is a social revolution the only one pending: there is a horror of great darkness abroad; Christianity is on its trial; and more than that, the most elementary belief in, and worship of, Almighty God. The judgment to come, the resurrection of the body, the life everlasting,—these fundamental articles of a Christian's faith have come to be pooh-poohed; and this, not only amongst profane persons and ungodly livers, but amongst people of reputation both for goodness and wisdom.

And how are the young girls to be prepared to meet this religious crisis? In the first place, it is unwise to keep them in the dark as to the anxious questions stirring. Their zeal and love will be quickened by the knowledge that once again Christianity and infidelity are in the way to be brought into agonising conflict at our doors. But let their zeal be according to knowledge. Lay the foundations of their faith. It matters less that the lines between Church and Dissent, or between High and Low and Broad Church, be well defined, than that they should know fully in Whom they have believed, and what are the grounds of their belief. Put earnest, *intellectual* works into their hands. Let them feel the necessity of bracing up every power of mind they have to gain comprehension of the breadth and the depth of the truths they are called to believe. Let them not grow up with the notion that Christian literature consists of emotional appeals, but that intellect, mind, is *on the other side*. Supply them with books of calibre to give the intellect something to grapple with—an important consideration, for the danger is, that young people in whom the spiritual life is not yet awakened should feel themselves superior to the vaunted simplicity of Christianity.

One more point: let them not run away with the fallacy that no one is responsible for what he believes, but only for what he does. Try this principle for a moment by applying it to our social relations—say, that no man is bound to believe in the fidelity of his wife, in the dutifulness of his child, in the common integrity of the people he has dealings with—and the whole framework of society is broken up. For, indeed, our whole system, commercial and social, is nothing else than a system of credit, kept up by the unbounded faith man reposes in man. That every now and then there is hue and cry after a defaulter, is only one way of proving how true are men in general to the trusts reposed in them. Does a countryman hide away his sovereigns in an old stocking because he puts no faith in banks? He is laughed at as a miser. Will he have nothing to do with his neighbours because he is mistrustful of them? He is a misanthrope, only fit to live by himself. And if the man who does not place due and necessary faith in his fellows, however much his trust has been abused, is an outcast, what is to be said of him who lifts up his face to Almighty God, his Maker, Father, Preserver, Redeemer, sole intimate Friend, and ever-present Judge, and says, "I do not believe, because I can neither see nor understand"?

I am not going out of my way to speak strongly as to the necessity of taking a firm stand here. For the sake of the children yet to be born, let the girls be brought up in abhorrence and dread of this black offence of unbelief. On points not vital, let them think gently and tolerantly, having a firm grasp of the truth as they hold it themselves, but leaving others to choose their ways of approach and service. But on questions that trench on the being, nature, and work of Almighty God, Father, Son, and Holy Ghost, and our relations of love and service towards Him, there is no room for toleration of adverse opinions: though we may have much cause to esteem the holders of such opinions. " His (creed) must be true whose life is in the right," is precisely one of those fallacies which young people should be taught to examine.

As for proofs, this is no question for proof. Every pulse that beats in the universe is, if we will have it so, a witness for God, being inexplicable without Him ; but who goes about to prove that the sun is shining ? At the same time, such works as Paley's *Natural Theology*, possibly, and Butler's *Analogy* most certainly, have their use, if only as showing how many plausible arguments have long ago been answered.

PURSUITS AND OCCUPATIONS

I have left little space to glance at the pursuits and occupations proper for young women at home. It is becoming rather usual on the Continent, and, to some extent at home, for the schools to instruct young ladies in the duties of household economy—an invasion, perhaps, of the mother's province. Every woman should understand, and know how to perform, every duty of cooking or cleaning, mending or making, proper to a house; and a regular, practical course of training under her mother's eye might well occupy an hour or two of the girl's morning. May I suggest the great use and value of a household book, in which the young housekeeper notes down exactly how to do everything, from the scouring of a floor to the making of an omelet, either as she has done it herself, or has watched it being done, with the little special wrinkles that every household gathers. Such an "Enquire Within" should be invaluable hereafter, as containing personal experiences, and should enable her to speak with authority to cook or housemaid who "Never *saw* it done like that, ma'am." The ordering of dinners, setting of tables, entire management for a short time of the affairs of a house, will all have place in this training in domestic economy.

Where there is still a nursery, the home daughter has a great advantage, for the right regulation of the nursery in all that pertains to cleanliness, ventilation, brightness, health, happiness is a science in itself; and where there is no longer one at home, it is worth while for her to get some practical knowledge of details at the hands of a friend who has a well-regulated nursery. As for sewing, every woman should know how to cut out and make all garments for herself and her children up to a full-grown dress, and it is worth while to learn how to cut out and make even that scientifically; so here is another art in which the young lady at home must needs serve her apprenticeship. At the same time, an hour's brisk needlework at a time is as much as should commonly be expected of her; for while almost every other sort of household occupation affords healthful muscular action, to sit long at her needle is not good for a young girl.

Besides, she has not unlimited time to sew; her education has only been begun so far, and must be kept up, and she must acquire habits of intellectual effort on her own account. She should have an hour or two in the morning for solid reading. English literature is almost an untrodden field for her; she has much history to read—ancient, mediæval, modern, —all of which would be read the more profitably in the light of current history. She has learnt to read French and German, and now is her time to get some acquaintance with French and German literature. She will probably find it necessary to limit the reading of *novels* to the best, those which have become classics, except on occasion of a bad cold, or toothache, or for an idle half-hour after dinner. It is very helpful to read with a commonplace book or reading-diary, in which to put down any striking thought in your author, or your own impression of the work, or of any part of it; but *not* summaries of facts. Such a diary, carefully kept through life, should be exceedingly interesting as containing the intellectual history of the writer; besides, we never forget the book that we have made extracts from, and of which we have taken the trouble to write a short review.

Two or three hours of the afternoon should be given to vigorous out-of-door exercise, to a long *country* walk, if not to tennis, cricket, etc. The walk is interesting in proportion as it has an object, and here the student of botany has a great advantage. At almost every season there is something to be seen in some out-of-the-way spot, to make up the list of specimens illustrating an order. The girl who is neither a botanist nor an artist may find an object for her walk in the catching of some aspect of nature, some bit of landscape, to describe in writing. The little literary effort should be both profitable and pleasant, and such a record should be a dear possession in after days.

It is evident that the young lady at home has so much in hand, without taking social claims into consideration, that she can have no time for dawdling, and, indeed, will have to make a time-table for herself and map out her day carefully to get as much into it as she wishes.

The pursuits we have indicated are all, more or less, with a view to self-culture ; but they will become both more profitable and more pleasant if they can be proposed to the girl as labours of love and service. Household duties and needlework will, of course, be helpful in the home; but all her occupations, and especially her music, even her walks and reading, can be laid under contribution for the family good, or for that of her neighbours, rich or poor. The girl who knows something of wild-flowers or birds, for example, is popular as a walking companion with persons of all sorts and conditions. Sunday-school teaching, cottage visiting, some sort of regular, painstaking, even laborious effort for the ignorant, the distressed, should be a part of every girl's life, a duty not to be put aside lightly for other claims. For it is only in doing, that we learn to do; through service, that we learn to serve; and it is more and more felt that a life of service is the Christian, and even the womanly, ideal life.

I shall notice, later, the importance of qualifying a girl, by means of definite training, for a particular line of service—for teaching, or nursing, or for general work in a parish, for instance; but in default of such training, as giving her an object in life apart from social success, the mother may do much to make "*Ich dien*" the motto of her daughter's life, marking out some special line of helpfulness into which she may throw her youthful energy.

> "Abou Ben Adhem (may his tribe increase)
> Awoke one night from a deep trance of peace,
> And saw within the moonlight of his room,
> Making it rich and like a lily in bloom,
> An angel writing in a book of gold.
> Exceeding peace had made Ben Adhem bold,
> And to the presence in the room he said,—
> 'What writest thou?' The vision raised his head,
> And in a voice, made all of sweet accord,
> Answered, 'The names of all who love the Lord!'
> 'And is mine one?' Ben Adhem asked. 'Nay, not so,'
> Replied the angel. Abou spoke more low,
> But cheerful still,—'I pray thee, then,
> Write me as one who loves his fellow-men.'
> The angel wrote and vanished. The next night
> He came again, with a great wakening light,
> And showed the names whom love of God had blessed,
> And lo! Ben Adhem's led the rest."

"Write me as one who loves his fellow-men!" is, indeed, the cry of the earnest-minded amongst ourselves; and to qualify her for some definite line of service, in the workhouse, the infirmary, amongst the blind or the mute, to give her some object in life beyond herself, and having no bearing on her own advancement, is, perhaps, the kindest and wisest thing the mother can do for her daughter.

OBJECTS IN LIFE—VALUE OF SPECIAL TRAINING

This consideration brings me to a question sufficiently puzzling to the heads of households: What is
to be done with the girls? About the boys there is
less difficulty—they go to college, or they go to learn
their profession; they are set to work at once, to
prepare for that "opening" which, it is hoped, will
introduce them to a profitable career.

Suppose a girl leave school in her eighteenth year;
—her eldest sister being already at home for good, her
mother's right hand, and so much identified with all
the interests of the family that her career is marked
out. The sense of leisure and irresponsibility is delightful at first, and every girl should have a taste of
it, just as a grocer is said to give his new apprentices
the run of the shop, that they may long no more for
figs and raisins. She plays tennis, goes to dances, is
allowed to go as much into society as her parents can
conveniently arrange for. In her leisure, she paints
a little, works a little, practises a little, reads a little
French and a good many novels. Her mother assigns
her some domestic duties, which she fulfils with more
or less care; but these are seldom important enough
to call forth all her energy and will. Perhaps she is
to sew for the family; but then, the stress of work
comes only now and then, in spurts, when everybody
helps, and to be regularly and laboriously employed
as a sempstress would be intolerable to a girl of
spirit and education. She is not exactly idle; her
occupations spread fairly well over the day, though
they might all be easily crushed into the spare hour
or two of a busy woman; she enjoys a good deal of

leisure and pleasure, and her parents look on good-naturedly, glad that she should have her day.

For a few months, perhaps for a year or two, this is delightful ; but in a year or two life becomes a burden. To dance with the same people, to play in the same set, to make or listen to the same talk month after month, becomes intolerable. But then, it is objected, she has her home-work, and additional duties can easily be made for her. Not so easily ; the mother of the family clings to her own duties, having discovered that, of the two delights of life, *work*—the duties of our calling—is to be preferred to *play*. Besides, the girl wants more than work— she want a *career*; she wants work that depends upon her, that cannot be done without her, and the doing of which will bring her honour, and, possibly, pay. Let her "improve her mind," you say? It is hardly the tendency of modern education to make girls in love with knowledge for its own sake, and what they do for *their* own sakes is too fitful and desultory to yield much profit or pleasure, unless the old spur is applied—the hope of distinction in some public examination.

Now, what is the poor girl to do under this craving for a career, which is natural to every adult human being, woman as much as man ? Hard things are said of the "girl of the period"; but she deserves more consideration than she gets. People do not allow that she has erred because there has been no such outlet for her energy as her nature demands. In the 'sixties,' say, there was, practically, but one career open to the young woman of the lower and upper middle classes. She must wait until the prince comes by, and—throws the handkerchief. The girl with more energy and ambition than modesty and breeding sees her opportunity here. What if that foolish prince should throw the handkerchief to the wrong maiden, and leave her out in the cold, with nothing to do, nothing to look forward to, all the rest of her life? The thing is not to be thought of; she will make it her business to let him know where his favours should fall. And then begins a career indeed, a "hunt," people call it, exhibiting a very ugly phase of young womanhood on which there is no occasion to dwell.

The well-brought-up girl will hardly own to herself that she dreams of this best of all careers for a woman, that of wifehood and motherhood. Maidenliness will not let her put it before her as the thing of which she lives in hope. Indeed, it is not so; her fate in this respect depends so entirely on the mood of some other, that it is impossible for her to allow herself in serious anticipation, though maiden meditation may dwell innocently upon Romeo and Juliet and their kind. Except for these sweet fancies, half illicit in the eyes of many a pure-minded girl, and not too wholesome, the future is a blank; she is in real need of something beyond

> "Human nature's daily food"

of common duties, pleasures, home affections. It is *natural* for the human brood, as for every other, to leave the parent nest; and when the due time comes, and the overgrown nestling has not taken flight, it is but a comfortless bird.

The girl wants a career, a distinct path of life for her own feet to tread, quite as much as does the boy. But the girl will be provided for, it is said, while the boy must be made able to support himself and a family by his labour of head or hands. That is not the point: people are beginning to find out that happiness depends fully as much upon *work* as on wages. It is work, work of her very own, that the girl wants; and to keep her at home waiting for a career which may come to her or may not, but which it is hardly becoming in her to look forward to, is, to say the least of it, not quite fair. The weak girl mopes and grows hysterical; the strong-minded girl strikes out erratic lines for herself; the good girl makes the most of such employments as are especially hers, but often with great cravings for more definite, recognised work.

The worst of it is, these home-bred daughters are not being fitted to fill a place in this workaday world at any future time. Already, amateur work is at a discount; nobody is wanted to do what she has not been specially trained for. Here seems to me to be the answer to the perplexing question, What is to be done with a family of grown-up-daughters? It is not enough that they learn a little cooking, a little dressmaking, a little clear-starching. Every one of them should have a thorough recognised training for some art or profession whereby she may earn her living, doing work useful to the world, and interesting and delightful to herself, as is all skilled labour of head or hands. It appears to me that parents owe this to their girls as much as to their boys. And valuable training in many branches of woman's work is to be had, at so low a charge as hardly to cost more than would keep a lady fittingly at home. Whether the girl makes use of her training, and practises the art she has acquired, depends upon circumstances, and—the handkerchief! But in no case is the training thrown away. To say nothing of the *special* aptitude she has acquired, she has increased in personal weight, force of character, and fitness for any work. It is not necessary to specify the lines for which women may qualify by thorough training—art, music, teaching, nursing, loftier careers for the more ambitious and better educated ; but may I say a word for teaching in ˙elementary schools—a lowly labour of quite immeasurable usefulness.

May I urge, too, the advantage of *training* for work which has been too long the refuge of the destitute— I mean, the truly honourable, and often exceedingly pleasant, post of governess in a family ? In proportion as parents awake to the necessity for all-round training for their children, this profession of governess will open a more and more delightful and remunerative career to the *trained* woman able to develop character on right lines, and to teach on rational methods.[1]

I fear the reader may think of that fox who left his tail in a trap, and advised all the foxes he met to cut off theirs—"so pleasant," says he, "to be without the incumbrance of a tail!" But, indeed, I do not speak without book on this subject, having had opportunities of learning the views of many women who have placed themselves under training, partly as feeling the need of the *discipline* it affords, and partly out of a great craving to take some active recognised share in the work of the world. The mistress of a house and mother of a family is—unless she be a lawless, self-indulgent woman—under a discipline of circumstances which should bring out whatever is strong and lovely in the female character; but in the case of grown-up

[1] Already this awakening has taken place so far that perhaps no woman's work is more in request or better paid than that of the *specially trained* governess.

daughters at home, the difficulty parents labour under is just that of keeping up wholesome discipline. They cannot be for ever struggling against the dawdling, procrastinating, self-indulgent habits girls will fall into when not under the stimulus of pressing duties; for parents must needs admit their grown-up daughters to a friendly footing which makes an over-strict government out of the question.

The young women want scope, and they want the discipline of work, their own work, for which they alone are responsible; not of home tasks, which may be done or left undone, or which are sure to be done by somebody if the right person neglect her duty. A year or two of home life, in the interval between school and such training as I propose, is very desirable, both that parents may enjoy their daughters, and the daughters their homes, and also that parents may have an opportunity of dealing with the crude characters the girls bring home from school. But with work of their own in view, the girls will live under the stimulus of a definite future, their present work being to make the very best of themselves with a view to that future. Here is a motive for effort, and the important thing is, to keep up the *habit* of effort, intellectual, moral, spiritual, bodily. Nor need such regular training and regular work stand in the way of matrimony. In the first place, early marriages are far less frequent than they were, so there is time to get in some special training and some special work before the final step be taken; and, in the next place, the girl who is only *occasionally* at home, with fresh interests, greater force of character, is a more attractive person than her sister, who has become a little stale because she is always on hand.

Forgive me if I make use of this opportunity to press home what may seem to the reader a one-sided view of an important question. I am by no means alone in the view I advocate; seeing that many enlightened men are causing their daughters to undergo as regular a professional training as their sons, not because their means are inadequate to portion the girls, but because they feel it a duty to open a career of usefulness to these as much as to the boys of their families. Besides, I know of no other way of answering the question, What is to be done with the girls? Families of grown-up daughters at home are simply in the way. They are in an anomalous position, with no scope to produce the best that is in them ; and unless they have an unusually wisely ordered home, some deterioration in character is almost a necessary consequence of the life they lead.

Part IV

"IT IS WRITTEN"

Some Studies in the Evolution of Character

"I too acknowledge the all-but omnipotence of early culture and nurture."—*Sartor Resartus.*

"Of a truth, it is the duty of all men, especially of all philosophers, to note down with accuracy the characteristic circumstances of their education, what furthered, what hindered, what in any way modified."—*Sartor Resartus.*

I

TWO PEASANT BOYS

I

Jörn Uhl[1] and *Wilhelm Meister* are books that
parents should read. To mention a book of yesterday in the same breath as a world's classic is bold,
perhaps foolhardy, but in the two we get the two sides
of the shield. Wilhelm Meister becomes, passively ;
circumstances play upon him, and he yields himself
to this formative play. Jörn Uhl also is the creature
of his circumstances, but only in so far as they give
impulse to his personality. Meister is, as we know,
a highly emotional being in whom rank sentiment
chokes out personality. The peasant boy, reared
in a rougher school, becomes a *person*, or rather, is
a person from the first. We get in these two the
hint of a line of demarcation which divides the
world into the people who, for one cause or another,
are at the mercy of circumstances, and those others
able to order their lives.

Jörn Uhl was the son of a peasant-proprietor
whose farm (in Schleswig-Holstein) had been in the
family some three hundred years. Klaus Uhl is a
man worth considering as a father. He is notable
for a hearty, jovial laugh, tells a good story, discusses

---

[1] *Jörn Uhl*, by Gustav Frenssen.

politics, drinks, plays cards, is a popular person among the fast spirits of the country-side, doubly popular because he is a sort of headman among them and can always claim the flattery of a ready laugh at his jokes.

His wife, a woman of another mould, dies in giving birth to a little daughter—Elsbe, her fifth child,—chiefly because her husband would not be persuaded to send for the doctor. At last he comes to weep over her as '*Mutter, Mutter*'; he has forgotten her in the relation of wife. She, a daughter of a peasant of the heath, brought the qualities of her own people into her husband's family. The three eldest sons took after their father, while the two younger children, Jörn and the little Elsbe, were Thiessens, of their mother's blood. Jörn was four years old when his mother died. The mother had the gift to attach to her, at any rate, one faithful friend, in Wieten, a serving-woman whom she charged with the care of her children.

This is how the story opens; and the scenes and circumstances of peasant life are bitten in as with an engraver's tool. Without any word to that effect, the reader feels that here is the little, bright-haired, straight-featured, handsome Jörn set down to a problem. Here are the factors of his life. What answer will come out?

This is why I venture to call this story of *Jörn Uhl* a companion piece to *Wilhelm Meister*. In both cases, we have a boy set down with the problem of life before him. Will he cry 'check' to circumstances, or will they checkmate him? This is the anxious question that presents itself now and then to every mother when she goes up for the last good-night;

to every father when the curious children gather round to see what he would show: and the children exhibit themselves in far more distinct and diverse colours than would so many neutral-tinted men and women.

The little Jörn's first essays at life afford delightful reading. Everything is so big—the house, the barn, the home-fields go on without end. Great big people come out of doors and go about their various work in a grave, puzzling way. There is no one just like Jörn but Spitz, and they two make experiments together. One day they both go into a ditch after a rat, and together are they fetched home, put into the wash-tub, whipped, and put to bed, where together they cry and comfort one another. Another day they think to make a friend of another young thing which they recognise as one of their kind—a little foal not long arrived. They know that the horse belongs to the grave, grown-up world, but the foal is another thing, and the two venture near to make acquaintance, Spitz, of course, making the opening remarks; but the mare kicks up her heels and they fly. Another day they peer down a cellar, a dark world which for them has no bottom; but beetroots and turnips come flying up at them, and, tumbling in, they find themselves on the head of a labourer. All the while the child was another Robinson Crusoe, and the world was his island. There was no one to tell him the meanings of things; Wieten was too busy, and no one else cared.

The little soul had to build its own habitation, fashion its own tools, find its own meat: 'so best,' says the author, and perhaps he is right. Little children must needs ruminate. We tease and distract them by our pestilent explanations, our continual calls upon attention already fully occupied, because we find it difficult to realise that even young children have need of a separate life. It is one thing to give a little child two or three lessons in attention in the day by inducing him to look a little longer at something he has already begun to regard with interest, but quite another to make him name a statue of Achilles or the portraits of the kings of England. Of course he can do these things; children are not stupid, but preoccupied, and the occupation they find for themselves is good for them. A clamorous forcing of his attention in many directions is apt to leave a child incapable of answering the demands which are rightly made upon him at a later date.

But little Jörn ran no risks of this sort. He and Spitz had it to themselves, running in many times a day to see that other soft young thing, the baby. And one day a strange thing happened; they found the baby standing at the door. It was very odd; but they took the little Elsbe into their company, and made their researches thenceforth in a party of three. By and by, Spitz fell to the second place, and became only a plaything where he had been companion and leader, and the children learned from each other. A little sister teaches a boy tenderness and valour, and learns from him confidence and love and that pride in him which makes a boy a hero.

Later, we get a group of three children sitting round Wieten's work-table of an evening. Fiete Krey, whose father and mother work about the place, has much to say. The Kreys, almost a clan in the village, are an ingenious folk given to petty trade and not bearing a very good name for honesty. Fiete has the family traits; he romances, tells of hidden pots of gold and of strange underground folk who guard the treasures. Wieten too tells of a rich merchant who threw all his money into a well, and of a little gray man in a three-cornered hat who sate at the bottom minding it. She tells, too, of one Theodor Storm, a student, who meant to write a book of the folk-tales.

All these things go to Jörn's education.

Here is a matter which sometimes causes uneasiness to parents: they are appalled when they think of the casual circumstances and chance people that may have a lasting effect upon their children's characters. But their part is, perhaps, to exercise ordinary prudence and not over-much direction. They have no means of knowing what will reach a child; whether the evil which blows his way may not incline him to good, or whether the too-insistent good may not predispose him to evil. Perhaps the forces of life as they come should be allowed to play upon the child, who is not, be it remembered, a product of educational care, but a *person* whose spiritual nurture is accomplished by that wind which bloweth whither it listeth.

Meanwhile, the father was not unaware of his fourth son, who had come to be known as a promising boy; but his concern was shown only by boastful talk in the ale-house. He should be a scholar—Klaus himself remembered tags of Latin learned at school,—should be a land-agent, should somehow bring grist to his father's pride.

One day Jörn went to school—such a pleasant

schoolhouse under the lindens, where the bees came
buzzing through the open windows. Lehrer Peters,
the old schoolmaster, was a kindly human soul, who
scanned the red heads of the Kreys and the fair
heads of the Uhls with the sense that the children
came to school with the makings of all they would
become. The young scholars made sentences that
day. "We have heard about King David," said
Peters. "Who is our king?" And a small child
replied: "Our king is called Klaus Uhl," for, was
not Klaus the head man of the village? Then an
unexpected thing happened; Jörn, the little new
boy, stood up flushed and wrathful, and said: "My
father is no king"; little Elsbe sobbing, "But my
father *is* a king." When the other children had gone,
the schoolmaster asked Jörn: "Why did you say
your father was not a king?" "He often can't
stand." "What? he can't stand!" "No, because
he is often drunk."

This is what the child had learned for himself,—
that a king must at least be able to control his own
life, and that self-rule is a sort of kingship. Already
had evil, passing through the alembic of a child's
mind, brought forth some knowledge of good. But
at what a cost! 'Experience teaches,' we say. We
say too, 'Experience makes fools wise,' but that is
an error. The fools are the people who get nothing
from experience but the confirmed habit of things
as they are. If they have done amiss and suffer
for it, why, they go on doing amiss, and suffer
again. If they see others do amiss, they practise
the ill-doing they see, taking no heed to penalties.
Fools of this sort, who do *not* learn from experience,
were Jörn's elder brothers.

It is because the little boy was no fool that he was able to draw that tragic deduction from his experience of life—"My father is no king." Experience truly teaches the wise-hearted, whether child or man, but at so heavy a cost that the lessons are apt to leave the learner bankrupt for the remainder of his days. Reverence and the sense of filial dependence were gone out of Jörn's life; so too was the love of his mother, with all its tender teachings; and the little Crusoe was isolated from all the natural good that the filial relation includes. How soon may it dawn upon a child that his father is no king, his mother no queen!

We elders are never safe. A child's eyes are ubiquitous. They see everywhere and all the time, but it is only at some small crisis in his life that the child's knowledge takes shape even in thought. Poor little Jörn! He had probably seen his father in a besotted state a thousand times without any inward comment; but this thought of a king reduced his vague ideas to clear knowledge—overwhelming, shameful knowledge.

It was the fact that they were aware of the child as a judge that caused the parents of an earlier generation to sit in state, august, unapproachable; but this was a futile endeavour to blind the child-judge who sees, however gradually, through all seeming, and arrives at the simplicity of being, worthy or unworthy. He knows what his parents *are* for better for worse, though it may be years before he realises that he knows.

It is instructive to compare the beginnings of Jörn Uhl with those of another peasant boy of a rather lower class. How did Diogenes Teufelsdröckh begin

the world in the village of Entepfühl; or rather, to
look through a transparent veil, how did Thomas
Carlyle begin in the village of Ecclefechan? First,
as to his father: "Andreas Futteral" was "in very
deed a man of order, courage, downrightness, that
understood Büsching's Geography, had been in the
victory of Rossbach and left for dead in the Camisarde
of Hochkirch." For Andreas had been grenadier-
sergeant and even regimental schoolmaster under
Frederick the Great. He was a diligent man who
cultivated a little orchard and lived on its produce
'not without dignity.' On evenings, he smoked and
read (had he not been a schoolmaster?), and talked to
neighbours about the wars and told how Frederick
had once said to him,—'Peace, hound!' as a king
should.

To begin with, Diogenes, or Gneschen, as they
called him, had a better chance of learning reverence
in the contemplation of an upright man, and obedience
from an old soldier, than fell to a son of that facile
good-fellow, Klaus Uhl. Then, Gneschen had a
mother, a notable housewife and kind and loving
mother who provided for the young child "a soft
swathing of Love and infinite Hope wherein he
waxes and slumbers, danced round by sweetest
dreams." To such a pair, living in a roomy
painted cottage surrounded by fruit-trees, with
flowers looking in at the windows, came "one
meek, yellow evening," a Stranger of reverend
aspect. He met the pair with grave salutation,
and deposited before them "what seemed some
basket overhung with green Persian silk, saying
only, 'Good Christian people, here lies for you an
invaluable Loan; take all heed thereof, in all care-

fulness employ it: with high recompense, or else
with heavy penalty, will it one day be required
back."

Here we get the true note of parenthood, the sense
of a loan, a trust, containing great possibilities and
involving great responsibilities. The mysterious
Stranger may indicate the advent of the august
Angel of Life; the roll of notes he left behind
for the nurture of the child may mean such things
as the love, integrity, dignity, simplicity of the
pair to whom the infant arrived; for such things
as these are possessions well expended on the
nurture of a child. Anyhow, these were not casual
parents like the one left to the little Jörn.

"Meanwhile the incipient Diogenes, like others, all
ignorant of his Why, his How or whereabout, was
opening his eyes to the kind light; sprawling out
his ten fingers and toes; listening, tasting, feeling;
in a word, by all his five senses, still more by his
Sixth Sense of Hunger, and a whole infinitude of
inward, spiritual, half-awakened senses, endeavouring
daily to acquire for himself some knowledge of this
strange universe where he had arrived, be his task
therein what it might. Infinite was his progress;
thus in some fifteen months he could perform the
miracle of—Speech!

". . . . I have heard him noted as a still infant,
that kept his mind much to himself; above all, that he
seldom or never cried. He already felt that time was
precious; that he had other work cut out for him
than whimpering." Thus the young Gneschen grew
in the paternal cottage, with a father in whom he had
"as yet a prophet, priest, and king and an obedience
that made him free."

As for his education, he listened to the talk of the old men under the shadow of the linden in the middle of the village. He played, and his plays were his lessons; for, says our author, "in all the sports of Children, were it only in their wanton breakages or defacements, you shall discern a creative instinct: the Mankin feels that he is born Man, that his vocation is to work. The choicest present you can make him is a Tool; be it knife or pen-gun, for construction or for destruction; either way it is for work, for change. In gregarious sports of skill or strength, the Boy trains himself to co-operation, for war or peace, as governor or governed: the little Maid again, provident of her domestic destiny, takes with preference to dolls."

Here is a thing to ponder, a word of wisdom, which should clear our nurseries of mechanical toys, and of all toys which have no use but that of being looked at. In this regard the two little boys, Jörn and Gneschen, had fairly equal opportunities. Both grew up in open places where they had the good of heaven and earth. We read how little Gneschen took out his porringer of bread and milk and ate it on the coping of the wall, from which he could see the sunset behind the western mountains. He made friends with cattle and poultry and much besides. While his sports made the boy active and sharpened his wits, "his imagination was stirred up and an historical tendency given him" by the reminiscences of his father Andreas, who had tales of battle and adventure to tell, wonderful to the child. "Eagerly I hung upon his tales, when listening neighbours enlivened the hearth; from these perils and these travels, wild and far almost as Hades itself, a dim world of adventure expanded

itself within me. Incalculable also was the knowledge
I acquired in standing by the old men under the linden-
tree: the whole of Immensity was yet new to me;
and had not these reverend seniors, talkative enough,
been employed in partial surveys thereof for nigh
fourscore years? With amazement I began to discover
that Entepfühl stood in the middle of a country, of a
world; that there was such a thing as History, as
Biography; to which I also, one day, by hand and
tongue might contribute."

It would appear that nature opens to all children,
one way or other, a perception of time past, History,
and of space remote, Geography, as if these ideas
were quite necessary nutriment for the mind of a
child; and what is to be said for a school education
that either eliminates this necessary food altogether,
or serves it up in dry-as-dust morsels upon which the
imagination cannot work?

These two, History and Geography, were let in
upon Jörn too, though by other ways. There were
the inscriptions upon the house-front telling of all the
Uhls for the past three hundred years; and there was
an old oak chest which gradually discovered its
significance to the little boy. As for Geography,
that was associated with the wide heath where his
uncle Thiess Thiessen lived, an odd, solitary peasant
of the heath who slept much among his piles of turf,
but who had also an intellectual outlet. His cherished
possession was an old atlas, and his whitewashed
walls were covered with his own rough scrawls of
journeys from China to Peru, from Hamburg, the
outlet of Schleswig-Holstein, to all places everywhere.
Here was Geography, as a child should get at it! Of
all our sins of omission and commission, none perhaps

are worse than the way we defraud children of those living ideas which are their right.

Here is a delightful description of how, and how slowly, a fundamental geographical idea reached the young Gneschen. (By the way, it should be enough to give chapter and verse, and not to quote at length ; but *Sartor Resartus* is not a new book, and, do people read any but new books?) " In a like sense worked the Post-wagon, which, slow rolling under its mountains of men and luggage, wended through our Village : northwards, truly, in the dead of night; yet southwards visibly at eventide. Not till my eighth year did I reflect that this Post-wagon could be other than some terrestrial Moon, rising and setting by mere Law of Nature, like the heavenly one; that it came on made highways, from far cities towards far cities ; weaving them like a monstrous shuttle into closer and closer union. It was then that . . . . I made this not quite insignificant reflection (so true also in spiritual things): *Any road, this simple Entepfühl road, will lead you to the end of the World!* " Even so said an Irish peasant the other day, when asked where a certain road led to.

Then, too, had he not the swallows which came year after year all the way from Africa and built in the ' cottage lobby,' and from these he learned, too, the sweet ways of the feathered nations. " Thus encircled by the mystery of existence; under the deep heavenly firmament ; waited on by the four golden Seasons, with their vicissitudes of contribution, —for even grim winter brought its skating matches and shooting matches, its snow-storms and Christmas carols,—did the Child sit and learn. These things were the Alphabet, whereby in after-time he was to

syllable and partly read the grand volume of the
World; what matters it whether such Alphabet be
in large gilt letters or in small ungilt ones, so you
have an eye to read it? For Gneschen, eager to
learn, the very act of looking thereon was a blessed-
ness that gilded all: his existence was a bright, soft
element of Joy; out of which, as in Prospero's Island,
wonder after wonder bodied itself forth, to teach by
charming."

Jörn, too, grew up in a world of wide spaces, and for
him also was the ministration of the seasons. But
neither of the little boys had a quite happy childhood.
Indeed, childhood is quite happy only from the point
of view of the elders. The pains of little children are
as acute as their pleasures, and, what is more, they
are eternal. Experience has not begotten hope, and
every grief and disappointment is final. Besides,
there probably grows about all children, as about
Gneschen, "a dark ring of Care as yet no thicker
than a thread and often quite over-shone," yet always
reappearing and always waxing broader. "It was
the Ring of Necessity whereby we are all begirt.
Happy he for whom the Ring of Necessity is
brightened into a Ring of Duty."

In this, Gneschen had an advantage over Jörn.
Tender care and wise teaching made the needs-must
of his life merge into the 'I can, I ought, I will' of
duty. It was not that Jörn did not learn duty; he
did, in that hard school of experience wherein he
learned the meaning of kingship; but duty remained
to him necessity, without the sense of joyful election
on his own part.

Thus, one day Wieten sends the three children in
the waggon on a picnic over the heath to the little

uncle, Thiess Thiessen; and on the way back they talk. Thiess says: "The best in the world is to live on the heath and sleep and eat *schwarzbrot* and pig's head; and little Elsbe cries: "Love is the best in the world." "No," says Jörn, "work is the best." How had he learned it? Day by day, with solemn, childish eyes, he had watched the fruits of idleness and neglect about the homestead; neglected cattle, neglected crops, neglected out-buildings taught their lesson to the wise-hearted child, and this was the creed he got out of it—work is the best thing in the world. He never forgot it; hardly for a day did he relax the plodding, patient toil that the neglect of others had laid upon him.

Another thing he learned: "Elsbe and I will *never* go into an alehouse." "But when there is a ball?" said Elsbe. "I, never in my whole life," said he. The little Jörn was left to develop himself without much fostering or much hindrance, whereas Gneschen says: "I was forbid much; wishes, in any measure bold, I had to renounce. Everywhere a strait bond of Obedience inflexibly held me down.—In which habituation to Obedience, truly, it was beyond measure safer to err by excess than by defect. Obedience is our universal duty and destiny; wherein whoso will not bend must break: too early and too thoroughly we cannot be trained to know that would, in this world of ours, is as mere zero to should, and for the most part as the smallest of fractions even to shall. Hereby was laid for me the basis of worldly Discretion, nay, of Morality itself. Let me not quarrel with my upbringing!"

But the protest is well founded. Passivity is not the sole quality to be cultivated in children. It is by their self-ordered activities they develop, and they require more scope for these than an orderly house affords. An attic, a garden, a yard, a field, wherein to do as they will, is necessary to the free growth of children. If we could rid ourselves of the notion that children are somewhat imbecile, incapable of understanding principles and ordering themselves wisely, a child in a family might grow up with as little sense of collision as most of us are aware of in regard to the laws of the State to which we belong. We obey without knowing it ; but when our obedience is challenged, we give it loyally.

For one other thing Diogenes blesses his parents in words so stimulating that they must be quoted :—

"My kind mother . . . . did me one altogether invaluable service : she taught me, less indeed by word than by act and daily reverent look and habitude, her own simple version of the Christian Faith. Andreas too attended Church ; yet more like a parade-duty, for which he in the other world expected pay with arrears,—as, I trust, he has received ; but my mother, with a true woman's heart, and fine though uncultivated sense, was in the strictest acceptation Religious. How indestructibly the Good grows, and propagates itself, even among the weedy entanglements of Evil ! The highest whom I knew on Earth I here saw bowed down, with awe unspeakable, before a Higher in Heaven : such things, especially in infancy, reach inwards to the very core of your being ; mysteriously does a Holy of Holies build itself into visibility in the mysterious depths ; and Reverence, the divinest in man, springs forth undying from its mean envelopment of Fear. Wouldst thou rather be a peasant's son that knew, were it never so rudely, there was a

God in Heaven and in Man; or a duke's son that only knew there were two-and-thirty quarters on the family coach?"

This intimate sense of the presence of God was not for little Jörn.

.   .   .   .   .   .

II

"Jörn shall study," said his father; "that is understood. He shall be a land-agent. Let us drink to Jörn Uhl, the land-agent." And they drank. So the notion got about the village that Jörn was destined for high things. He went to school to Lehrer Peters to be prepared for the gymnasium. It must have been good to see him on the sofa with the old teacher, the little lad with fair hair standing on end, and deep-set, eager eyes devouring the book he held; an English book it was, for Lehrer Peters was a man of notions. He himself knew a little English, and held that English was the key to all wisdom, and indeed to the meaning of the world. A little Latin also was got in, but that was by the way.

Here follows a pretty episode. A charming child, Lisbeth Junker, the schoolmaster's niece, woos Jörn to go out fishing with her in the master's absence; and while they sit dangling their lines Jörn overhears a conversation between the schoolmaster and the magistrate, and gathers from it that his father's affairs are in a bad way. This is how another of life's lessons came to Jörn, and very admirably does the old schoolmaster bring it home to the boy, who owns frankly that he has overheard the talk. He tells him a tale of the successful career of an ancestor of Jörn's, and ends with a wise word of 'that great thinker, Goethe'—that what you inherit from your fathers you must labour in order to possess. This seed of thought sank deep. Thenceforth the little boy felt that he was responsible when there was no other to take responsibility. The child's eye kept the farm-labourers at work; and two horse-dealers, who came to traffic with his brothers, were abashed by his gaze.

But how is a person to prepare for the gymnasium with so many affairs on hand?

The time came when he must go to the neighbouring town to try his chances. Thiess Thiessen took him and his books in the waggon. The boy went in at the great gates; and Thiess, meanwhile, made acquaintance with an old shoemaker, who cheered him by saying that of five who go in, only one comes out successful. "But," says Thiess, "Jörn is clever, sits the whole day over his book and sees and hears nothing; he must succeed." But, alas! Lehrer Peter's English teaching somehow did not qualify him for a pass in Latin, and Jörn and Thiess went home crestfallen. This was the end of the boy's definite schooling.

His religious teaching fared no better; the preparation for confirmation should have been much to him, but Jörn was told of justification by faith, that he should do no murder, and the like. The confirmation classes, though conducted by a diligent and kindly man, were a source of torment to him because he did not understand the teaching. By the way, his confirmation is a very definite era in the life of a German boy (or girl). So soon as he is fourteen he leaves school (if he be a child of the people), and, before he takes up any employment, is under the instruction of his pastor for six weeks, and works three hours a day in the church, besides writing and learning at home.   Before his confirmation, he may not even run an errand for a neighbour for the usual penny. The practical and purposeful Jörn knew all about the concerns of the Uhl and of the whole village, but knew nothing of either the sin or the mercy about which he was taught.   The list of sins began too far down, with theft, robbery, and murder, and the mercy came all too soon to satisfy his young sense of justice, — as soon as a man should throw his sins upon the Lord.   God appeared to him an unpractical judge, who kept his books in fine order in his office and allowed himself to be deceived by the people without.

Meantime Jörn took his place steadily, of his own accord, as a farm labourer.   He would do what he could to right matters in the neglected homestead. His step became heavy through following the plough in the heavy furrows; he had little to say, because he was more used to cattle than men; it seemed that his intellectual life had gone out, and he was in a fair way to become as one of the farm-hands.   This is what the schooling of life had brought to Jörn Uhl.

Young Teufelsdröckh also goes to school and learns to handle his 'earliest tools'—his class-books. He cannot remember ever to have learned to read, which is true of many young scholars.   He speaks of his education got in schools as 'insignificant.'   He learned what others learned, seeing no use for it.   His schoolmaster did little for him, and knew it, but thought him a genius, and said that he must be sent to the gymnasium and afterwards to a university. Meanwhile he read, eagerly as Cervantes, any scrap of page or printed paper he came across, including 'stall literature' bought out of his copper pocket-money and sewed into volumes by his own hands.

He got something out of this random reading, bits of history and bits of fable, real, both of them, out of which his mind got its necessary food. Now, here is a point worth attention. How seldom do we hear of a famous man who got that food for his mind which enabled him out of his school studies! And how often, on the other hand, do we read of those whose course of life has been determined by the random readings of boyhood! We go on blindly and stubbornly with our school curriculum, as if this were a fact of no significance, because, say we, the boy will have chances after his school-days to get such pabulum as he needs; but life is not long enough to afford the waste of some dozen years, its freshest and most intelligent period. And, what is more, the boy who has not formed the habit of getting nourishment out of his books in school-days does not, afterwards, see the good of reading. He has not acquired, in an intellectual sense, the art of reading, so he cannot be said to have lost it; and he goes through life an imperfect person, with the best and most delightful of his powers latent or maimed. Why in the world should we not give children, while they are at school, the sort of books they can live upon; books alive with thought and feeling, and delight in knowledge, instead of the miserable cram-books on which they are starved?

In spite of his school, Gneschen developed some power of thought:—"It struck me much" (he was in his twelfth year), "as I sat by the Kuhbach, one silent noontide, and watched it flowing, gurgling, to think how this same streamlet had flowed and gurgled, through all the changes of weather and of fortune, from beyond the earliest date of history "—a type of the thoughts, original so far as they are concerned, which strike all children of average intelligence.

Things went no better with Diogenes at the gymnasium; he was home-sick, the boys were rough and rude, he hated fighting and thought it disgraceful to be beaten, but also disgraceful to fight; so he wept a good deal, which did not help him with his school-fellows. Then, as for the teaching he got; Greek and Latin, he says, were mechanically taught, while, "what they called history, cosmography, philosophy and so forth, no better than not at all." Still, he learned something by watching the craftsmen who came in his way, and from some odds and ends of reading he lighted upon at his lodgings.

He complains that his teachers were hidebound pedants with no knowledge of boys' nature or of anything but their lexicons. "Innumerable dead vocables (no dead language, for they themselves knew no language) they crammed into us, and called it 'fostering the growth of mind';" and he asks how can a mechanical gerund-grinder foster the growth of mind, which grows, not like a vegetable, by having 'etymological composts' laid upon it, but like a spirit, by contact of spirit, 'thought kindling itself at the fire of living thought.'

His years at the gymnasium brought him one idea, fertile for good and evil—"*I was like no other.*" Here we have one of those words of profound educational insight with which *Sartor Resartus* abounds. There comes an epoch in every young life when the person discovers himself to be an individual. He perceives that he is like no other. It is this notion working in them which makes the captious girl and headstrong youth 'neither to have nor to hold'; and 'education' leaves young people absolutely unprepared for an era so important in their lives. The arrogant young man is apt to suppose he is individual in all that he is, and, by consequence, that in everything he is superior. No wonder he is unmanageable and infallible! But give him a ground-plan of human nature, let him know what he has in common with all men, and he is able to understand and to make use of his individual quota for the general good.

In due time Teufelsdröckh goes to the university. Being fairly perfect in 'dead vocables,' he believes he is set down "by the living Fountain there to superadd Ideas and capabilities." But, alas! it was true for him as for others that 'the pear-tree he had climbed at twelve he was still climbing at twenty.' Also, grinding poverty oppressed and distracted him, for he had lost his father.

He discovers that his university is the worst in the world for his needs. Among other defects, where all was defective, he tells us that "we boasted ourselves a Rational University; in the highest degree hostile to Mysticism; thus was the young vacant mind furnished with much talk about Progress of the Species, Dark Ages, Prejudice, and the like; so that all were quickly enough blown out into a state of windy argumentativeness; which by the better sort had soon to end in sick impotent Scepticism; the worser sort explode in finished self-conceit, and to all spiritual intents become dead."

This invective discovers a mistake in our educational methods. From the time a child is able to parse an English sentence till he can read Thucydides, his instruction is entirely critical and analytic. Does he read "The Tempest," the entrancing whole is not allowed to sink into, and become a part of him, because he is vexed about the 'vexed Bermoothes' and the like. His attention is occupied with linguistic criticism, not especially useful, and, from one point of view, harmful to him because it is distracting. It is as though one listened to "Lycidas," beautifully read, subject to the impertinence of continual interruptions in the way of question and explanation. We miss the general principle that critical studies are out of place until the mind is so 'throughly furnished' with ideas that, of its own accord, it compares and examines critically. "The hungry young," says Teufelsdröckh, "looked up to their spiritual Nurses; and, for food, were bidden to eat the east-wind"—"vain jargon of controversial Metaphysic, Etymology, and mechanical Manipulation falsely named science." Worse happened to him. Besides his wants and distresses—want of money, sympathy, hope—this manner of education resulted in 'fever paroxysms of doubt,' and he tells of cries for light in the silent watches of the night, of distresses of mind and heart, which it took long years to soothe, under "the nightmare, Unbelief."

This malady of unbelief, again, is common to serious minds, educated to examine all things before they *know* the things they criticise by the slow, sure process of assimilating ideas. If we would but receive it, we are not capable of examining that which we do not *know*; and knowledge is the result of a slow, involuntary process, impossible to a mind in the critical attitude. Let us who teach spend time in the endeavour to lay proper and abundant nutriment before the young, rather than in leading them to criticise and examine every morsel of knowledge that comes their way. Who could live if every mouthful of bodily food were held up on a fork for critical examination before it be eaten?

Meantime, Teufelsdröckh got what served him, not out of the class-rooms but out of the chaos of the University library. "The foundation of a literary life was hereby laid: I learned, on my own strength, to read fluently in almost all cultivated languages, on almost all subjects and sciences; further, as man is ever the prime object to man, already it was my favourite employment to read character in speculation, and from the Writing to construe the Writer."

To Jörn, who had the makings of a man of science as had the other of a philosopher, all intellectual avenues save one were closed. In that chest, itself a page of history, he found an old book on astronomy (Littrow's). He had always liked solid knowledge, and, later in life, he explained that he had in childhood been so overfed by Wieten and Fiete Krey upon romantic legends that he had no more appetite for poetry or fiction. Littrow was his solitary outlet; in course of time, he was able to indulge himself in the luxury of a telescope, the one luxury of his life; he contrived a revolving roof to an old arbour; made observations and recorded them on his own charts; and found in the heavens solace and relief from the manifold distresses of life. So, in spite of hindrances, we may consider that the two arrived at education. The one had reached the infinite solace and content of books; the other found for himself a single intellectual pursuit upon which the whole force of his mind could spend itself. But it is a pitiful thing when his education leaves a youth without the power or habit of reading, and also without an absorbing intellectual interest. Some men, as these two, get such gains in spite of their schooling; but how good it would be if we could devise an education which should be not only serviceable in making a living, but should enable young people to realise, use, and enjoy fulness of life! "The life is more than meat."

We read next, how Teufelsdröckh tried at various points to open that oyster of the world, and how Jörn Uhl was compelled to drive doggedly at a single point, and how each of them imagined, "it was with Work alone, and not also with Folly and Sin, in myself and others, that I had been appointed to struggle," and how folly and sin overcame them both.

Jörn Uhl forgot, just for once, his childish vow never to enter a *Wirtshaus*. He drank and was ashamed; and, in his shame, was thrown into a worse temptation—he learned the meaning of lust. But the woman was older than he, and had come out of the same fire herself, and taught him—Chastity. This lesson he learned so well that, later, he would not touch the hand of the woman he was about to marry until he had arranged for their nuptials.

We cannot follow Teufelsdröckh through his love-sicknesses and sorrows; but we know how it went with him, on the whole. To both young men life was a dour, hand-to-hand conflict, both set their teeth and fought it out, and both carried to the end the hardening or the softening, the sweetening or the souring of the lessons that had arrived to them during their education. For the most part, these two learned in the hard school of experience. For the one, Nature herself was a hard mistress, though passionately beloved ; but each accomplished his 'pilgrim's progress' by the aid of things and of the ways of men ; it is distressing to note how little help either got from direct teaching.

The problem before us all is, how far direct teaching and training may help in the evolution of character ; and perhaps few things should be of more use to us than the study of such veracious records as we have in *Sartor Resartus* and *Jörn Uhl*. It were profitable to consider what might have been done here, and here, and here, for the guidance, help, and inspiration of either lonely and courageous young pilgrim. I venture to call these two veracious records, though *Jörn Uhl* is a novel and *Sartor Resartus* offers us much the same thing, that is, facts seen through a veil of romance; because we perceive that both are essentially true, and are profitable for our instruction in righteousness.

We have been told so much of the sournesses and sorenesses of Thomas Carlyle that we are in danger of forgetting how much we owe to the philosopher who, more than any other, has put hope and purpose into the adverse conditions of modern life; and, what is more to our present purpose, we overlook the lesson that the gloom and bitterness we condemn were the *inevitable* results of the upbringing sketched for us in the assumed experiences of Diogenes Teufelsdröckh ; and that the strong virtues we admire came also out of that upbringing. So too of Jörn Uhl. Things went well with him in the end ; but it took all the skill of the wise wife whom he loved to tide him over periods of dour gloom not unlike those which fell upon Carlyle.

This is (roughly) how the brave record ends :—
" Your life, Jörn Uhl, has not been an insignificant

one. Your boyhood was tranquil, your youth, lonely; and you wrestled bravely and single-handed with the riddles of life; even if you could guess only at a few of them, your labour was not in vain. You went to the front for the land that lies about this well; you have been hardened by fire and frost and have made progress in the most important study—that of distinguishing things according to their value. You have learnt to know the passionate love of woman, and in that you gained the second great experience that life can give. You have buried Lena Tarn as well as your father and brothers, and in those hours of human grief you have peered into the eyes of knowledge and have become humble. You have fought with adverse fate and not given way; you plodded on, though it was long before help came. You worked your way into knowledge with clenched teeth and a lofty courage at an age when most men expect to repose. And, now that building and measuring and the like have been your work and joy for some years, you have not got into a groove: you take thought for all the land on each side of your measuring chain, and even consider the books which a friend of yours called Heim Heidreter writes.

"What shall a man write about, Jörn, if a life of so much meaning is not worth recording?"

II

A GENIUS AT 'SCHOOL'

" Minds like Goethe's are the common property of all
nations."—*Carlyle.*

I

EVERY intimate and penetrating book has something
of the nature of an autobiography. If it do not tell
us what happened to the writer in the actual circumstances, it reveals what, in his idea, would have come
to pass under such and such conditions. If this be
true, how is it possible for one man to produce, not
fifty men and women, as Browning claims to have
done, but hundreds of actual persons behaving as they
must because of the character that is in them? To
realise this possibility is indeed as amazing and
confounding as a fixed regard upon the Milky Way.
Does it mean that all things are possible to all men?
Anyway, Goethe confessedly images himself more or
less in all his written work ; and one failure especially,
that of moral instability, is writ large for our instruction in " Wilhelm Meister."

It may not be unprofitable to compare this hero
with another of whom we possess the *journal intime*,
our old friend and favourite Arthur Pendennis. How
far " Pendennis " is consciously an autobiography we
need not inquire, for Thackeray takes no pains to tell

us. Goethe, on the contrary, is at the greatest pains to trace the influences that result in himself, not only in his *Dichtung und Wahrheit*, an Autobiography, but in "Werther," "Wilhelm Meister," "Faust"; he is at pains to tell us, in fact, over and over again, that all he wrote was a record of himself. He tells us of the astrological influences under which he was born, and of the incidents of his birth, and he analyses his own nature with immense care, traces this to his father and the other to his mother, further traits to great-grandfather and great-grandmother. As Goethe says, he got his tall, strongly built frame and a certain earnestness in living from his father, a 'man of laws' who had also a taste for art: he married a wife not half his own age, who felt that she and her son were better mated in years and tastes than were she and her husband: "I and my Wolfgang were both young."

Catherine Goethe was a person of distinction, a correspondent of various learned ladies who, like herself, belonged to the *Kultur Kampf.* She appears to have been a delightful woman, full of gaiety, feeling, and imagination. "Joyousness," she writes, "is the mother of all virtues; when we are content and cheerful we wish to see all people gratified and gay, and do all we can to make them so." And again: "I have it by God's grace that no living soul ever went from me dissatisfied. I love humankind, old and young feel it." She tells us that she tried to reform no one, saw the good side of her neighbours, and left the bad to Him who made men, and "by this means I am content and happy." All this sounds well; but in practice it meant that Madame was an eclectic who chose only what she would out of her life; for example, she must not on any account be perturbed—

a sentiment shared by her great son. She would say, we are told, on hiring a servant: "You shall tell me nothing terrifying, disquieting, or disagreeable, whether it happens in my own house, the neighbourhood, or the town. Once for all, I will know nothing of it. If it concerns me, I shall hear it soon enough. If it does not concern me, I have nothing to do with it. Even if a fire were to break out in the street where I am living, I will not hear of it sooner than I can help." It was not that she could not feel, but that she would not. During her son's acute illness in 1805, she would not allow herself to be told of what was going on. When it was over, she said: "I have known it all along. . . . Now we may again talk about him without my feeling a stab in the heart at every mention of his name"; 'stab in the heart'—in the phrase we find her excuse. She would not 'dree her weird,' would not endure the share of poignant feeling that fell to her.

To her influence and example, as well as to the nature inherited from her, we owe the limitation which must always distress the disciples of Goethe. Finding him so great, it is to them 'a stab in the heart' that he has not the added greatness of one who cared for his country and his kind. If only he had let himself care, when his country was going through one acute crisis after another! If only he had helped when men looked to him as the one wise man! But his mother saw about that. Anyway, she has left a lesson to mothers of the future. The idea of personal culture is so fascinating, and appears under so bewildering a disguise of pseudo-virtue, that high-minded women are apt to be deceived. They believe that to cultivate their minds and conserve their feelings is the best they can do not only for themselves but the world, on the principle that, if every man sweep before his own door, the street will be clean; and they bring up their children with the same desire for and effort after personal culture, and the same aloofness from the lives of other men. It is well we should clear our thoughts on this subject, and recognise, once for all, that personal culture is hardly a legitimate aim. We are allowed to seek knowledge for the sake of knowledge, culture of body and mind for the sake of serviceableness; and, recognising this, we give our lives an impersonal aspect. We look at pictures and read books for the sake of the pictures and the books, and not at all for our sakes. Our children carry forward this larger view of life. They feel, think, and labour without sparing as occasion calls upon them; they live, that is, the common life, and are not stranded in an inlet of individual culture.

We hear of the little Goethe's horror of ugliness as early as his third year,—" The dark child must be taken away. I can't endure it"; and here we get the key to much that came after. He was never taught to endure as a child, because his mother understood and shared his sensibility; and therefore endurance, the manly and cheerful acceptance of the inevitable, was never made a part of his life. Who will not endure must needs evade, and we find, let us say, Wilhelm Meister evading obligations as they occurred with a hardihood worthy of a better cause. We are shy of criticising a poet—above all, one of the world's few great poets. I once heard a distinguished man, who had had the honour of knowing Goethe, lecture upon him. His praises were fervent; and why not? But he could not bring himself to blame the poet for any failure, and said at the end to a friend, 'Have I not whitewashed him well?' Now, Goethe was too great for this process. He has offered himself as a beacon to mankind, indicating not only harbourage but rocks ahead; and we do not dishonour a great genius by considering why, in certain aspects, he was less than other men; how he might have become greater all round.

His grandmother's large room upstairs was the favourite playing place for himself and his little sister Cornelia, always tenderly cherished by her brother; and one Christmas Eve this grandmother invented an amusement which gave direction to the boy's whole after-life. This was the famous puppet-show. We get full details of the incident in *Wilhelm Meister*. "How often," Wilhelm's mother is made to say, "have I been upbraided with that miserable puppet-show which I was unlucky enough to provide for you at Christmas, twelve years ago! It was the first thing that put these plays into your head." "Oh, do not blame the poor puppets; do not repent of your love and motherly care! It was the only happy hour I had enjoyed in the new, empty house. I never can forget that hour; I see it still before me; I recollect how surprised I was, when, after we had got our customary presents, you made us seat ourselves before the door that leads to the other room. The door opened; but not as formerly, to let us pass and repass: the entrance was occupied by an unexpected show. Within it rose a porch, concealed by a mysterious curtain. All of us were standing at a distance; our eagerness to see what glittering or jingling article lay behind the half-transparent veil was mounting higher and higher, when you bade us each sit down upon his stool and wait with patience. At length we were all

seated and silent; a whistle gave the signal; the
curtain rolled aloft, and showed us the interior of the
Temple, painted in deep red colours.   The high priest
Samuel appeared with Jonathan, and their strange
alternating voices seemed to me the most striking
thing on earth.   Shortly after entered Saul, over-
whelmed with confusion at the impertinence of that
heavy-limbed warrior who had defied him and all his
people.   But how glad was I when the little, dapper
son of Jesse, with his crook and shepherd's pouch and
sling, came hopping forth and said : ' Dread king and
sovereign lord! let no one's heart sink down because
of this; if your Majesty will grant me leave, I will go
out to battle with this blustering giant'!   Here ended
the first act, leaving the spectators more curious than
ever to see what further would happen, each praying
that the music might soon be done.   At last the
curtain rose again.   David devoted the flesh of the
monster to the fowls of the air and the beasts of the
field ; the Philistine scorned and bullied him, stamped
mightily with both his feet, and at length fell like a
mass of clay, affording a splendid termination to the
piece.   And then the virgins sang : ' Saul hath slain
his thousands, but David his ten thousands !'   The
giant's head was borne before his little victor, who
received the king's beautiful daughter to wife." [1]

Here we get the first indication of a career, the
moment of vocation which came to the poet-child,
as to many another, casually and without warning.
Henceforth he lived in the dramatising of situations
that came in his way, in the conception of situations
worthy of being dramatised, and we are able to understand how, until the end of his life, the direction of

[1] Carlyle's Translation.

the princely theatre at Weimar was his congenial and delightful occupation. We get many details in *Wilhelm Meister* showing how the child became possessed more and more completely by this one idea; how, prying about as children will, he found, laid by in the store-room, the puppets which had given him such joy; how he begged his mother to give them to him; how he contrived various costumes for them, and caused them to play many parts; how by and by he wrote plays for the puppets to act, speaking their several parts himself with such just expression and delicate enunciation that his sterner father, who looked askance at this new delight, felt that it was after all an instrument of education.

Many parents, who do not imagine their children to be embryo poets, are a little perplexed by the delight they take in any manner of acting, from Punch and Judy up, and they wonder how far it is well to encourage a taste which may come to interfere with serious pursuits. Children are born poets, and they dramatise all the life they see about them, after their own hearts, into an endless play. There is no reason why this natural gift should not be pressed into the service of education. Indeed, it might be safe to go further: the child who does not dramatise his lessons, who does not play at Richard and Saladin, who does not voyage with Captain Cook and excavate with Mr Flinders Petrie, is not learning. The knowledge he gets by heart is not assimilated and does not become part of himself.

Therefore it is well that children should, at any rate, have the outlet of *narration*, that they should tell the things they know in full detail; and, when the humour takes them, 'play' the persons, act the scenes that interest them in their reading. On the other hand, there is the danger that their representation of facts may become more to them than the facts themselves, that the show of things may occupy their whole minds. For this reason it may be well not to indulge children with anything in the form of a stage or stage properties, not with so much as a puppet-show. They will find all they want in the chair which serves as a throne, the sofa which behaves as a ship, the ruler which plays the part of rapier, gun, or sceptre, as occasion demands. In fact, preoccupation with tawdry and trivial things will be avoided if children are let alone : imagination will furnish them with ample properties, delightful scenes, upon the merest suggestion of reality. Bottom the weaver and his crew furnish the prototype for children's plays,—

"This lantern doth the hornéd moon present,"

and there is a hint of Shakespeare's earnest in this broad jest, for do we not get the same idea amplified in the prologue to *Henry V.*?

II

Young Goethe's father, who delighted in teaching, instructed his children himself; and there are still exercises of the boy preserved in the Frankfort library, in German, Latin, Greek, and French, written between his seventh and ninth years. These exercises show that the manner of instruction was immediate and interesting; the father dictating what had struck himself—some news of the day or some story of 'old Fritz'; or the boy chose his own subject. He never seems to have gone to school, except on one occasion, when the family house was being rebuilt and the children were sent out of the way. Their school experience appears to have offended the two fastidious children: they were not accustomed to the turbulent life of a school, and possibly, in this first experience of a public of his own age and status, was sown the seed of that indifference to the public welfare which continued with Goethe through life. But it is easy to err in emphasising this seeming defect in the poet's character; is it not conceivable that his philosophic mind put in the balances the sorts of service it was possible for him to render, and that he recognised the impossibility of bestowing upon mankind any gifts comparable with those he has left us?

Possibly it was while he was at school that he learned to hate grammar—and, curiously enough, on the very grounds which made this subject repellent to Herbert Spencer; he could not put up with arbitrary rules. Both thinkers might have been the better for some grammatical grind; both, indeed, took their education into their own hands, as is rather the way of persons of genius.

If the analysis of language teased him, the analysis of human nature occupied young Goethe at a very early age. He tells us a curious anecdote in which he appears in the attitude proper to a child, that of curious interest and suspended judgment. He and some young friends joined in a verse competition:—
" And here occurred something strange, which long troubled me. I could not help regarding my own poems, be they what they might, as the best. But I soon perceived that my competitors, who produced very poor things, were in the same case, and thought no less of themselves; nay, what struck me as still

more curious, a good, though for-work-incapable, lad, who got the tutor to make his rhymes, not only held these to be the best, but was fully convinced he had himself made them, as he in perfect honesty declared to me."

Already, in his eighth or ninth year, has he observed, and that without censure or comment, one of the most baffling complexities of human nature—that the attempt to appear other than we are is rather an intellectual than a moral vice, and that the hypocrite is commonly a person who, through bad intellectual habits, is able to deceive himself. This reminiscence of Goethe's childhood reminds us that the clear-sighted child, not blinded by habits of conventional usage, is with us, taking curious and amazed, if unconscious, note of all our small hypocrisies of opinion and action.

It is good to know that the sort of books all children love were dear to this poet-child. Telemachus, he tells us, had 'a sweet and beneficent influence upon him'; and that Anson's *Voyage round the World* combined for him 'the dignity of truth with the rich fancy of fiction,' and that he delighted in *Robinson Crusoe*, in folk-tales and fairy-tales.

It was a fitting thing that Goethe's home was in an ancient city, rich in traditions and associations, in all of which he took passionate delight. What was it not to him to stand in the hall in which emperors had been crowned, on the spot where once was a castle occupied by Charlemagne himself! How good, too, to think as he looked up at the vault of the Rathaus, how, for ages past, the fathers of the city had deliberated there! Then there were the pictur-esque houses of the Römer-Platz, and, not least significant, the stately old dwelling with projecting gables occupied by the Goethes themselves. These things he tells us of at length in his *Dichtung und Wahrheit*, wherein he gathers up at great length the impressions of his early childhood ; and, certainly, Frankfort, with its long historic perspective and stirring modern life, proved itself 'meet nurse for a poetic child.'

A child's first impressions of his native place are such a precious and rare possession that it will repay us to follow this boy in the pursuit of such ideas as his *Vaterstadt* had to offer him.

"It was just about this time that I first awoke to my *Vaterstadt*, as I wandered up and down, more and more freely and uncontrolled, now alone, now with my playfellows. In order to some extent to explain the impression which these solemn and revered surroundings made upon me, I must begin with the impression I received of my birthplace as it gradually disclosed itself to me in its many parts. Above all I liked to walk on the Mainz bridge. Its length, its strength, its handsome appearance made it a noticeable structure; it was also a very notable memorial of that foresight in years gone by which the world owes to its burghers.

"The beautiful river drew my gaze with it up and down stream, and when the golden cock on the cross on the bridge glittered in the sunshine, I had a delightful sensation. We then usually went through Sachsenhausen, and, for a kreuzer, enjoyed the ferry across. Then, again, on this side, we stole along to the wine market, gazed at the cranes at work unloading goods, but were especially entertained by the arrival of the market boats, whence we saw many strange figures descend. Then we went into the city, and, every time, paid our respects to the *Saalhof*, which was, at any rate, on the very spot where the castle of Charles and his successors is said to have stood. We lost ourselves in the old trading quarter, and only too gladly found ourselves in the throng that gathered round the church of St Bartholomew on market days.

"... I remember, too, the horror with which I fled past the closely packed, narrow, and hideous meat-stalls. The Römerberg was a quite delightful place to walk in. But what most drew the attention of the Boy were the many little towns within the town, the fortresses within the fortress; for example, the walled cloisters remaining from earlier times, and other more or less castle-like buildings transformed into dwellings and warehouses."

Frankfort had at that time no modern architecture of importance, but everywhere was evidence of 'old, unhappy, far-off times, and battles long ago.' Forts, towers, fortifications, moats, enclosed the new town, and all spoke of the necessity for providing for the common safety in troublous times. "A certain inclination towards the antique took fast hold of the boy, which was especially nourished and favoured by old chronicles and woodcuts, as, for example, those of Grave relating to the siege of Frankfort: to this another taste was added, that of observing the common circumstances of life in all their natural complexity, without any regard to interest or beauty. One of our favourite walks, which we tried to take several times in the year, was the round of the city walls. Gardens, courts, back buildings stretch to the Livinger; and we saw many thousand people in their domestic, narrow, shut-off, hidden conditions of life. From the ornamental show gardens of the rich to the orchards of the burgher who grows for his own needs, from thence to the factories, bleaching grounds, and similar workshops, to the churchyard itself (for a little world lay within the town boundary) we wandered on past a most varied, most wonderful, ever-changing spectacle, of which our childish curiosity was never weary.

"Within the Römer, . . . everything that concerned the election and coronation of the emperors had the greatest charm for us. We knew how to get round the keepers in order to get permission to go up the gaily painted imperial staircase, otherwise shut off by an iron gate. The Hall of Election, hung with purple, decorated with gold fringes, inspired us with awe. The door-hangings—on which little children or genii dressed in imperial colours and bearing the royal insignia play a wonderful part—we examined with great attention, and longed to see a coronation with our own eyes.

"It was only with great difficulty they got us out of the imperial hall once we had succeeded in slipping in, and we considered those our truest friends who could tell us of the deeds of the emperors whose half-length figures were painted at some height all round. Of Charlemagne we heard many a tale, but the historic interest began for us with Rudolf of Hapsburg, who by his courage put an end to so much strife. Charles the Fourth also drew our attention to himself. . . . Maximilian we heard praised as the friend of man and of the burghers, and that it was prophesied that he would be the last emperor of his house; which was, alas! indeed the case, for after his death the choice lay only between the King of Spain,

Charles the Fifth, and the King of France, Francis the First."

All this intimacy with his native town 'the Boy' would seem to have got before his seventh year, or possibly a little later, during the period in which the family house was being rebuilt, and the children were with friends—a time when they seem to have been left more to their own devices than was customary.

This knowledge of the *Vaterstadt* appears to have been picked up by the way—from children like themselves, for example, who had heard it from curators, workpeople, and the like. Where there is avidity for any sort of knowledge, it comes from chance sources. It is lamentable that this kind of lore is not much sought after by English children; and, seeing that every English county, and almost every town, is wonderfully rich in associations, historical and personal, there must be some reason why we are wanting in the local patriotism with which most Continental nations succeed in imbuing their children. I have heard a father in a valley of the Harz telling his little boy of five that here was the scene of Tilly's famous march; and, of course, the child saw the valley filled with armed men with waving plumes on pawing horses: he would never forget it. Again, a small street-urchin in Bruges will tell you where such and such a picture by Memling is to be found; or at the Hague you meet a working man taking his children round the picture-galleries, and explaining, you do not know how or what, but certainly the children are interested. Now, this sort of interest is as though it did not exist for, let us say, eighty per cent of British-born children. There appear to be two or three reasons for our defective education in this respect. In the first place,

we have been brought up to believe in what is
'useful' in education: it may help us to gain a
living if we can read and write and cast accounts;
may help us in society if we can play and sing and
chatter French; or in a career, if we can scrape up
enough classical and mathematical knowledge to win
a scholarship. But where's the good of knowing
what happened in the past, even at the next street-
corner! What's the good of having an imagination
furnished with pictures that open out in long perspective, and enrich and ennoble life?

It is the old story; utilitarian education is profoundly immoral, in that it defrauds a child of the
associations which should give him intellectual
atmosphere.

Another notion that stands between us and any
vital appreciation of the past is, that—'we are the
people!' We are cocksure that we know all that is
to be known, that we do all that is worth while;
and we are able to regard the traditions and me-
mentoes of the past with a sort of superior smirk, a
notion that, if the book-writers have not made it all
up, this story of the past is no such great thing after
all: that 'a fellow I know' could do as much any
day! There are few things more unpleasant than
to see the superior air, and hear the cheap sneers,
with which well-dressed people, not to say 'Arry
and 'Arriet, disport themselves in the presence of
any monument of antiquity they may make holiday
to go and see. We have lost the habit of reverence.

A third, and perhaps more amiable trait, tells
against our due delight in the past. It is strongly
borne in upon us that bragging is odious. We do
not choose to make much of our private possessions,

and unconsciously apply the same principle to whatever might tend to magnify the past we own as a people. It is well we should know that this sort of knowledge of, and intimacy with, the associations of the past is every child's right, whatever be his class. Once we perceive the defectiveness of the education we give children in this respect, we shall no doubt find ways to remedy it.

III

Another fragment of his early education Goethe describes in words that must be quoted in order to do justice to the strength of the impression made on the little boy's mind :—

"In the house, my gaze was chiefly attracted by a row of Roman views with which my father had decorated an ante-room. Here I daily saw the Piazza del Popolo, the Colosseum, the Piazza of St Peter's, St Peter's, exterior and interior, the Castle of St Angelo, and much else. These pictures made a deep impression on me, and my father, otherwise a very laconic man, was often pleased to volunteer descriptions of the subjects. His love for the Italian language, and for everything concerning that land, was very outspoken. He often showed us a little collection of marbles and natural objects which he had brought away with him, and he spent a great part of his time in writing up a diary of his travels."

Here we get a hint as to what may be done for a child by the pictures we surround him with. This row of engravings and his father's talk about them gave Goethe practically a second fatherland. The speech of Italy, the sun of Italy, the past of Italy, became a home for his thoughts; and we know how profoundly his late long sojourn in Italy affected his style as a poet—for good or ill.

Our first idea is that all we can do for children is to give them a correct feeling for art; to surround them, for example, with the open spaces and simple, monumental figures we get in Millet's pictures: we cannot do better, but we can do more. Some, at any rate, of our pictures should be like the little windows, showing a landscape beyond, which the Umbrian Masters loved to introduce. That is just what the children want, an outlook. Every reminiscence of travel in the way of post-card or photograph will almost certainly bring about some preoccupation of a child's mind with the country his parents have seen and known; and will, as certainly, end in the child's seeking these same places when he becomes a man, not so much because his parents have been there, as because his own childish imagination has been there, and because, there, he has furnished a home for his thoughts.

IV

We find that public events, which must needs rouse reflection in all men, had their share in the education of 'the Boy': notable amongst these was the extraordinary calamity which, he tells us, deeply, for the first time, troubled his peace of mind. On 1st November 1755 occurred the earthquake of Lisbon, falling as a terrific shock upon a peaceful world. The earth shook, opened, and a large, beautiful city, with its houses, towers, walls, churches, royal palaces, and 60,000 of its people, was swallowed up by the gaping earth, while smoke and flames enveloped the ruins.

"'The Boy' who heard all this talked over was not a little troubled. God, the Creator and Upholder of heaven and earth, as the explanation of the first article of the Creed so wisely and mercifully declares, had shown Himself in no fatherly guise in rewarding the just and the unjust with destruction. In vain the young spirit sought to free itself from impressions, the more difficult to get rid of, since wise men and scholars could not agree as to the way in which such a phenomenon should be regarded."

Then he tells us that the following summer gave him another opportunity of becoming acquainted with the angry God of the Old Testament. A terrific hailstorm broke the windows of the new house, flooded the rooms, and sent the maids, shrieking, to their knees, that God would have mercy upon them. His faith was doubly shaken; he doubted both the fatherhood of God and the filial confidence of men— a seed-thought to bear fruit in the future.

Unforeseen and unpreventable natural calamities cannot occur without stirring profound reflections in the minds of thoughtful children. They think more and not less of such things than their elders, because to them they are new. A child's faith may be undermined, and no word said, by the news of some such catastrophe, and the casual way in which it is talked about; but after all, such occurrences are opportunities rather than hindrances. Every day of our lives we are face to face with the 'providential' and with the unaccountable; we cannot make the one idea fit the other; and in these contradictions consists for us much of the 'mystery of godliness.' It might be well to bring a child to face the fact of mystery when first his mind is greatly agitated by some public or private calamity. We do not know; we are not meant to know; we have our limitations. If we understood everything, there would be no room left for faith in God, because we should only believe what we could quite well see and understand. But it is just possible that the sudden loss of all these precious lives may mean that life and death are not the great and final things in the eyes of God that they are in our eyes. We are sure that people go on existing; and how they do so, we must trust to our Father, because He is *our* Father and *theirs*. Such opportunities for the exercise of a strong faith should be a means of fortifying rather than enfeebling the religious life.

Later, we get a curious account of how 'the Boy,' dissatisfied with the religious teaching he got, determined to make a religion for himself, and, like many another child, made for himself an altar (out of a lacquered music-stand of his father's), and offered natural productions thereupon over which a constant flame was to burn, signifying how man's heart rises in desire for his Maker. The flame was produced by burning pastilles, lighted at a burning-glass heated by the sun. But, at the second sacrifice, the altar caught fire, and the poetic child was diverted from the notion of inventing his own religion.

Through hard work, he tells us, he soon learned to understand what his father, and the teachers he employed, would have him learn; but he was not grounded well in anything. Grammar, as we have seen, he disliked; but he forgave the Latin grammar, because

the rhymes assisted his memory. The children had a
rhymed geography, too, which helped them to retain
facts and names ; but that following of Anson's voyages
with finger on the globe, together with their father's
travels, probably constituted their real knowledge.

'The Boy's' gifts of language and rhetoric were
greatly cherished by his father, who made many plans
for the future, turning on these gifts. He should, for
example, go to two universities—Leipsic first ; the other
he should choose,—and then he should travel in Italy :
whereupon the father would talk of Naples—talk the
children delighted in more than in prospects too far in
the future to attract them.

The great folio Bible, Comenius' *Orbis Pictus*, Gott-
fried's *Chronicle*, with cuts, taught them the principal
facts of the world's history. Fables, mythology, and
Ovid's *Metamorphoses*, the first book of which he
diligently studied, all went to the nourishment of the
boy.

V

His seventh year (1756) brought a new public
interest to the boy, the opening of the war which, he
tells us, had for the next seven years great influence
on his life. Frederick the Second, king of Prussia, had
with 60,000 men fallen upon Saxony ; and, instead of
leaving the war to account for itself, had issued a
manifesto showing why he invaded Saxony. This
astute move divided men into two parties, and the
Goethe family was divided like the rest. The grandfather, who had assisted at the coronation of Francis
I. and received a golden chain from the Empress,
took, with several of the family, the side of Austria.

His father, whose sympathies had been with the unlucky Charles VII., adopted the cause of Prussia. There followed endless feuds in a hitherto united family, for all other interests gave place to the passionate partisanship stirred up by the war; and, "so was I," he says, "also Prussian, or, to speak more exactly, Fritzisch; that was what made us Prussians: it was the personality of the great king that worked on all minds. I rejoiced with my father over our victories, wrote with delight songs of triumph, and with even more delight songs of derision upon our opponents, however feeble the rhymes.

"As the eldest grandson and godson, I had, since childhood, dined with my grandparents on Sunday; and the hours spent with them were the happiest of my week. But now the food revolted me, for I had to listen to the most horrible calumnies upon my hero. Here another wind blew, here was another manner of speech than at home. My affection, indeed even my respect, for my grandparents was lessened. I could not disclose any of this to my parents; my instinct, as well as a warning from my mother, forbade me. So I was thrown back upon myself, and as in my sixth year, after the earthquake at Lisbon, I became somewhat sceptical of the goodness of God, so now, on account of Frederick the Second, I began to doubt the justice of public opinion. I was by nature reverently inclined, and it took a great shaking to make my faith waver on any matter worthy of reverence."

How far, we are inclined to ask, should children be allowed to share in the party spirit and party strife on questions of Church and State which agitate their elders? Probably we are all agreed that young

children should be kept out of this sort of turmoil.
We keep the little ones in the kingdom of heaven;
and, certainly, the virulence and bitterness of party
do not belong to the blessed state. For another
reason, too, we should do well to reserve before the
children our opinions on burning questions. We
naturally wish them to embrace our own views; but,
if too great an emotional pressure has been put upon
them as children, their tendency when they are older
is to react in the opposite direction. They are apt to
become indifferent or hostile where once they had
been jealous and bigoted. Perhaps this is why we
hear now and then of the children of Unitarians
becoming Roman Catholics, of the Radical son of a
Tory father, and the like. We must, for all reasons,
refrain ourselves before the children; and, indeed, it is
not bad for us to have their moderating influence
among us. But a boy must, sooner or later, take
sides, and must take the side he has a mind to, be it
right or wrong; to do so is part of his initiation.

We are surprised that 'the Boy,' in the glow of his
poetic sensibility, did not embrace the cause of Maria
Theresa, the good and gracious empress, who
certainly had a claim on chivalric devotion. But
here, again, we may read between the lines. It was
not only that his father's sympathies were with
Frederick; it was that that astute monarch had
stated his case, and a statement is, of its nature, convincing to the logical mind. This is a point we are
apt to miss in dealing with questions of religion and
the philosophy of life. We leave it to the dissentients
to state the case, and the first statement almost
inevitably carries conviction. Perhaps this is why
atheistical teaching spreads so rapidly among intel-

ligent artisans. For the first time they have received the intellectual compliment of a logical statement. As, probably, most statements can be proved to the hilt, the mind of the neophyte is stirred with sudden joy. '*I have thought,*' he says to himself, for perhaps the first time; and his reason enjoys the satisfaction of logical demonstration. No wonder that it is not easy to shake what are, in such a case, primal convictions; and especially is it difficult to supplant them by means of emotional appeals. Pride of intellect is legitimate. Where we err is, in not enlisting it on the side of right thinking and right living. We seldom trouble ourselves to offer young people the intellectual grounds for any opinions we propose to them; everything is casual; and then we are discomforted when children of this world, wiser than we, make an appeal to the *mind* in behalf of views which are repugnant to us, and which we believe to be wrong.

Another point to be noted in this connection is the cocksureness of the young person. All young persons are cocksure, not at all because they are foolish and arrogant, but because they are unaware of the fact that equally reasonable and equally intelligent persons are capable of holding opposite views on any given question. In this, as in so many other ways, we feel the lack of what must be the rational basis of a sound education—that is, an ordered study of human nature.

Goethe's remarks on the subject are profoundly instructive :—" Thinking now carefully over the matter, I find here the germ of the indifference, indeed even contempt, of the public which influenced a period of my life, and was only late brought within bounds

through greater insight and cultivation. The con-
sciousness of party injustice was uncomfortable enough
even then—was, indeed, injurious, for it accustomed
the Boy to a barrier between himself and those he
loved and valued.

"The battles and events quickly following each other
left the parties neither rest nor peace. We took a
malicious pleasure in stirring up again every imagined
evil, and magnifying every trick of the opposition ;
and so we went on tormenting each other till a
few years later, when the French took possession of
Frankfort and brought real discomfort into our
houses."

The elders of the house, fearing, perhaps, the mischief that a zealous young partisan might do in a
divided town, kept the young people more at home,
and devised schemes for their amusement and occupation. The grandmother's puppet-show was once
more in use and plays on a larger scale were produced. One boy friend after another was brought
in to see the show, and thus, says Goethe, he made
many friends. But boys are restive, and the young
actors were obliged to fall back on a younger public,
with their attendants to keep them in order. We
get a detailed account of this period in *Wilhelm
Meister*—of the plays the young poet wrote, to the
wonder of his companions, of how these plays never
came to a point and disgusted the author, of the
elaborate staging attempted, and much besides.

"I surrendered myself to my imagination ; I re-
hearsed and prepared for ever, built a thousand
castles in the air and saw not that I was at
the same time undermining the foundation of
these little edifices." He it was who made the

necessary equipments for the boy actors, manufactured the swords, gilded and decorated the
scabbards, furnished helmets with plumes of paper,
made shields, even coats of mail.   "We marched about
the courtyards and gardens, and smote fearfully upon
each other's shields and heads.   Many flaws of discord
rose among us, but none that lasted."   The other boys
were happy in this warlike display ; not so 'Wilhelm.'
" The aspect of so many armed figures naturally stimulated in my mind those ideas of chivalry which for
some time, since I had commenced the reading of old
romances, were filling my imagination."   He was
particularly influenced by a translation of *Jerusalem
Delivered* which he came across, and lived long in the
atmosphere of the poem.   Of Clorinda he says :—
" The masculine womanhood, the peaceful complete-
ness of her being had a great influence upon my
mind, just beginning to unfold itself. . . . A hundred
and a hundred times have I repeated to myself the
history of the mournful duel between Tancred and
Clorinda."

" However strongly I inclined by nature to the party
of the Christians, I could not help declaring for the
Paynim heroine with all my heart, when she engaged
to set on fire the great tower of the besiegers.   And
when Tancred in the darkness met the supposed knight,
and the strife began between them under that veil of
gloom, and the two battled fiercely, I could never
pronounce the words—

> ' But now the sure and fated hour is nigh,
>   Clorinda's course is ended, she must die !'

without tears rushing into my eyes, which flowed
plentifully, when the hapless lover, plunging his

sword into her breast, opened the departing warrior's helmet, recognised the lady of his heart, and, shuddering, brought water to baptise her. How did my heart run over, when Tancred struck with his sword that tree in the enchanted wood; when blood flowed from the gash, and a voice sounded in his ears, that now again he was wounding Clorinda; that destiny had marked him out ever unwittingly to injure what he loved beyond all else! The recital took such hold of my imagination, that the passages I had read of the poem began dimly, in my mind, to conglomerate into a whole; wherewith I was so taken that I could not but propose to have it in some way represented. I meant to have Tancred and Rinaldo acted; and for this purpose, two coats of mail, which I had before manufactured, seemed expressly suitable. The one, formed of dark-gray paper with scales, was to serve for the solemn Tancred; the other, of silver and gilt paper, for the magnificent Rinaldo. In the vivacity of my anticipations, I told the whole project to my comrades, who felt quite charmed with it, only could not well comprehend how so glorious a thing could be exhibited, and, above all, exhibited by them." [1]

VI

Thus, for the second time, circumstances compelled the young poet on the lines of his vocation. We hear, too, of his success as a story-teller, and the youth of Frankfort wondered at his tale of *The New Paris*.

At this time 'the Boy' appears to have had lessons with other youths; but things did not go well with him.

[1] Carlyle's translation of *Wilhelm Meister*.

The teacher was harsh and cruel, and the use his best pupil made of his persecutions was to set himself definitely to bear pain without wincing. He tells us, too, how, on one occasion, three of the most ill-conditioned of his comrades fell upon him. He bore their cruel slashing of his legs with rods until the clock struck the hour which should dismiss the boys; then he turned upon the three and came off victor. In the end this attempt at companionship at lessons fell through, and he was kept more at home. He appears to have been entirely friendly with his boy comrades, but took rather an *en haut de bas* attitude which was no doubt exasperating to his less gifted companions. Perhaps, had he worked steadily at the gymnasium of his native town, things would have gone otherwise with him. He would have learnt something of the give and take of life, how far to bear and when not to bear, and, especially, how to bear with good-humour. He would have learned, too, that other boys have brains, would have laid a foundation of sound scholarship, and would not in the end have had to confess that he had not been grounded in anything.

All of this is true, at any rate, of an ordinarily clever boy; but we cannot predicate about a poet. It is true that we should not have had Milton had not the scholar been superadded to the poet. Byron and Shelley, on the other hand, are quoted as showing how little effect Eton and Harrow had upon poets that were to be; and perhaps it is a fact that, the more original the mind, the less it is capable of working in grooves, and the more tiresome are grammatical and even mathematical studies. But it must not be supposed that what may be all right for a genius is the best thing for persons of ordinary intellectual powers. The fact is, the genius cannot accept of the intellectual discipline of the schools, not so much out of lawlessness, as because his constructive mind is for ever busy in evolving a mental discipline of its own. It is in this sense that a genius is a law unto himself. He is not lawless, but has singular powers of self-education. The parents of the young genius will probably do him an injury if they do not give him the chance of the school-training in habits of clear-thinking and right judgment, as well as in the invaluable power of sustaining relations with his fellows—a power often wanting in persons of casual education. They need not fear the undue fettering of the gifts they prize in their son. Your genius has an amazing and sufficiently irritating way of evading that which bothers him; and assuredly he will be thankful in after days for any such tincture ot scholarship as his masters are able to get into him.

Goethe himself throws as much light as may be on the subject of the evolution of the man from the child.

"Who is able to speak worthily of the fulness of childhood? We cannot watch the little creatures play before us without delight and admiration, for indeed the promise of childhood is usually greater than the fulfilment, as if Nature, among other of her tricks, here also specially designs to make sport of us. . . . .

"But growth is not merely development: the various organic systems which go to make a man, spring from each other, follow each other, change into each other, press upon each other, even swallow each other up, so that after a certain time there is scarcely a trace left of many activities, many indications of power. Even if, on the whole, the talent of a man appears to

have a certain bent, it would be hard for the greatest
and most experienced philosopher to trace it with any
degree of certainty; and yet it is quite possible to
perceive the underlying indication of a tendency."

Among the conditions which moulded 'the Boy,'
was undoubtedly the restless temper of the burghers
of Frankfort during the seven years of the war.   Even
when the town was not directly affected, every family,
every citizen, as we have seen, took sides.   Frankfort,
divided as it was already by three religious parties,
was peculiarly disturbed.   At first Goethe's father,
notwithstanding his (Fritzisch) sympathies, continued,
with the few friends he had gathered about him, to
live his life of quietness and culture.   We get the
names of a whole row of the beautifully-bound works
of poets whose names are little known to-day, outside
of Germany at any rate; these the father read
constantly and knew well, and so did the boy, who
could recite many passages for the pleasure of his
elders.

But all of these recognised poetry as an art in which
the form was of at least as much consequence as the
substance; and upon this formal character of poetry
the elder Goethe insisted with passionate intensity
when an intimate friend, who was greatly influenced by
Klopstock's *Messias*, endeavoured to win his sympathy.
But the lover of poetry which conformed to given
rules could not away with Klopstock, who not only
wrote in unrhymed hexameters, but was somewhat
reckless about metre.   The friend retired from the
controversy and read his Klopstock on Sundays; but
he had gained disciples—the mother and children
borrowed the volume and got it by heart during the
week days.   We have an amusing scene when the

mystery of these secret readings transpired. The
father of the family was being shaved, and the two
children sat on stools somewhat out of sight and
harangued each other in such strong language, Satan
being one of the speakers, that the barber lost his
presence of mind and upset the bowl of lather over
his patron.

VII

The year 1759 was eventful for all the families in
Frankfort, for then began the French occupation
which lasted for a couple of years. Herr Goethe was
especially afflicted. His new, or rather his restored,
house was not yet completed, and, behold, billeted
upon him were Count Thorane, the King's Lieutenant,
with his staff. He could not reconcile himself to
this invasion. The very first night, on the occasion of
the distribution of the rooms, the Lieutenant made
overtures of good-will. There was chance mention
of the decoration of one of the reception-rooms, and
Thorane, who was interested in matters of art, insisted
upon seeing the pictures immediately, admired them,
inquired who were the artists, and did his best to keep
the careful hand of a master upon the treasures of the
house. Notwithstanding this community of tastes,
the elder Goethe could not accommodate himself to
the new situation. He became more and more morose,
and difficulties were barely smoothed over by the
efforts of the house mistress, who set herself to learn
French from a common friend, who represented to the
Count the difficulties of the situation.

But the children had fine times. The Lieutenant
had a sort of civil jurisdiction over the troops, and

there was a constant coming and going of officers and men ; and as the children were always peering about on the common stairway, they got to know a great deal about military matters and many military persons. The young Goethe made himself a *persona grata* with the Count in a remarkable way. He, at this time a child of ten, knew the haunts and homes of the artists of the city,—those artists to whose work his father had introduced the Lieutenant. Nay, more, the boy had been in the habit of attending auctions, and had always been able to describe, rightly or wrongly, the subjects of the pictures for sale. He had written an essay containing suggestions for twelve pictures illustrating the history of Joseph, and some of these had been painted. In a word, the young Goethe, child as he was, appears to have been regarded as a connoisseur; and Thorane not only took him about with him, but took his advice regarding decorative pictures for the château of his eldest brother, for which he was arranging.

A sort of little studio was set up in the house, where one and another artist worked for the great man, and these seemed to have liked to have the boy with them. This anecdote is interesting as offering a hint of the marvellous versatility of the poet, who would have been great as a scientist, and conceivably as an artist, had not poetry laid compelling hands upon him.

It would seem as if rather familiar intercourse with such a man as Count Thorane must in itself have been an important factor in the education of Goethe. He appears to have been the type of French officer with whom history has made us familiar, a man of dignified and reserved manners, who maintained good-

humoured relations with the persons under him partly
by means of his shrewd and caustic wit. One circumstance appears specially to have impressed the
boy. For a day, perhaps days, at a time this
accessible chief was invisible. It appears he was
subject to fits of hypochondriacal depression, and while
they lasted he would see no one but his valet—an
impressive piece of self-control.

"But now it seems necessary to set forth more
circumstantially and to explain how, in the midst of
such events, I got hold of French, more or less easily,
though I had not learned it. My inborn gifts came
to my aid, so that I easily grasped the sound and ring
of a language; the movements, accent, tone, and other
external peculiarities. Many words were familiar
from my knowledge of Latin, Italian helped still
more, and in a short time I heard so much from
servants and soldiers, sentries and visitors, that though
I could not start a conversation, I could at least
understand questions and answers." But he tells
us that all this was nothing compared with the help
which the theatre brought him. His grandfather
had given him a free pass, and every day found him
there, against the will of his father, but with the con-
nivance of his mother. At first his entertainment
consisted only in catching the accent and watching
the gestures of the players. Then he found a volume
of Racine at home, and hit upon the plan of learning
long speeches by heart and delivering these, so far as
he could, as he had heard them, though without understanding their drift.

And now he made a friend—a nice boy connected
with the theatre. The two became inseparable
companions, for in the dearth of boy companion-

ship the stranger managed to understand young
Goethe's French, and by aid of familiar intercourse
with him 'the Boy' made progress that surprised
his friend. The two haunted the theatre, and presently found their way into what served as a green-
room, where Goethe saw (hardly comprehending
much) what he described as taking place in the
scratch company whose doings he chronicles in
Wilhelm Meister. He and his friend discussed many
things, and "in four weeks (I) learned more than
could have been imagined ; so that no one knew how
I suddenly, as if by inspiration, had acquired a foreign
language."

Possibly, when the *entente cordiale* has become
acclimatised, let us say, children belonging to the
two countries may come to visit each other's families,
and more French may yet be learned in a month
from the companionship of a nice French boy than
the best master in the world would succeed in teaching in a year. The desire to communicate with each
other would doubtless bring about the power.

The French boy, whom he chooses to name
Derones, introduced young Goethe to his sister, a
grave maiden, who did not forget that she was much
older than he ; otherwise, no doubt, we should have
had the first of a long series of love interludes. But
he complains that young maidens treat boys younger
than themselves as if they were their aunts, and his
offerings of fruit and flowers made little impression.

By and by the two young friends must needs fight
a duel ; provocation was there none, but that did
not matter. Derones called young Goethe out, and
they went to a lonely place and wielded their mock
swords, and the honour of the Frenchman was satis-

fied when he stuck his dagger into a ribbon on the
enemy's equipment; and they went to a coffee-house
and received each other into a closer friendship than
ever.

These days of the occupation of Frankfort offered
continual festival to the children and young people.
Theatre and ball, parade and march drew the children
hither and thither, and the life of a soldier seemed
to them very delightful. The fact that the King's
Lieutenant dwelt in their house made the Goethe
children familiar, by sight at any rate, with all the
persons of distinction in the French army.

But the war had other things in store. " A camp
of the French, a flight, a defence of the town, intended
only to cover a retreat in order to hold the bridge, a
bombardment, plundering—all this excited the imagination and brought sorrow to both parties." Easter
week of 1759 saw the event. A great stillness pre-
ceded the storm. The children were forbidden to
go out of the house ; and after some hours, waggon-
loads of the wounded on both sides were brought
into the town, proclaiming that the action was over.
By and by the victorious Count Thorane returned on
horseback ; the children sprang towards him, kissed
his hands and showed their joy, which appeared to
please him, and he ordered that a collation of sweet-
meats should be made for them to celebrate the
event. But the father behaved quite otherwise. He
met the victorious General with insult and violence :
the consternation in the household was great, for it
appeared certain that its head would be committed to
prison; but the intervention of a friend saved the
bitter and somewhat eccentric man, and things went
on as before.

VIII

The children's interest in the theatre continued; many half-historical, half-mythological pieces were played then, and it came into 'the Boy's' head that he himself could write such a piece. He did so, made a clean copy, and laid it before his friend Derones, who read it with great attention, and, in answer to a modest question, conceived that it was not impossible that the piece should be played; but, first of all, he would go over it carefully with the author. "Although my friend was otherwise easy-going, the opportunity, long wished for, of playing the master seemed now to have come. He read the piece attentively, and while he sat down with me to correct a few trifles, he so altered the piece in the course of this performance that scarcely one stone was left upon another. He crossed out, added, took away a character, substituted another; in fact, he carried on the wildest career in the world, so that my hair stood on end. He even grudged to have to allow me any authorship whatever; for he had so often told me of the three unities of Aristotle, of the regularity of the French drama, of probability, of the harmony of the verse, and the rest, that I must acknowledge him as builder and founder of my play. He abused the English and despised the Germans; in fact, he brought the whole dramatic litany before me as indeed during my life I have heard it constantly repeated."

The poor boy took back his work in pieces and tried in vain to put it together again. Once more he had a fair copy made of the piece as it stood originally and showed it to his father; this time he got something in the shape of a reward; for his father no longer grumbled when he came home from the theatre.

His friend's opposition made the boy think. He determined not again to have his work shipwrecked on theories which he did not understand, so he read Corneille's work on the Unities. He read, too, in great perplexity, the criticisms and counter-criticisms on *The Cid*, and found that even Corneille and Racine were obliged to defend themselves from the attacks of the critics. He laboured honestly to understand what they would be at, and this famous law of the three unities became as distasteful to him as he had already found grammatical rules. Again he was a law unto himself; nor did he, for many years, reconsider his decision.

In course of time Count Thorane was transferred to another post, and the Chancellor Moritz took his place in the Goethe household. All was fish that came to the young Goethe's net. The Chancellor had a brother, the Councillor of the Legation, whose love for mathematics amounted to a hobby, and who helped the boy in this study, which he considered was of use to him in the drawing lessons which now occupied an hour daily. Of his drawing master he says, "This good man was indeed only half an artist: we had to make lines and place them together, and out of these, eyes, noses, lips and ears, and at length whole faces and heads were to grow; but there was no thought of either natural or artistic form. We were tormented for a time with this *quid pro quo* of the human figure, and were thought at last to have been carried so far that we received the so-called 'Passions' of Le Brun to copy; but these pictures did not appeal to us. We went on to landscapes, to

all those things which are practised in the usual
system of teaching without aim and without method.
At last we attained to close imitation, and dropped
into exactness of line without troubling ourselves
about the worth or artistic value of the original."

Then, as now, art was supposed to be assisted by
mechanical devices. Then, as now, children were
taught to draw, not from objects, but from drawings
of those objects; that is, they were and are taught to
imitate *lines* rather than to receive and record impressions of *things*. The father, who held that
nothing was so stimulating to young pupils as for
their elders to learn with them, also laboured at this
unprofitable copying; and with an English pencil on
fine Dutch paper he not only copied the lines of the
composition but the strokes of the engraver. "Everybody must learn to draw," the Emperor Maximilian is
reported to have said; a maxim which the elder Goethe
had seized upon with the avidity of one feeling in
the dark for guidance in the puzzling and difficult
business of education.

Charlotte Brontë tells us how Lucy Snowe exercised
herself in this same laborious way, and conceived that
she was learning to draw; and probably Lucy's experience is a reminiscence of "Currer Bell's" own efforts.
We are not told that Charlotte Brontë ever learned
to draw, but we know that all his life Goethe had a
great hankering after this art; and as an old man
we still find him copying a detail of some picture, line
by line, shade by shade. It would appear as if we
are always handicapped by the faults of our education,
not merely in a general way, but subject by subject,
method by method, we are only able to go on with
that which has had a *living* beginning in our youth.

It was always the intention for the children to learn music ; but not until the boy took the matter in hand himself did the right man appear to teach them. He chanced to hear a companion taught by a master who had little jokes for every finger, facetious names for every line and note, and for the moment this took with even so able a boy as the young Goethe. However, the jokes came to an end so soon as the teacher was employed ; and the music lessons were deadly dry and dull, until that enterprising educationalist, the father, set up a young man who had been his secretary, and who spoke French well, and could teach it, as a schoolmaster; for the town was not satisfied with the public teaching, and there appeared to be an opening for private enterprise. This young man set to work to learn music so zealously that in a few weeks he had accomplished wonders; and not only so, he became acquainted with a maker of first-rate instruments, which he introduced to his house. This man's enthusiasm gave that impetus to the family in the direction of music for which they had been waiting.

IX

"The more I was allowed to work in this way the more I wanted to, and even my leisure hours were spent in all sorts of wonderful occupations. Already, since my earliest days, I had felt a strong impulse towards finding out about natural objects.

" I remember that as a child I often picked flowers to pieces to see how the petals were fixed in the cup, and even plucked birds to see how the feathers were fastened into the wings. Children should not be blamed for this, for even naturalists often think they will learn more from rending and parting than from connecting and uniting, from the dead than from the living.

" An armed loadstone, sewn up daintily in a piece of scarlet cloth, must needs one day experience the result of such desire for discovery. For the secret attractive power which it not only exercised on the little iron bar attached to it, but had this further quality that it increased in strength, could daily bear a heavier weight,—this secret virtue filled me with delight, so that I spent a long time in merely wondering at this power. At last I thought I should make a closer acquaintance with it if I took away the outer covering. This was done without making me any wiser, for the naked iron taught me nothing further. I took this off also and held the bare stone in my hands, with which I was never weary of experimenting with filings and needles, experiments from which my young mind drew no advantage but a manifold experience. I did not know how to put the arrangement together again, the parts got destroyed, and I lost the striking phenomena as well as the apparatus."

An electric machine, too, the property of a friend, was a source of much interest to the children, and a further means of awakening the boy's scientific imagination.

Two occupations laid upon them by their father fell as hardships upon the young people. The one was the care of silkworms, to the rearing of which a room was appropriated; but it was difficult to keep the worms in health under such artificial conditions, thousands died, and the removal of these and the efforts to keep the rest cleanly and in good condition fell to the children. The other task which they did not love was connected with the views of Rome, the source of so many early impressions. The engravings which had been so long exposed on the walls of the old house were no longer in a condition to decorate the new one, and the task which fell to the children was to keep the sheet, to which a copperplate was attached, constantly moist for a considerable time, until it could be easily removed from that which was mounted upon it. As there were a good many engravings, this was not a slight labour, and the reader hails with pleasure a mention of tiresome tasks which *must* be performed. That such tasks were rare is evident enough; but the meaning of *must* can only be learned by means of a duty which it would be agreeable to shirk.

"Lest we children should lack anything of all that life and learning have to give, it happened at that time that an English language master presented himself, who undertook to teach English to anyone not quite raw to language study in four weeks—enough, that is, to enable him to continue his study by himself. He asked a moderate fee; the number of pupils for the lesson was of no consequence.

"My father resolved on the spot to make the attempt, and took lessons with me and my sister from this expeditious master.

"The lessons were faithfully given and there was no lack of repetition, and for the four weeks some other studies were laid by. The master parted from us and we from him with satisfaction. As he stayed in the town and found plenty of employment, he came to see and help us from time to time, thankful that we were among the first who had trusted him, and proud to show us as models to the others."

It would be pleasant to know if this unnamed English teacher anticipated the conversational methods of to-day.

But new acquisitions were new responsibilities, for the father was anxious that the newly acquired English should be kept up as fully as the other languages at which the children had worked; and now we get from 'the Boy,' weary of many grammars, each with many lists of exceptions, a scheme which, though we had not the wit to originate, we might at any rate follow with advantage.

"Thereupon the thought occurred to me of settling the matter once and for all, and I invented a story about six or seven brothers and sisters who, scattered over the world at some distance from each other, mutually exchange news of their various conditions and sentiments." The eldest brother gives in good German news of all the circumstances and events of his journey. The sister, in a feminine manner, with full stops and short sentences, tells now him, now the others of the family, what she has to say as to her domestic life, as well as of her love affairs. One brother studies Latin, and writes very formal Latin, adding occasionally a postscript in Greek. Another brother, an agent in Hamburg, had to manage the English correspondence; a younger brother, in Marseilles, the French. As for Italian, one brother, a musician, was making his first essay in the world; and the youngest, cut off from the other languages, had taken refuge in Juden-Deutsch, and with his fearful lingo threw the others into despair. "The idea made my parents laugh. For this extraordinary arrangement I had to find a *format*, and I studied the geography of the places where

my creations lived, and invented for these bare
localities all sorts of human interests, in fact whatever
had any relation to the character and business of my
people.   In this way my exercises became much more
voluminous, my father was more contented, and I
perceived much more quickly what was necessary in
the way of revision and completion."

X.

There is an unfortunate tendency at the present
time to depreciate knowledge, which is indeed the
chief instrument of education.   Bible knowledge
especially is discountenanced for several reasons.
The utilitarian asks, "What is the use of teaching a
child the more or less fabulous 'history' of the
earlier books and the insignificant later records of
one of the least among the nations?" while religious parents are inclined to pick and choose and
teach only such parts of the Bible as seem to them
likely to give the religious impulse.   To-day we are
confronted with the new difficulties raised by the
Higher Criticism.   "How far," we ask, "is it safe
to offer Bible knowledge to a child when we have
by no means come to the end of the critical study of
the Bible, and he may, later, hear what we have
taught him controverted point by point?"   If we
could only know how such knowledge affects a
child; could we know how the critical acumen, with
which clever children are endowed, plays of itself
round the sacred text; and could we know what is
left of solid possession after childish scepticism has
had full play!

Goethe offers us precisely such a test case in *Aus*

Meinem Leben. He gives us the minutest details of his own Bible studies, tells us with what temper he came to these studies, and how, by degrees, his Bible knowledge became the most precious of his intellectual possessions. This is how it came about. As a child of about ten or so he was already embarrassed by the possession of several languages which his father expected him to keep up, so he hit, as we have seen, on the plan of keeping a family diary, the brothers and sisters writing each in the language of the country where he or she lived. He had some knowledge of Juden-Deutsch, and one brother was set to correspond in that tongue.

This brilliant idea, as is the way with ideas, produced after its kind. The boy's synthetic mind found the Juden-Deutsch fragmentary and unsatisfactory. He must needs add Hebrew to his list of languages, and his father succeeded in securing lessons from Dr Albrecht, the Rector of the Gymnasium. This Rector seems to have been a man of original mind, whimsical, satirical, little understood by his fellow-townsmen. Naturally, he took to the young genius who came to him to be taught.

The Hebrew lessons went delightfully, no doubt, to both master and pupil, and the impression made upon the latter by the Hebrew Scriptures is of singular interest to us to-day when the question of teaching Old Testament history to children is much agitated. The boy was already able to read the Greek of the New Testament, and appears to have been in the habit of following, in the original, the Epistles and Gospels as they were read in church. Of course, a boy of his power, with both a logical and a scientific turn, ferreted out difficulties enough. "For already the contradictions between tradition and the actual and possible had struck me much, and I had put my tutors in many a corner as to the sun which stood still for Gibeon, and the moon which did likewise in the valley of Ajalon, to say nothing of other improbabilities and inconsistencies. All this was now stirred up again, for while I sought to master Hebrew, I worked entirely with the Old Testament, and this studied through, no longer in Luther's translation, but in the interlinear version of Sebastian Schmid, printed under the text, which my father had procured for me. Reading, translation, grammar, copying and repeating words seldom lasted half-an-hour; then I began immediately to attack the meaning of the passage; and although we were working at the first book of Moses, I introduced the discussion of many points which I remembered in the later books. At first the good old man tried to dissuade me from such exertions, but after a time they seemed to entertain him. He continued his tricks of coughing and laughing, and however much he coughed, as a hint to me that I might compromise him, I persisted, and was even more insistent in setting forth my doubts than in getting them answered. I became ever more lively and bolder, and he only seemed to justify me by his behaviour. I could get nothing out of him but, now and again, a laugh which shook him, and ' foolish rascal, foolish rascal.'"

All the same, his master was not blind to the boy's difficulties, and was willing to help him in the best way. He referred him to a great English 'Bible-work' in his library, which attempted the interpretation of difficult passages in a thoughtful and judicious way. The German divines who translated the book

had improved upon it. Various opinions and inter-
pretations were cited, and, finally, a line was taken
which preserved the dignity of the Book, made
evident the grounds of religion, and gave free play
to the human understanding. Now, when the boy
brought out his doubts and questions towards the end
of a lesson, the master pointed to the Commentary.
The pupil took the volume and read while his master
turned over the pages of his Lucian, and sagacious
comments were answered only by the master's peculiar
laugh. " In the long summer days he let me sit as
long as I could read, often alone, and later he let me
take one volume after another home with me."

It would be good to know all about that Commentary which satisfied so keen a young mind. Anyway,
we can commend and imitate the wisdom of Dr
Albrecht. Of all ways of attempting to arrive at
truth, perhaps discussion is the most futile, because the
disputants are bent upon fortifying their own doubts,
and by no means upon solving them. The will unconsciously takes a combative attitude, adopts the doubt
as a possession, a cause to be fought for ; and reason
is, as we know, ready with arguments in support of
any position the will has taken up. But, give the
young sceptic a good book bearing on the questions
he has raised, let him digest it at his leisure without
comment or discussion, and, according to his degree
of candour and intelligence, he will lay himself open
to conviction. The silence and the chuckle of this
good professor are worth remembering when we are
shocked by the daring announcements of the young
sceptics who belong to us. So, too, is the wise
passiveness which put a solution of his difficulties in
the boy's way, but made no attempt to convince him.

" Man may turn where he will ; he may undertake whatever he will ; but he will yet return to that road which Nature has laid down for him. So it happened to me in the present case. My efforts with the language, with the contents of the Holy Scriptures, resulted in a most lively presentation to my imagination of that beautiful much-sung land, and of the countries which bordered it, as well as of the people and events which have glorified that spot of earth for thousands of years."

Those timorous but not unbelieving parents who hesitate to make their children familiar with the Old Testament Scriptures because of the difficult problems they suggest, or of the lax morality they now and then record, or because of a hundred vexed questions concerning authorship and inspiration, will find this episode in the young Goethe's education very full of interest and instruction. Here was a boy prone to doubt, quick to criticise, whose eager intellect tore the heart out of whatever subject was presented to him, and who appears, from his own confession, to have made merry over certain scientific difficulties which the Bible narrative offered ; but what was the net result? This : that nowhere, so far as I know, does there exist a more valuable defence of Bible teaching than Goethe has drawn up from his boyish reminiscences.

" This little spot was to see the origin and growth of the human race ; from there, the first and only news of the primeval history of the world was to reach us ; a setting was presented to the imagination, simple and easy to be conceived, and adapted to manifold and wonderful wanderings and settlements. Here, between four named rivers, was chosen out of the whole habitable earth a little, wholly pleasant spot for the youth of man. Here he was to develop his activities, and here meet the fate that was allotted to his posterity—to lose his peace in striving after knowledge. Paradise was closed; men increased and grew more wicked; God, not yet accustomed to the evil deeds of this race, became impatient and annihilated it. Only a few were saved from the over-whelming flood; and hardly had those awful waters gone down, when there, before the eyes of those grateful saved souls, lay the familiar ground of their fatherland. Two rivers of the four, the Euphrates and Tigris, flowed yet in their beds. The name of the first remains, the second is indicated by its course: it could not be expected that exact traces of Paradise would remain after such a catastrophe. Now the new human race began for the second time; it found various means of getting food and work, chiefly by collecting great herds of tame beasts and travelling with them in all directions. This manner of life, as well as the increase of the families, soon made it necessary for the peoples to part. They could not resolve at once to let their relations and friends journey away not to return, so they hit upon the plan of building a high tower, which should from a distance show them the way back. But this attempt, like their first endeavour, failed. They were not to be happy and wise, numerous and united. God sent confusion amongst them; the building was stopped, the people were scattered; the world was peopled, but divided. But our gaze is fixed upon, our concern remains with, this region. At last, the founder of a race goes out again from here who is so happy as to stamp a decided character on his posterity, and by this means to unite them for all time, a great nation, inseparable through all changes.

"From the Euphrates, not without the divine guidance, Abraham wanders to the west. The desert offers no insurmountable barrier to his journey; he reaches the Jordan, crosses the river, and spreads over the beautiful southern region of Palestine. This land was already in other hands and fairly well populated. Mountains, not too high, but rocky and unfruitful, were cut through by many well-watered, pleasant valleys; towns, encampments, single settlements lay scattered over the plain on the sides of the great valley whose waters flow into Jordan. Though the land was inhabited, built upon, the world was still big enough; and men were not careful as to space, nor necessarily active enough to make themselves masters of adjacent country.

"Between their possessions lay great spaces, by which grazing herds could easily pass up and down. In such spaces Abraham and his 'brother' Lot encamped, but they could not stay long on these pastures. The very condition of a land whose population fluctuates, and whose resources are never in proportion to its needs, brings unexpected famine, and the immigrant suffers with the native, whose own supplies he has lessened by his chance presence. The two Chaldean brothers went to Egypt; and thus the stage is brought before us on which for some thousands of years the most important events of the world took place. From the Tigris to the Euphrates, from the Euphrates to the Nile, we see the earth peopled; and in this spot a man, known and loved of Heaven, and already honoured by us, goes up and down with his herds and possessions, and in a short time increases abundantly. The brothers come back, but, compelled by necessity, decide to part. Both indeed journey on to southern Canaan; but while Abraham remains at Hebron, near the plain of Mamre, Lot goes to the valley of Siddim, which—if our imagination is bold enough to give the Jordan an underground outlet, so that we should have dry ground where the Dead Sea at present lies—must appear to us a second Paradise; so much the more so because the inhabitants and surrounding nations, notorious for their effeminacy, lead us to the conclusion that life to them was comfortable and merry. Lot lived amongst them, but was not of them. But Hebron and the plain of Mamre appear before us as the important spots where the Lord spoke with Abraham and promised him all the land as far as his eyes could see in four directions.

"From these quiet dwellings, from these shepherd people who walk with angels, entertain them as guests and converse with them, we must turn our eyes again to the East and think of the settlement of the neighbouring tribes, which was probably like that of Canaan. Families held together, they united, and the manner of life of the tribe was settled by the locality which they held or had seized. On the mountains which send down their waters to the Tigris we find the warlike peoples who already very early foreshadow the brigands and war-lords of the future, and who give us in a campaign, stupendous for those times, a foretaste of wars to come. . . . . . Now the prophecy of unending heirs was renewed, a prophecy ever enlarged in scope. From the waters of the Euphrates to the river of Egypt the whole extent of land is promised; but as Abraham has no heir, fulfilment seems doubtful. He is eighty years old and has no son. Sara, with less trust in the gods than her husband, becomes impatient; she desires, according to oriental custom, to have offspring by a maid. But scarcely is Hagar given over to her lord and there is hope of a son when division enters the house. The wife treats her own substitute ill, and Hagar flees in order to find a better position with another tribe. By divine guidance she is led back and Ishmael is born.

"Abraham is now ninety-nine years old; the promise of numerous posterity is again and again repeated, and at last both husband and wife begin to be contemptuous; and yet to Sara comes the hoped-for good and she brings forth a son, who is called Isaac. The history of the human race rests on a regulated growth. The most important world-events must be traced to the domestic life of the family, and therefore the marriage of the father of the race gives us pause for reflection. It is as if the Godhead which loves to guide the fate of man wished to set forth as in a picture every aspect of marriage. Abraham having lived so long with a beautiful and much-sought-after but childless wife, finds himself in his hundredth year the husband of two wives, the father of two sons, and at this point his domestic peace goes. Two wives together, as well as two sons of two mothers in opposition, make matters impossible. The one who is less favoured by law, by descent, by disposition must yield. Abraham must sacrifice any feeling for Hagar and Ishmael; both are forsaken, and Hagar is compelled against her will to set forth again upon the road she had taken in her wilful flight, at first, as it seems, to the destruction of herself and her child; but the angel of the Lord, who had before sent her back, saves her again, this time that Ishmael may become a great people, and that the most improbable of all promises should be more than fulfilled. Two parents far on in years and a single late-born son: surely here, indeed, is cause for domestic peace and earthly happiness! But no. Heaven is preparing for the patriarch the hardest trial yet. But we cannot enter upon this without many previous considerations.

" If a natural universal religion were to rise, and a special revealed religion were to develop from it, these lands in which our imagination has lingered, the manner of life, the very people themselves, were the most entirely suited for it; any way, we do not find in the whole world anything more favourable.

" If we assume that the natural religion rose earlier. in the mind of man, we must grant the clearness of perception which belongs to it, for it rests upon the conviction of a universal providence which rules the whole world. A particular religion leads belief to a special providence which the Divine Being extends to certain favoured men, families, tribes and peoples. This could hardly be developed from the human spirit. It implies tradition, descent, custom, carried forward from the oldest times. . . . . The first men seem closely related, but their divers occupations soon part them. The hunter was the freest of all, and from him the warrior and ruler is developed. Those who wielded the plough and devoted themselves to the soil built dwellings and barns to hold their possessions, and could think well of themselves, because their circumstances promised permanence and safety. The shepherd at his post seemed to have the most limited and yet boundless possessions. The increase of flocks went on for ever, and the land on which they fed extended its boundaries on all sides. These three callings seem at first to have looked at each other with contempt and suspicion; and because the shepherd was hated by the townsfolk, he kept his distance from them. The hunter disappears from our eyes into the mountains, and only appears again as the brigand. The first fathers belong to the shepherd ranks. Their mode of life in the wide stretches of desert and pasture gave their minds breadth and freedom; the vault of heaven under which they lived, with its stars at night, gave them a sense of awe and dependence, and they were more in need than the active, resourceful hunter, or than the secure, careful, home-keeping ploughman, of the unshaken belief that a god went beside man, that he visited them, took their part, guided and saved them.

"One more consideration before we go on with the history. However human, beautiful, and cheering the religion of these first fathers appears, there are traces of savagery and cruelty out of which men rise, or into which they may again sink. That hatred should be avenged by the blood, by the death of the defeated enemy is natural; that a peace should be concluded between the rows of the dead is readily imagined; that man should think of confirming a covenant by the slaughter of animals is a natural consequence; also, there is nothing to wonder at in the fact that mankind should try to appease and win over by sacrifices the gods, who were always regarded as taking sides, as their opponents or helpers. . . ."

Here follows a very interesting disquisition upon the ideas which men expressed by means of sacrifices, to introduce the story of the supreme sacrifice demanded of Abraham, the final test of his faith.

"Without a shudder Abraham blindly sets himself to carry out the command; but, to God, the will is enough. Now Abraham's trials are over, for they cannot be heightened. But Sarah dies, and this gives opportunity for Abraham, as in a figure, to take possession of the land of Canaan. He must have a grave, and this is the first time he looks round for the possession of land on this earth. A double cave towards the grove of Mamre he may have already sought for. He buys this, with the adjoining field, and the legal forms which he observes show how important this possession is for him. It was more so than perhaps even he could imagine, for he, his sons and grandsons, were to rest there, and the claim to the whole land, as well as the ever-growing inclination of his descendants to settle here, were thus founded in the most special way.

"From this time the manifold scenes of domestic life come and go. Abraham still keeps himself isolated from the inhabitants of the land; and even if Ishmael, son of an Egyptian woman, has married a daughter of the people, Isaac must marry with his own kin and one of equal birth.

"Abraham sends his servant to Mesopotamia, to his kin whom he had left behind. The wise Eleazer arrives, unrecognised; and in order to take the right bride home, he tests the serviceableness of the girl at the well. He asks for water, and, unasked, Rebecca waters also his camels. He makes her a present; he offers for her, and she is not refused to him. So he takes her to his master's house and she is betrothed to Isaac. Here also heirs were long expected.

Rebecca is only blessed after some years of trial, and the same division which resulted from the two mothers in Abraham's double marriage springs here from *one*. The two boys, of opposite characters, already strove beneath the mother's heart. They reach the light of day, the elder lusty and strong, the younger delicate and wise; the former his father's darling, the latter his mother's. The strife for precedence, begun already at birth, continues. Esau is calm and indifferent as to the birthright which fate granted him, but Jacob does not forget that his brother forced him back. Watchful for any opportunity of gaining this longed-for advantage, he trades with his brother for the birthright, and is beforehand in getting his father's blessing. Esau, in a rage, swears he will kill his brother. Jacob flees, in order to try his fortune in the land of his ancestors.

" Now, for the first time in so noble a family, appears a trait which hardly bears dwelling upon—that of gaining by cunning and strategy the advantages denied by nature and circumstances. It has often been remarked and discussed that the Holy Scriptures do not in any way set forth our first fathers and other men favoured by God as models of virtue. They also are men, various in character, with many deficiencies and failings, but there is one special quality in which men after God's own heart may not be wanting—it is the unshaken belief that God hears and cares for them and theirs.

" A universal, natural religion requires no special belief; for the conviction that a great governing, ordering, ruling personality hides behind nature in order to make it possible for us to comprehend Him— such a conviction forces itself upon everyone ; even, indeed, if a man drop the clue which leads him through life, he will be able to pick it up again at any time. Quite otherwise is it with a particular religion which tells us that this Great Being distinctly interests Himself for one person, one family, one nation, one country. This religion is founded on faith which must be unshaken if the religion is not to be entirely destroyed. Every doubt is fatal: a man may get back to conviction, but not to faith. This is the reason of the endless trials, the tardy fulfilment of oft-repeated promises, by which the living faith of the patriarchs is brought into play.

"Jacob also had his share of this faith; and if he does not gain our respect by his strategy and deception, he wins it by his lasting, unbroken love for Rachel, whom he wins for himself as Eleazer had won Rebecca for his father. In him is the promise of a numerous posterity first fulfilled; he was to see many sons around him, but his heart suffered many pangs on their account and that of their mothers.

"Seven years he served for his loved one, without impatience or any hesitation. His stepfather, like him in cunning, like-minded in thinking the end justifies the means, deceived him, serving him just as he had served his brother. Jacob finds a wife whom he does not love in his arms. It is true that in order to pacify him Laban gives him also the one he loves, but on the condition of seven more years of service; then follows disappointment after disappointment. The unloved wife is fruitful, the loved one has no children, and she, like Sara, desires motherhood by a maid; but the first wife grudges her even this advantage, and she also gives a maid to her husband; and now the good father of the race is the most persecuted man in the world ; four wives, children by three, and none by the beloved wife ! But she at last is favoured and Joseph comes into the world, a late-born child of sorrowful love. . . . . There is strife. Jacob flees with all his possessions and encounters the pursuing Laban, partly by luck, partly by cunning. Now Rachel presents him with another son, but she dies at his birth; the son of sorrow, Benjamin, lives ; but the old father is to suffer yet greater pain at the apparent loss of his son Joseph.

" Perhaps someone may ask why I set forth here in such detail this universally known history, so oft repeated and expounded. This answer may serve : that in no other way could I show how, with the distractions of my life and my irregular education, I concentrated my mind and my emotions in quiet activity on one point ; because I can in no other way account for the peace which enveloped me, however disturbed and unusual the circumstances of my life. If an ever-active imagination, of which the story of my life may bear witness, led me here and there, if the medley of fable, history, mythology, and religion threatened to drive me to distraction, I betook my-self again to those morning-lands, I buried myself in the first books of Moses, and there, amongst the widespreading shepherd people, I found the greatest solitude and the greatest company."

Here we have set forth a full and sufficient reason for giving children a profound acquaintance with the Old Testament Scriptures. It will be said that in Goethe's case such an acquaintance did not result in religion. No, he was never religious in the usual sense of the word ; and at the time when he recites the above confession of faith—the faith acquired in his child-

hood, and probably little affected by after events—
he had paid that momentous visit to Italy, had
returned to the classicism of his earliest years, and
classic paganism had become so strong in him that
he practically ceased to be a believer in God as we
understand the phrase.   But religion has two aspects.
There is the attitude of the will towards God, which
we understand by Christianity: in this sense Goethe
was never religious, any more than he was moral in the
accepted sense.   How to set his will right towards the
relations of life, whether human or divine, formed no
part of his manifold culture.   But religion has another
aspect: that conception of God which comes from a
gradual slow-growing comprehension of the divine
dealings with men.   This repose of the soul, this fresh
background for the thoughts, Goethe tells us he got
from his study of the books of Moses; tells us, too,
that he could have got it in no other way (and,
indeed, he tried all ways); and in all the errors of
his wilful life this innermost repose appears never to
have left him.   "His eyes were tranquil as those of
a god," says Heine; and here is revealed the secret
of that large tranquillity.   Here Goethe unfolds for
us a principle of education which those who desire
their children to possess the passive as well as the
active principle of religion would do well to consider;
for it is probably true that the teaching of the New
Testament, not duly grounded upon that of the Old,
fails to result in such thought of God—wide, all-
embracing, all-permeating—as David, for example,
gives constant expression to in the Psalms.

Let us have faith to give children such a full and
gradual knowledge of Old Testament history that
they unconsciously perceive for themselves a pan-

oramic view of the history of mankind—typified by
that of the Jewish nation—as it is unfolded in the
Bible. And we need not be frightened off this field
by the doubts and difficulties that clever children will
raise. Let us, as did that good Dr Albrecht, not try
to put down or evade their questions or pretend
to offer them a final answer, but introduce them
to some thoughtful commentator (what, we wonder,
was that 'big English book' to which Dr Albrecht
referred his pupil?) who weighs difficult questions
with modesty and scrupulous care. If we do this, difficulties will assume their due measure of importance;
that is to say, they will be lost sight of in the gradual
unfolding of the great scheme whereby the world was
educated.

XI

As my point is to indicate how the education
of the boy told in the life of the man, it is not
necessary to follow further these most instructive
records *Aus Meinem Leben*. Nowhere else, so far as
I know, have we a minute, almost impersonal consideration of all the influences that went to the making
of a man. That this was a man of genius, a great
poet, is not important to us from the educational
standpoint; the noticeable fact is that no single fragment of his education, hardly a book that he read or
hobby that he pursued, above all, hardly a single subject
in all his numerous studies, but bore directly and obviously on the man that he became. But there is another side to the question: with all his intellect, his
mighty genius, he possessed nothing as a man the seed
of which had not been sown in the course of his educa-

tion. The examples of both parents, the unresting efforts of his father, were all in the direction of culture; and he died with the exclamation, "More light!" The very subjects of his study as a boy, *and no other subjects*, fired and stimulated him to the end. His English put him in sympathy with Shakespeare, who became a passion and power in his life. His scientific interests remained with him to the end. He is allowed to have been in some respects a precursor of Darwin: he it was who discovered that all plant forms are modifications of the leaf, and arrived at the certainty that there must have been an original plant from which all plants were developed. The cathedral of Strasburg led him in his student days to the study of Gothic architecture, and in late life to the study of architecture in Italy. We hear of him saying, towards the end, that there were other contemporary poets, that there had been greater poets than he, but that no other person had promulgated his theory of colour. He spent his time in Rome in drawing, learning perspective, instructing himself in architecture, practising composition in landscape, and modelling the human form, limb by limb. His drawing never came to more than a taste for the art, but he himself perceived that the value of his study lay in teaching him to appreciate the work of others. His study of music was a parallel case of painstaking endeavour. In his eightieth year we find him taking daily music lessons from Felix Mendelssohn, and the lessons were of a kind we should do well to imitate: he would retire into a dark corner and listen for an hour to the playing of Mendelssohn. He rather shrank from Beethoven, but his master insisted on introducing him to the great composer, without any very marked result. But in his notes on these two subjects of study, as throughout the autobiography, we find repeated what we might well take as a canon of education in these subjects; that is, that a power of appreciation in both arts is of more value to many, perhaps to most of us, than the power of production, and should be as deliberately and as regularly cultivated.

The puppet-show of his childhood developed, as we know, a ruling penchant, if not passion, of his life; and the direction of the theatre at Weimar in middle life and old age was removed in degree but not in kind from the management of the puppet-plays of his early boyhood.

The enormous industry, or rather the multifarious occupations of his boyhood were continued until the closing years of his life; and even then he rejoiced that he had learned to play cards at Frankfort, because "a day is infinitely long, and you can get so much into it." Card games he regarded as a means of making himself pleasant in society; as did the late Professor Jewett, whose parting counsel to a child of his acquaintance was, " Be a good girl, my dear, read the Waverley novels and learn to play whist "; but it is a question whether the risk of developing the gambling instinct, common to us all, is not to be set against the social equipment which a knowledge of card games affords.

Again, as a child he was brought up upon the classics. The first Book of Ovid's *Metamorphoses* appears to have been the first book he appropriated in an intellectual sense; and though he is strongly attracted by the romanticism of the period, again and again he reverts to his old faith. We find him, while at the University of Leipsic, exchanging all his collection of modern authors with a fellow-student for a few volumes of the classics, in which for a period he lived entirely. Later, he is brought under the dominion of Shakespeare, whom he hails as his father and invokes as his inspiration; and his greatest work, no doubt, belongs to the period when he discarded the trammels of the 'Unities,' and surrendered himself to the guidance of Nature. But the old predisposition returned upon him after his two years' sojourn in Italy, and astonished Germany was required to assist at a complete overthrow of former theories.

We have just seen, too, how his Bible studies remained with him as a green background for all his thoughts. In a word, no single branch or department of his early education but bore fruit *in kind* all through his life and to extreme old age.

If we look, on the other hand, at the records of most English men of renown, we find their school studies have passed into oblivion, as matters that had no serious effect upon their after career. The random reading that they do for themselves becomes a power in their lives, but their set studies simply do not count. This is a point that invites reflection. Goethe's education was, as we know, casual and very faulty. We have heard him lament that he was thoroughly grounded in nothing, and yet this defective education enriched him with the seed thoughts which produced his after development in every kind. Was it that he came to each study, even on account of the very imperfection and inadequacy of the teaching equipment, as if it were a fresh field in which his own intellect had ample play? If so, it behoves us perhaps to add this freshness of outlook, this scope for the individual, to the disciplinary value of our ordered school studies.

It is perhaps a fact that each of us should, as was Goethe, be able to discern the crop yielded by every sowing of our childhood's studies. Instead of which, we put away our school-work as if its intention had been entirely disciplinary and it would be idle to look for the maturing of any seeds of knowledge sown in the days of childhood or school-life. Surely this is a lamentable and reckless waste of intellectual gains.

Another not less vital lesson presents itself in this invaluable record. There is another side to the shield. Everything which had been initiated in Goethe's education came to conspicuous development; but, also, nothing which had been overlooked in his education arrived to him in after life. The indiscipline of his early education remained always as a defect of character, as well as lost ground which he failed to make up in his university career. Neither at Leipsic nor at Strasburg did he distinguish himself. The provincialisms, both of manner and accent, which he owed to his upbringing in a burgher family in Frankfort, were not only a constant detriment to him, but affected, so to speak, his pose of character. He always remained impressed with the fact that only persons of noble birth enjoyed the possibility of complete culture; an idea which he did not lose, notwithstanding his intimacy with the grand-ducal family at Weimar. The circumstances of his birth were no doubt fixed, but his own outlook upon these circumstances depended upon the family point of view. Had some idea of manhood other than that of culture been always present to his thought, comparisons of this sort would not have occurred to him, nor would he have been distressed or annoyed by a sense of inequality.

This consideration brings us to the grand omission in the education of this highly cultured boy. Of religious impressions, presented with enough freshness and power to reach him, he got, as we have seen, vivid ideas from the Mosaic books, and, so far as he tells us, nothing more; nothing, we should imagine, from the atmosphere of his home, his parents being occupied with the single ideal of culture. The enthusiastic reading of Klopstock's *Messias* appears to have left none but a literary impression. His moral education, like that of most of us, seems to have been pretty much left to chance. He appears to have received no instruction and few impressions as to his relations with, and duties towards, the persons with whom he came in contact, his country or his kind. He does not appear to be aware that he has the power of regulating his emotions, or that his moral life should be under the direction of his will. Hence, Goethe as a man is disappointing. He is like a city laid out on a grand scale, but only half built according to the plan, and the rest left waste or overrun with wretched shanties. Goethe should have been a great man as well as a great poet. He had every possibility of greatness, moral as well as intellectual; and we find him running to waste in endless puerilities of the affections, transient loves, inconstant friendships, personal aims, illiberal thoughts upon public questions other than those which affected his art. A man of mighty intellect, who should have been a great example and a great teacher of his kind, is hemmed in by narrow limitations, marred by moral defects. We are inclined to say—'But a poet is not to be judged as other men; his emotional nature runs away with him; we cannot always look for the poet and moralist in one, so let us take what we get and be thankful.' This manner of reasoning, and the careless living that proceeds from it, arises from the notion that morals and religion are independent of intellect, are, in fact, matters with which the mind is little concerned. When we perceive that the truly moral life depends upon the breadth of the intellectual outlook, upon strenuousness of intellectual effort, we shall understand that taking pains in these directions also is the concern of genius.

Probably there never was a great man who lent himself more to support the theory that genius itself is the faculty of taking pains; he had the most extraordinary patience and talent for detail; and, that he did not employ these gifts in building up a moral greatness equal to his greatness as a poet, seems to be solely the result of a defective education which did not present this manner of effort to him in his eager childhood and boyhood. What his early education did not initiate his mature life failed to accomplish.

In another point of view, too, this educational study should be profitable to us. However far back Goethe goes in recovering recollections, we never find him less than himself. He is always capable of an immense number of interests, of an immense number of studies carried on at the same time, but never interfering with one another; of æsthetic insight, of the power of generalising, of taking delight in poetic form; in fact, all that the man became the child *was*, not only potentially but actively. Here is where we err in our dealings with children. We regard them as persons of immature and feeble intellect, and deliberately deprive them of the scope and activities proper to an able and active mind. Every child has not in him the makings of a Goethe, but every child has the degree of power to deal with knowledge which will belong to himself as a man. His limitations are not those of incapacity, but of ignorance and of *physical* feebleness. Therefore our business is to feed him daily with the knowledge proper for him—in small portions, because he is a child, but of the finest intellectual quality, because he is a person—rather than to furnish him with the tools for dealing with knowledge, or even to make him an expert in the use of these tools : and of all the knowledge which a child should get, the knowledge of God is first in importance, and the knowledge of himself, next. It is not necessary to send forth any normal child as a moral or intellectual runagate.

III

PENDENNIS OF BONIFACE

"When, like a heavenly sign
Compact of many golden stars, the princely child did shine."—
(*Iliads*, Book Six (Chapman's Trs.).)

I

ARTHUR PENDENNIS is as real a person as Wilhelm
Meister, and, as a companion study, is not without
instruction for us. What an Admirable Crichton he
is, to be sure! He carried himself down Main Street
with a lordly grace, for was he not the Prince of
Fairoaks! The young lords themselves were content
to be his followers, and of so fine a nature was he
that he did not distinguish between gentle and simple.
How princely his tastes were in wines, repasts, trinkets,
and how many tastes he enjoyed! Horses, books,
pictures, nothing came amiss to him so long as it
was of the best. His copious shelves were filled with
rare editions and choice bindings, his walls hung with
rare prints (first proofs, of course). Nay, Alcibiades
himself could not have outdone him in the elegance
of his personal habits. The perfumed bath was a
necessity to him as to his witty prototype, especially
after any contact with the *canaille*, in the persons of
less distinguished men. Then, too, what a name he

had for intellectual prowess: " Pendennis could do anything *if*"—momentous syllable—" *if* he would only work." But, really, why work? He had tried the schools—— " During the first term of Mr Pen's academical life he attended classical and mathematical lectures with tolerable assiduity; but discovering before very long time that he had little taste or genius for the pursuing of the exact sciences, and being perhaps rather annoyed that one or two very vulgar young men, who did not even use straps to their trousers, so as to cover the abominably thick and coarse shoes and stockings which they wore, beat him completely in the lecture-room, he gave up his attendance at that course, and announced to his fond parent that he proposed to devote himself exclusively to the cultivation of Greek and Roman literature. . . . Presently he began, too, to find that he learned little good in the classical lecture. His fellow-students there were too dull, as in mathematics they were too learned for him. Mr Buck, the tutor, was no better a scholar than many a fifth-form boy at Grey Friars —might have some stupid humdrum notions about the metre and grammatical construction of a passage of Æschylus or Aristophanes, but had no more notion of poetry than Mrs Binge, his bedmaker; and Pen grew weary of hearing the dull students and tutor blunder through a few lines of a play, which he could read in a tenth part of the time they gave to it."

We know the rest. The time came when this golden youth got somewhat haggard, absent-minded, and cynical. By the way, is debt only one cause of cynicism, or is it our chiefest and bitterest grievance against the world that it does not understand our prerogatives, does not see that we have a right to the free enjoyment of our elegant tastes, no matter at whose cost? This is a blundering world. A day of ignominy is at hand for the Prince of Fairoaks. After a brilliant and admired career, regardless of the schools, he, Pendennis of Boniface, no less, is *plucked*, runs out of Oxbridge like a beaten cur, with a pack of creditors at his heels.

He picks himself up, we know, at last (at the cost of those pinched and impoverished ladies, his mother and Laura), because he has some good stuff in him. He finds his feet and a friend, and earns his bread; and is, at last saved, as by fire, by the two women who loved him. But he never loses the cynicism of the whipped cur; and a certain brand of the world, which he bore when he went to college, remains with him to the last. It is well for those who have the bringing up of golden lads and girls to bear in mind always that the leopard does not change his spots. Our facile faith in a regeneration to be brought about somehow, at school, at college, by a profession, by family ties, by public work, is really born of our laziness. That which will be done *somehow* for young people, we do not take the trouble to do ourselves; we shift our responsibility, and the young bear our sins and their own till the end of the chapter.

The literary parent of 'Pen' takes great pains to tell us how it all came about; and such things are, if we will receive it, written for our instruction; but it would be interesting to know how many parents and masters could stand a searching examination upon the lessons proposed to us by Thackeray alone upon the upbringing of youth.

In the first place, Arthur was the Prince of Fairoaks; and what, indeed, was Fairoaks? It was a petty estate, worth about five hundred a year; but any dunghill is high enough to crow from if we have a mind to; and the author's shrewd wit, and keen but not unkindly satire, make great play about this princely family, whose ancient glories, like their family portraits, were more or less faked up, but as firmly believed in as if Debrett were the authority.

The Pendennises are by no means solitary as the bringers-up of pseudo-princes. It begins often enough with the 'princely heart of innocence,' manifested by the little son in the way he carries his head, the fearless glance of his eye, and the frank simplicity with which he takes possession of the world which is indeed his. The parents look on and admire, and begin to suspect that this fine bearing of their child's is a family, and not a human, inheritance. A certain sense, not of greatness or scope, but of superiority, is a part of the child's nurture; and when he leaves home, either he behaves himself *en prince*, as did young Pendennis, at anybody's cost who will pay the piper; or he awakes to the humbug of the thing, and becomes unduly depressed and reckless; or, like the young Goethe, who never got over a certain sense of disqualification on account of his burgher birth, he attaches undue importance to class distinctions.

At the very outset of a child's career there is a rôle waiting for his parents. This is how a person arrives to us:—

"Those pure and virgin apprehensions I had in my infancy, and that divine light wherewith I was born, are the best unto this day wherein I can see the universe. .... Certainly Adam in Paradise had not more sweet and curious apprehensions of the world than I when I was a child.

" All appeared new and strange at first, inexpressibly rare and delightful and beautiful. I was a little stranger, which at my entrance into the world was saluted and surrounded with innumerable joys. My knowledge was divine; I knew by intuition those things which, since my apostasy, I collected again by the highest reason . . . All things were spotless and pure and glorious; yea, and infinitely mine, and joyful and precious . . . I was entertained, like an angel, with the works of God in their splendour and glory; I saw all in the peace of Eden. . . .

" The corn was orient and immortal wheat, which never should be reaped nor was ever sown. I thought it had stood from everlasting to everlasting. The dust and stones of the streets were as precious as gold: the gates " (of Hereford, where he was born) " were at first the end of the world. The green trees, when I saw them first through one of the gates, transported and ravished me; their sweetness and unusual beauty made my heart to leap, and almost mad with ecstasy, they were such strange and wonderful things. The Men! O what venerable and reverend creatures did the aged seem! Immortal Cherubims! And young men glittering and sparkling angels, and maids strange seraphic pieces of life and beauty! Boys and girls tumbling in the street were moving jewels: I knew not that they were born or should die. But all things abided eternally as they were in their proper places. Eternity was manifest in the Light of the Day, and something infinite behind everything appeared, which talked with my expectation and moved my desire. The City seemed to stand in Eden, or to be built in Heaven. The streets were mine, the temple was mine, the people were mine, their clothes and gold and silver were mine, as much as their sparkling eyes, fair skins, and ruddy faces. The skies were mine, and so were the sun and moon and stars, and all the world was mine; and I the only spectator and enjoyer of it."[1]

Or, to quote from the same writer's verse:—

"How like an angel I came down!
How bright are all things here!
When first among His works I did appear
O how His glory did me crown!
The world resembled His eternity,
In which my soul did walk;
And everything that I did see
Did with me talk.

. . . .

The streets were paved with golden stones,
The boys and girls were mine,
O how did all their faces shine!
The sons of men were holy ones,
In joy and beauty they appeared to me,
And everything which here I found,
While like an angel I did see,
Adorned the ground."[1]

Now, if such be the child's natural estate, what is our part? Parents are right enough in thinking that this fine sense of dignity, this luminous intelligence, grace their child, should help him through life, and are by all means to be preserved. But they make a fool of the child when the magnification of his family are the method they adopt. Whatever elements of dignity and greatness do exist in a family will have, we may be sure, enormous influence

[1] Thomas Traherne (1636–1674).

on its young scions; and the less said the better.
But young Pendennis was brought up in an atmosphere of spurious dignity, none the less false because
it was believed in by 'our family.' As a consequence, he was always superior to his situation,
and, indeed, that is a human propensity which needs
not be accentuated : at school, at college, in the
world, notwithstanding a kindly and generous nature,
he was never quite genial and simple, and when he
had outgrown 'airs,' he took on the superiority of
the cynic.

How fine a start, on the other hand, would the
child have whose parents recognised his distinction
as that of a human being ; for this, after all, is no
common state; it *is* distinction in each case. And
what a world of persons, sweet and serviceable, we
should have if each child were brought up to be all
that is in *him* !

II

Is it ill-natured to suggest, as second amongst the
causes which sent Pen astray, the influence of that
consummate personage, Major Pendennis? How
great he is in his own line, how absurd and how
respectable; how one likes him in spite of himself,
and how convincing is the neatness and finish of his
unworthy code! Is the title of the novel in truth
a conundrum, and which of the Pendennises is the
hero ? This is the reader's point of view ; but what
if we had been brought up to reverence this old
worldling, had been placed solemnly under his
guardianship? What if, on our first going forth
into life, such an one accompanied us as Mentor?

"God bless you, my dear boy," Pendennis said to
Arthur, as they were lighting their candles in Bury
Street before going to bed. . . . "I beseech you,
my dear Arthur, to remember through life that with
an *entrée*—with a good *entrée*, mind—it is just as easy
for you to have good society as bad, and that it
costs a man, when properly introduced, no more
trouble or *soins* to keep a good footing in the best
houses in London than to dine with a lawyer in
Bedford Square. Mind this when you are at
Oxbridge pursuing your studies, and for heaven's
sake be *very* particular in the acquaintances which
you make. The *premier pas* in life is the most important of all. Did you write to your mother to-day?
—No?—Well, do, before you go, and call and ask
Mr Foker for a frank—they like it. Good-night.
God bless you."

We find the old fellow's twaddle exquisitely absurd,
but all the same we lodge his maxims in our memory;
they may be of use some day. As for Pen, he was
with the man whom his family had delighted to
honour all his life, the man who had succeeded in
that emprise upon which all young people set out—
the conquest of the world; especially that enchanting
social world of which young persons dream.

We elders are hardly aware of the ingenuousness
of the young mind, of the ignorance and simplicity
of youth; and, at the same time, we fail to realise the
reverence in which young people hold us just for our
experience' sake. They say pert, clever, and flippant
things, and we take it for granted that they are up to
everything,—are, in fact, more men and women of the
world than we simple elders; so we produce our
little share of worldly wisdom,—they must not think

us quite simpletons,—and they are far more taken in than we suppose. They seize upon every scrap of talk which shows familiarity with the ways of the world—the rather wicked world, be it said—and from these construct a whole which is, in truth, widely different from our simple experience.

Dr Portman, the excellent rector of Clavering, will not be behindhand. He, too, has seen the world. Pen must order his wine, and that of the best, from a London vintner; and he does, and improves on his instructions. The Major praises a little dinner given in his honour, supposing the occasion to be a rare one. "Poor Pen! the worthy uncle little knew how often those dinners took place, while the reckless young Amphitryon delighted to show his hospitality and skill in *gourmandise*. There is no art than that (so long to learn, so difficult to acquire, so impossible and beyond the means of many unhappy people!) about which boys are more anxious to have an air of knowingness. A taste in and knowledge of wines and cookery appears to them to be the sign of an accomplished *roué* and manly gentleman."

What is to be done? The young folk *will* have a knowledge of what they call 'life.' If we offer them our scraps of, perhaps, secondhand experience, they generalise and conclude that we are not really the worthy and perhaps rather saintly persons they had taken us for. We, too, have had experiences, they think, of the sort they mean to try. Here we perceive the cause of the incomprehensible attractiveness of bad companions—they know life. Here are words of wisdom worth pondering :—" What young men like in their companions is what had got Pen a great part of his own repute and popularity—a real or supposed knowledge of life. A man who has seen the world, or can speak of it with a knowing air — a *roué*, Lovelace, who has his adventures to relate—is sure of an audience among boys. It is hard to confess, but so it is. We respect that sort of prowess. From our school-days we have been taught to admire it."

The young man who has a motive stronger than those which assail him because he is a youth among youths, if it be only that of winning academic distinction, gets through somehow. But a good many young fellows of parts, power, and generous temper, men like Pen himself, come to grief; and it is a serious question, what can be done to fortify these against the special temptations that belong to their time of life. Excellent help is to be found in novels. Here is the very knowledge of life the young person craves; the personages of the novel play their parts before him, and he is admitted to greater intimacy with them than we often arrive at with our fellows; there is no personal attack upon the reader, no preaching. If the novelist moralise a little here and there, it is but to relieve his own feelings. He is not preaching to the young reader, to whom the lessons of life come home with illustrations never to be forgotten. It is told that Mr Meredith was accused by a neighbour of caricaturing him in the character of ' Willoughby Patterne,' and that he replied—' Why, I am Willoughby Patterne, everybody is Willoughby Patterne! We are all Egoists.' In like manner, every young man who reads of Arthur Pendennis, or Edward Waverley, or Fred Vincey, or, alas, of Tito Melema, or of Darsie Latimer, George Warrington, or Martin Chuzzlewit—the list is endless, of course— finds himself in the hero. Novels are our lesson-books only so far as we give thoughtful, considerate reading to such novels as are also literature. The young person who reads three books a week from Mudie's, or elsewhere, is not likely to find in any of them 'example of life and instruction in manners.' These things arrive to us after many readings of a book that is worth while; and the absurdity of saying, 'I have read' Jane Austen or the Waverley novels should be realised. We do not say 'I have read' Shakespeare, or even Browning or Tennyson; but to 'have read' any of the great novels is also a mark of ignorance.

How many parents see to it that their sons and daughters read, mark, learn, and inwardly digest this one novel *Pendennis* before they go to college, or otherwise go out into life? It is stupid to disregard such a means of instruction; and yet, judicious parents either 'disapprove of novel reading for their young people,' or let them read freely the insipid trash of the circulating library until they are unable to discern the flavour of a good book. 'But,' says a good mother, 'I disapprove of novels for another reason besides that they are a waste of time. I have striven to bring up my family in innocence, and wish to keep them still from that very knowledge of life which novels offer.' There is a good deal to be said for this point of view; but the decisions of life are not simple, and to taboo knowledge is not to secure innocence.

We must remember that ignorance is not innocence, and also that ignorance is the parent of insatiable curiosity. But I do not offer a plea for indiscriminate novel reading. Novels are divisible into two classes—sensational, and, to coin a word, reflectional. Narra-

tions of hairbreadth escapes and bold adventures
need not be what I should call sensational novels ; but
those which appeal, with whatever apparent innocence,
to those physical sensations which are the begetters of
lust,—the 'his lips met hers,' 'the touch of her hand
thrilled him in every nerve' sort of thing which
abounds in goody-goody storybooks, set apart in
many families for Sunday reading, but the complete
absence of which distinguishes our best English novels.
To read that a girl has been betrayed by no means
affects an innocent mind ; but to allow oneself to thrill
with the emotions which led to the betrayal is to get
into the habit of emotional dram-drinking—a habit
as enervating and as vitiating as that of the gin-shop.
By the reflectional novel I mean, not that which
makes reflections for us, after the manner of a
popular lady-writer of the day.   He who would save
us the trouble of reflection ministers to the intellectual
slothfulness which lies at the bottom of the poverty
of our thoughts and the meanness of our lives.   The
reflectional novel is one which, like this of *Pendennis*,
awakens reflection with every page we read; offers
in every character and in every situation a criterion
by which to try our random thoughts or our careless
conduct.   If we bear in mind that the obvious
reflection proposed to us is as vicious in its way as
the sensation suggested, we shall find that this test—
the property of arousing reflection—eliminates all
flimsy work, and confines us to the books of our
great novelists.

We must record another step of this young 'rake's
progress' in Thackeray's own words.   To comment
is, here as elsewhere, as superfluous as it is impertinent.
"Mr Bloundell playfully took up a green wineglass

from the supper-table, which had been destined to
contain iced cup, but into which he inserted something still more pernicious—namely, a pair of dice,
which the gentleman took out of his waistcoat pocket
and put into the glass.   Then giving the glass a
graceful wave, which showed that his hand was quite
experienced in the throwing of dice, he called Seven's
the main, and whisking the ivory cubes gently on the
table, swept them up again lightly from the cloth,
and repeated this process two or three times . . . .
Presently, instead of going home, most of the party
were seated round the table playing at dice, the green
glass going round from hand to hand, until Pen finally
shivered it after throwing six mains.   From that
night Pen plunged into the delights of hazard as
eagerly as it was his custom to pursue any new
pleasure."

III

Pen was, like young Goethe, a mother's boy; the
son of a fonder, sweeter, less humorous mother; but
he, too, was the son of parents of unequal age, and
was his mother's companion.   We get charming
glimpses of this companionship.   There was that
evening when the two walked on the lawn of Fairoaks,
and watched the trees in the opposite park of Clavering put on a rich golden tinge, and the little river run
off brawling to the west, where was a sombre wood
and the towers of the old abbey church.   "Little
Arthur's figure and his mother's cast long blue
shadows over the grass; and he would repeat in a
low voice (for a scene of great natural beauty always
moved the boy, who inherited this sensibility from his

mother) certain lines beginning, 'These are Thy
glorious works, Parent of Good; Almighty, Thine
this universal frame,' greatly to Mrs Pendennis's
delight.   Such walks and conversation generally
ended in a profusion of filial and maternal embraces,
for to love and to pray were the main occupations of
this dear woman's life; and I have often heard
Pendennis say, in his wild way, that he felt that he
was sure of going to heaven, for his mother could
never be happy there without him."

What a pretty picture, and how every mother's
heart responds! Just so would she have it with her
little son. He should love her, and through her
should learn to love the best and the highest—Nature,
and the God of Nature. And the embraces, how
sweet to the mother's heart! We read later how,
during his childhood and youth, Arthur thought of
his mother as little less than an angel, as a super-
natural being, all wisdom, love, and beauty; and
indeed she was, not only a perfectly well-bred and
handsome woman, but, pure and heavenly-minded in
no common degree. If she had faults, they were the
rather insane family pride which produced the young
'prince' and her inordinate worship of that same prince.
It is a curious fact, which would seem at first sight to
challenge the justice with which the world is governed,
that the small failings of the good, those very failings
which appear to lean to virtue's side, and are scarce
discernible from virtues by the people who fall into
them—these faults of the good appear to produce a
more abundant crop of misfortunes than the glaring
vices of the unworthy: to whom much is given, of
him much will be required. The careless mother who
spends her days in pleasure-seeking will sometimes

have more duty-doing children than that mother whose only fault is that she loves her family, not wisely but too well. But nothing is in more urgent need of rectification than our moral code. Thackeray, tender as he is to Helen Pendennis, speaks of this same family pride and mother-rapture as "this unfortunate superstition and idol worship"; and frankly tells us that these were the causes of "a great deal of the misfortune which befel the young gentleman."

We have already considered the pride which made a prince of Arthur; and is not every mother's son a prince, and is it not the hardest thing in the world to see our son as others see him? It is less easy to understand that the maternal fondness, the unrestrained mutual embraces of mother and child, are also a danger, because they exceed that temperance, soberness, and chastity which is our duty. By and by this excess of tenderness becomes a counterfeit coin. The mother offers it to her child, and the child to his mother, in lieu of the only sterling currency amongst us—our duty. Do we not find Helen, later, hanging over her son as he lolls on the sofa reading a French novel, and handing him a cigar, which she lights, although she detests and condemns smoking? Nay, does he not tell her himself that he knows she would burn the house down to give him pleasure?

> "I could not love thee, dear, so well
>   Loved I not honour more,"

is true of mother-love as well as of other affections. This holy passion, too, is for service, and not for gratification; and the boy who knows that his mother will do anything for him, knows also that he stands in the place of duty, is more to his mother than her duty to him and to others; he grows up without learning the meaning of two chief words in our use—*must* and *ought* are to him terms capable of being explained away.

And this pious mother did her son a greater injury yet: she taught him religion, it is true, but the religion she taught was a sentiment, and not a duty. The boy loved the sound of the church-going bells, the echo of psalm and canticle, as he loved to watch the sunset from the lawn. Sacred poems and hymns, too, he loved to learn at his mother's knee. All holy associations were with him. But what Helen failed to teach him was his *duty* towards God; and is not this just where many a tender mother fails? She is so anxious to present the beauty of holiness, the love of the All-Father; she herself takes such joy in the sentiment of religion, that, that 'stern Daughter of the voice of God,' whose mandate is the only one that human beings obey in the face of resistance, is not allowed a hearing. Religion, service to God, is made to the child a matter of his own election and delight, and not a duty which he has no choice but to fulfil. He is taught that he *may* love and serve God, but not that he *must* do so; that this is the one duty he is in the world to fulfil. Parents have a unique opportunity to present the thought of duty to their children; and if they let this occasion pass, it is in vain to try to make up by religious feeling, sentiment, emotion. All these are passing phases, and do not belong to that tie which binds us to our God. Pen, we know, failed to say his prayers on that first evening in London when he was going up to Oxbridge with his uncle; and later, Laura tells him that she dare not inquire what he has kept of his faith.

IV

Like Goethe, again, Pen was a person of casual
education. It is quite open to contention that persons
thus educated do a good deal of the work of the
world ; that, indeed, men and women of great parts
and original mind are often persons who have managed
to evade the regular routine of the schools. Like
Pen, they have got out of working through that
Greek play, line by line and word by word, on which
'the Doctor' set such store, and have, like him, read
ten times as much in the time. Allowing the genius
to be a law unto himself, we must be on the watch
lest the ordinarily clever boy slip the yoke; indeed,
as we have seen in Goethe's case, the genius might
well have been the better for the common grind.
Pen, anyway, would probably not have run that
disastrous course at Oxbridge had he acquired the
habit of working under rule and towards an end.

It is well to consider this matter at a time when
we are casting about rather wildly to find out what
education is, and what it is to effect. There is certain
knowledge, no doubt, which it is shameful not to
possess, and, wanting which, the mind is as limp, feeble,
and incapable as an ill-nourished body. There is also
a time for sowing the seed of this knowledge, an intellectual as well as a natural springtime ; and it
would be interesting to examine the question, how far
it is possible to prosecute *any* branch of knowledge,
the sowing and germination of which has not taken
place in early youth. It follows that the first three
lustres belong to what we may call the *synthetic* stage
of education, during which his reading should be
wide and varied enough to allow the young scholar

to get into living touch with earth-knowledge, history, literature, and much besides. These things are necessary for his intellectual life, and are especially necessary to give him material for the second stage of his education, the *analytic*, which, indeed, continues with us to the end. It is in this second stage -that the value of the classical and mathematical grind comes in. It produces a certain sanity of judgment, and therefore a certain capacity for affairs, an ability for the examination of questions, which are rather the distinguishing marks of the public schoolman,—not merely the university man, that is another matter, but the man who has ground through that Greek play which both Pen and the young Goethe contrived to get out of. Whatever be the faults of the public school, it is not a manufactory of 'cranks'; and the danger of a transition period like the present is that it may produce a crop of these persons of unbalanced judgment and undisciplined will.

> "'O friend,' said he, 'hold up your mind; strength is but strength of will;
> Reverence each other's good in fight, and shame at things done ill.'"

This exordium of "Atrides" might well be the motto of our public schools; it sums up with curious exactness that which they accomplish,—the steady purpose, public spirit, and fine sense of honour which adorn our public services, recruited for the most part from our public schools.

But these fine qualities, of which we are proud, may co-exist with ignorance; and ignorance is the mother of prejudice and the obstinate foe of progress. The task before us in setting in order the house of our national education is a delicate one. We must guard those assets of character which the education of the past affords us, and recover, if we may, the passionate love of knowledge for its own sake which brought about an earlier Renaissance. To regard education as disciplinary only is as though a man sowed ploughs and harrows instead of seed-corn; but an eager, wilful, desultory pursuit of knowledge brings with it serious risks to character. There is much talk of reading in these days, of the use of public libraries to further education, and young students are taking up this cry of 'general reading.' We hear of 'three books a week' as a usual thing, and rather a matter of pride. But this, again, comes of our tendency to depreciate knowledge, and to lose sight of its aliment-ary character. If we perceive that knowledge, like bread, is necessary food, we see also that it must be taken in set portions, fitly combined, duly served, and at due intervals, in order to induce the digestive processes without which, knowledge, like meat, gives us labour rather than strength. In other words, desultory reading affords entertainment, and perhaps an occasional stimulus to thought. Casual reading —that is, vague reading round a subject without the effort *to know*—is not in much better case: if we are to read and grow thereby, we must read *to know*, that is, our reading must be study—orderly, definite, pur-poseful. In this way, what I have called the two stages of education, synthetic and analytic, coalesce; the wide reading tends to discipline, and in the disciplinary or analytic stage the mind of the student is well nourished by the continued habit of wide reading.

Arthur Pendennis made a failure of his college career, and only a qualified success of his after life,

through one other cause which affects most young
students. He went to college absolutely without
moral instruction other than that of certain virtuous
traditions and tendencies imbibed from his parents,
together with tendencies quite other than virtuous.
But no map of life had been presented to his view
showing the heights whose ascent should reward the
wayfarer with a noble outlook, the pitfalls and
morasses in which many a gallant young traveller disappears. This, too, belongs to the disrespect in which
we, as a nation, hold knowledge. To know is not
synonymous with to do; but we should not leave our
young people to stumble on right action without any
guiding philosophy of life; the risks are too great.
We who bear the name of Christ do not always give
ourselves the trouble to realise how His daily labour
was to make the Jews *know*; how '*ye will not understand*' was the reproach He cast upon them. Even
with the example of our Master before us, we take
small pains to make our young people realise the
possibilities of noble action that lie in them and in
everyone. We give them certain warnings, it is true,
for fear of ruin and loss of reputation, but do we warn
them against that deadly dull failure which is implied
in a career of commonplace success? Pen was
'plucked'; but how many a man who takes his
degree, let us say, does so through the continual
prodding of a petty ambition, without drawing from
his labour knowledge or love or strength of will towards
duty! If the worlds you conquer be those of academic
distinction, why, there is no spirit in you for further
labours, unless as more such worlds present themselves.

In some ways the Greeks had a more adequate
view of education than ourselves: they seem to have

held that, along with gymnastic and music, philosophy is the chief concern of every youth. "A freeborn boy," says Plutarch, "must neglect no part of the cycle of knowledge, but he must run through one (subject) after another, so that he may get a taste of each of them—for to be perfect in all is impossible—but philosophy he must pursue in earnest. I can make this clear by a figure: it is delightful and entertaining to travel through many cities, but only profitable to linger in the best.

"The philosopher Bion has well said: 'As the suitors of Penelope, when they could not obtain her, made free use of all that belonged to her, so also they who find philosophy too hard occupy themselves with other branches of knowledge, worth nothing by comparison. For this reason, philosophy must be put first in all education.

"For the nurture and development of the body men have invented two instruments, the study of medicine and gymnastic, of which one makes for the health of the body, the other for its strength. But for the sicknesses and sorrows of the soul, philosophy is the only cure.

"Through philosophy, man arrives at the knowledge of what is good and what is bad, what is just and what is unjust; most especially he learns what he should endeavour after, and what he should avoid; how he should order himself towards God, towards father and mother, towards his elders, towards the laws, towards strangers and superiors, towards his friends, towards wife and child and slave. She teaches humility towards God, reverence for parents, respect for the aged, obedience to law; to be in submission to authority, to love friends, to be chaste towards women. She teaches tenderness towards children and gentleness towards slaves; she exhibits to us the highest good, that in happiness our joy be measured, and in misfortune our grief restrained; in order that we be not as the beasts, unrestrained in desire as in rage. These are, I hold, some of the benefits we owe to the teaching of philosophy. For to be modest in good fortune, to be without envy, gentle in mind, to know how to extinguish evil desires, is wisdom; and the ruling of an angry spirit is the sign of no common understanding."[1]

The functions which Plutarch claims for philosophy we ascribe to religion, and by so doing we place life on a higher level. There is this fundamental difference between the two: while philosophy instructs, religion both instructs and enables. But it is a question whether that science of life or art of living which philosophy should teach had not better be made a distinct study, with its own methods, classifications, rules of progress, under the sanction of religion, and tried at every step by a religious standard.

As it is, the moral and philosophical training we give is random and scrappy to a pitiable degree. The very sincerity of our dependence upon God has resulted in a criminal ignorance about ourselves, our possibilities and our risks, and this in despite, as I have said, of the teaching of our Master. No one person should be launched upon life without an ordered knowledge of himself; he should know, for example, that he has certain appetites, servants, whose business is the upkeep of the body, and, when the time comes, the propagation of the race; that the

[1] *Opera Moralia* (trs. from Plutarch's *Ausgewählte moralische Abhandlungen*, translated by Dr Otto Güthling).

manly part is never, in small things or great, to yield
ourselves to the rule of any one of these appetites,
which are so constituted that, treated as servants, they
serve with diligence and obedience, but allowed to
encroach, rule with relentless tyranny.   To know such
matters in detail may not save a youth, but should
certainly give him pause—give him that moment in
which to listen to the divine Counsellor who is able
to save him.

Then, how many youths go into the arena of life
armed with the knowledge that they are equipped
with desires whose chief function seems to be to provide for the nurture of the mind and the propagation
of ideas, in much the same way as the bodily appetites
have their particular uses?   How many know that to
become the slave of a single desire, as ambition or
emulation, for example, results in as truly, though not
as obviously, ill-balanced and ill-governed a person as
does the inordinate gratification of any one appetite?
How many know that health is a duty, and not merely
an advantage; that a serviceable body, strong and
capable, is a debt we owe to ourselves, our kin, and
our kind?   A few are aware of the advantage of, at
any rate, a fit body ; but how many know that to
possess an alert, intelligent, and reflective mind is also
among our duties?   How many are aware of the incalculable joys of knowledge, of imagination, of
reasoned thought, and that these are a patrimony in
readiness for each of us?   Do young people, again,
realise that they enter on life with two great affections
capable of ordering all the bonds which unite them to
their fellow-men in just degree—capital, as it were, for
an outlay of continual serviceableness ?   Do they know
how conscience may be played with, how reason may

be suborned, how the right function of the will may give place to unreasoning wilfulness? Have they adequate thoughts of the Supreme relation? Are they aware of owing aught to man or to God? Does not our teaching of religion fall short just because we have allowed ourselves to become ignorant of ourselves? And are we not therefore in danger of losing that conception of God which should keep us in due equipoise? Are we not so much in the habit of hearing of the love and care and saving power of our God that we accept ourselves as the objects of His infinite tenderness, and gradually lose the point of view which makes men heroes and saints in the service of a Master? In a word, do we not implicitly teach our youth that *meat is more than life*, that getting on is the chief thing, that having is more that being or doing? No doubt there are noble youths who somehow seem to get themselves into right relations, as there are noble men and women to live with whom is continual inspiration; but, perhaps, these would be usual, and not exceptional, if we could arrive at a profounder and truer outlook upon life. Everything that need be taught to a youth is no doubt explicit or implicit in the Christian religion, but I cannot help thinking that we should make more progress in the way of that perfection which is commanded us if we set ourselves to the study of life with the method and purpose we give to other studies—pursuing this, however, with the sense of quite peculiar divine support and direction.

IV

"YOUNG CROSSJAY"

A GOLD thread running through a sombre stuff, a streak of sunlight in a lurid sky,—something like these is the fitful appearance of young Crossjay in that rather dreary study wherein a 'Patterne' English gentleman is exhibited, resting, fold upon fold, upon himself, every serpentine movement, stealthy, sudden, even vindictive, betraying the wiles and ways of the *Egoist*. But it is not as a mere foil to Sir Willoughby that Crossjay is introduced. He, with his frank outgoing boy nature, does, indeed, show up by sharp contrast the unhappy, self-involved, self-concerned, and self-adoring man. But Mr Meredith is a profound student of that one of the 'mysteries' which we call education. He has made a study of boys and of the way to handle them ; and has set forth in big letters so that they who run may read, in more than one book, how *not* to handle them.

But we take no heed; we discuss the plot of this novel or that, allow the author to be a master of style, quote him against persons who say we have no great novelists now, have remarks to make about the characters. What we do not perceive is, that philosophy as found written in books of philosophy to-day, has become more or less academic; she no longer "cries at the gates, at the entry of the city, at the coming in at the doors, Unto you, O men, I call; and my voice is to the sons of men."

She has become an affair of the Schools. Men meet with her there, not to their souls' profit so much as for the joy of intellectual gymnastic.

But philosophy keeps to herself still two or three resorts from which we may hear her voice, ' Unto you, O men, I call.' The poets entertain her; through them she still calls to men ; but her message is often implicit, and only the attentive ear may hear. Those who do hearken at the coming in of this door get oracles of price, luminous words for the interpretation of their days.

In the novel, however, she is explicit, takes up every one of the functions which we have seen Plutarch assign her; unfolds ourselves to us as poor things, most likely, and flashes a search-light upon our innocent little ways, our much-to-be-condoned moods. Also, as philosophy is for our instruction in life, and as our chief business is the bringing up of the generation to follow, the great novelists offer us a key to the vexed problem of education.

Young Crossjay is an example of this. We are told that a 'real and sunny pleasure befell Lætitia' when young Crossjay Patterne came to live with her. The phrase is delightfully just, as of course, seeing whose phrase it is. A real and sunny pleasure gleams out of every page on which Crossjay appears. The reader smiles at the mention of him as we do when a charming child crosses our path. This is how it came about. Sir Willoughby was, as we know, a mighty orb, environed by satellites, and with the gift of drawing into his sphere and causing to revolve round him whatsoever body chances to pass his way. Such a body is his cousin Lieutenant Patterne of the Marines : that he should not be of the regular Services was a mere eccentricity of English blood and ways, quite a pleasant thing to talk about, when he had distinguished the name of Patterne by an heroic action. So he is duly invited to Patterne Hall, and on a day when Sir Willoughby was spreading his glorious tail of many eyes upon the lawn before an admiring audience, and more, before the lady of his choice, he spies in the distance a rather common-looking thickset man carrying a valise, whom he discovers, by quick intuition of the folded creature, to be that cousin of his in the Marines. 'Not at home' is the answer when the footman produced the Lieutenant's card. And upon this answer turns the fiery trial between young Crossjay's lower and his higher nature, upon which much of the story hangs.

'Charming' is not at all the epithet most people would apply to Crossjay. " He was a boy of twelve, with the sprights of twelve boys in him "; and again "a rosy-cheeked, round-bodied rogue of a boy, who fell upon meats and puddings and defeated them with the captivating simplicity of his confession that he had never had enough to eat in his life." And he told of his four sisters and three brothers, 'all hungry!' How he came to live with Lætitia must be recalled to the reader. This lady was one of several persons who had been drained of their vitality by the absorbing egoist, who drew his sustenance from the vital forces of those about him. Vernon Whitford, as the reader will remember, was a cousin of Sir Willoughby's, who declined to be absorbed, and who received a small salary from him for his help in managing the estates; and it seems that this man, as outgoing a person as Crossjay himself, had heard of Captain Patterne's large family, knew, no doubt, of that 'not at home,' and felt it a shame which he must obliterate. So he went off to Devonport and brought back Crossjay, because, we are told, "Vernon was one of your men that had no occupation for their money, no bills to pay for repair of their property, and an insane desire to spend!" He had thought to have the boy at the Hall that he might prepare him for the Navy, but he counted without his host. Sir Willoughby would run no such risk. The boy's hair would be red, he said, his skin eruptive. So Vernon arranged for him to live at the Dales' cottage, and that was how this 'sunny pleasure' came to Lætitia. "The pranks of the little fellow and his revel in a country life, and muddy wildness in it, amused Lætitia from morning to night." She taught him in the morning when she could catch him, and Vernon in the afternoon if he could catch him, but there was the *if.* The boy was not only idle, but he hated knowledge as it was to be got out of books; and 'but I don't want to' was his answer to all persuasions. He had to be dug out of the earth, with a good deal of it upon him, when his lesson-hours arrived.

This steady hatred of books would seem rather a bad symptom in young Crossjay, only we get a key to it later on. When Clara Middleton, that 'dainty rogue in porcelain,' arrives on the scene, she and the boy become great friends, and she takes his idleness seriously to heart. Like a wise pedagogue, she set herself to find out what he did like. Having raced him and beaten him without panting, to his vast

surprise, she was in a position to bring him to his
bearings. He is asked to own that girls are better
than boys, that they can run faster, that they learn
their lessons, and so on. 'But,' says he, 'you can't
make soldiers or sailors of them, though.' But she
quotes Mary Ambree to him, and Mistress Hannah
Snell of Pondicherry, and other little-known heroines,
to say nothing of Joan of Arc and Boadicea ; and it
all ends up in a serious talk. "'Somebody spoils you :
Miss Dale or Mr Whitford?' 'Do they?' was the
answer. 'Sir Willoughby does?' 'I don't know about
spoil ; I can come round him.'" Here we have the
secret many a child discovers about Father or Mother,
master or governess ; and we ask ourselves—'How is
it the young urchins can come round us?'

We pat ourselves on the back and say—'Oh, I'm
a good-natured fellow, I know; I can't be hard on the
young monkeys.' Now, it seems to me, Crossjay has
been evoked just that we may not deceive ourselves
in this matter. It is not because of some amiable
trait in us that children can come round us, but
because we are tarred with the same brush as that
most fatiguing and intolerable person in all fiction—
Sir Willoughby Patterne. It would be a wholesome
and rather solemn exercise for those of us who have
to deal with young folk to get by heart all the
'Willoughby and Crossjay' scenes in the novel.
Who knows but the best of us might cry 'Lord, is it
I?' before he is half-way through. By such light
touches as this talk with Clara are the grave problems
of education brought up for solution and—this is the
point—*offered with a key*.

A few pages back we have been told that Crossjay
was steadily "opposed to the acquisition of knowledge

by means of books." But a few questions about Nelson, and he produces knowledge got out of books promptly, ready as the guns of a good ship. He has not been told or taught the knowledge of naval history he shows; 'he'(that is, Vernon)'bought me the books' is all the account he gives of it. There are, then, two sorts of knowledge to be had out of books, that which he is 'opposed to' and that which he takes to; and here, in what seems no more than a pretty, gracefully told incident, we have the rock indicated upon which our good ship, National Education, comes to grief. We offer children in books the knowledge they are 'opposed to,' and not that which they take to.

'It does not do to make education too interesting,' we say; 'they must learn to grind, to work against the grain'; but we forget about that horse who won't be made to drink; and the boy *never* takes into him that knowledge which, according to Crossjay, 'I don't want to.' He certainly does get it into that Lethe of the mind we call the verbal memory, out of which it can shortly be reproduced on call without having undergone any 'mind-change,' untouched by ideas, unwarmed by imagination, mere dead matter, an excretion of the mind. This is what we gain for our pains in getting into a boy that knowledge which he 'does not want to' learn. No wonder he throws it all up as soon as he can, and has a sick distaste for more of the kind.

But is there any knowledge he *does* want to know? Plainly, Crossjay anyway found such knowledge in books, and had it pat, telling, and to the point as gunnery practice. He was being coached for the Navy entrance examination, so probably the two sorts of books dealt with the same subjects. It is not the subjects a boy hates. He wants to know about other lands and other times, about great persons, and, in fact, about everything we want to teach him. He would rather get his knowledge out of books than have it poured into him by speech; the book is more terse, graphic, satisfying to the mind than the talk of any but very rare people. The boy has really an immense appetite for knowledge, and when he does not want to learn, it is because he does not get the right books.

We give children a diet of facts, either condensed or diluted, unaware that the mind has really no use for facts uninformed by intelligence. It takes ideas to evoke ideas, intelligence to awaken intelligence, and the heavy compendiums of the schoolroom are of no use in education. An encyclopædia is another matter, because it is when our intelligence has been awakened, our curiosity excited, that we consult it, and no school (or family) should be without a good encyclopædia, which every scholar is free to use. If we could awake to the right use of the right books in education, we should find that, as Goethe said, 'a day is infinitely long,' and we should cease to hear of an overcrowded curriculum. By the way, Nemesis is upon us: we have brought up children so long on a diet of facts that we have come to believe what we teach. We travel with Baedeker instead of the old, red, Murray's handbooks, and are becoming informed and bored rather than intelligent and alert travellers. Our notion of history is—ordered facts; though the narrations of three persons who have seen the same thing happen round the corner might show us that there is nothing so little to be depended upon as circumstantial evidence, whether historical or other. Books are a weariness to us, and no wonder, seeing the manner of books we elect.

But there's a good time coming. Crossjay would have been a good candidate as the entrance examination for the Navy is conducted to-day. He liked and knew how to get knowledge of a sort of which the world is learning the value. He knew the habits of birds, where to look for their eggs; all about fish, and how to catch them; how to manage rabbits. He had soon tramped the country about for an extraordinary number of miles. Someone had shown him a collection of stuffed birds of every English kind, and after once seeing, he could describe "goat-sucker owls, more mouth than head, with dusky dark-spotted wings like moths, all very circumstantial." We are awaking to the use of nature-knowledge, but how we spoil things by teaching them! We are not content that children should know the things of nature as we know our friends, by their looks and ways, an unconscious comprehensive knowledge which sinks in by dint of much looking, but we set them to fragmentary scraps of scientific research. They intend investigation, and lose the joy of seeing. Their attention is concentrated upon this or that, and they lose the all-round alertness which is the chief equipment of the nature-student. We shall awake some day and find that nature-study, as we have taught it, adds not at all to the joy of life. The child of the future will feel no thrill at the disclosure of the red under the tail of a little brown bird; now, every small boy likes to know such things, and it will be a weary day when we have ' nature-studied ' such knowledge out of existence.

Crossjay has his loyalties, as what boy has not? He has a passion for our Naval Service, and can be

even got through the lesson-grind for the sake of it.
Then, 'my father's the one to lead an army'; and
here comes in a problem which he pondered, boy-
fashion, bringing it out again and again, to the dismay
of his friends, always in the same words, always leading up to the same climax ('ten miles in the rain'),
never apparently coming to a conclusion, but turning
the thing over in his mind, it seems, until some day
the conclusion should arrive.   That, too, is the way
of young people: they observe, they retain, they hold
moral questions in solution, so to say, until some
crisis or some slight event precipitates a conclusion,
which remains from henceforth part of their moral
outfit, for better, for worse.   Here is Crossjay's
moral problem :—" My father's the one to lead an
army ! . . . .   I say, Mr Whitford, Sir Willoughby's
kind to me, and gives me crown-pieces ; why wouldn't
he see my father, and my father came here ten miles
in the rain to see him, and had to walk ten miles
back and sleep at an inn ? "

But we may postpone the consideration of Sir
Willoughby; for the present, it is enough to see why
he was not among Crossjay's loyalties.   Vernon Whitford, however, was, notwithstanding all his cousin's
gay attempts to present him as a dour taskmaster.

Crossjay tells Clara Middleton that he would go to
the bottom of the river for him.   The boy is shrewd,
too ; all boys are ; he believes that Whitford is paying
for him by way of making up for that grievous sending of his father back in the rain.   How that offence
rankled, and how justly angry the boy was !   Then,
as for Clara, why, he was her knight, chivalric in his
obedience (to the loss of his dinner !), giving her
unbounded love, admiration, and reverence, along

with a gay comradeship which she encouraged. They both loved wild-flowers, and games and open dealings, birds and all living things. Here was foundation enough for friendship!

We get, in connection with this friendship, a peep into boy nature that it behoves us to regard. Clara was reclining on the grass, with half-closed eyes, as she talked to him. We are told that had she been sitting up he would have sprung at her and kissed her.

Here we get a nice boy's unconscious reverence for the holy mystery of sex; and few things are more offensive and more likely to be disastrous than the way we set ourselves to dissipate this heaven-implanted reverence in our rash attempts to give knowledge of matters which are not for the mind. Chivalry, honour, delicacy and obedience, impassioned obedience, to the divine law, these are the chords to play upon if we are to have pure youths and maidens. But we must believe that chivalry and chastity are there, and are not foreign ideas to be introduced by our talk; and this is where many a parent fails. He is aware of evil in his child, and makes deadly allowance for it; and his suspicions create the very evils he dreads. We know how Helen Pendennis believed the worst of her son when the worst was not there, in order, one would think, that she might make occasion for self-sacrifice. It is well we should understand that suspicion also is sin, and begets mistrust and offence.

I think we should have the Utopia our hearts desire if we realised what springs of good are in our children waiting the right touch. Crossjay, who is no more than an ordinary, nice boy, has, we observe, everything he wants for noble living excepting

knowledge, and certain habits of mind and body.
How like a man of honour he behaves after the talk
he overhears when he awakes under the sofa-rug:
with a burning sense of the wrong done to his lady,
he has the shrewdness and delicacy of a gentleman.
He knew that this offer made to another lady was a
matter not to be talked about, a matter requiring
action, too, beyond his own powers. Here we get
a hint as to why it is so good for boys to go to school.
They get freer play for common-sense, shrewdness,
discrimination, gentlemanly feeling, in the school
democracy than they can find under the home
autocracy, be it ever so benign.

Thus we get Crossjay presented to us with consummate art, a 'human boy,' to quote the immortal
Mr Chadband. We find the 'human boy' delightful,
and perceive all that he is as a person; and we see
also the safeguards he needs that he may have room
for due development.

We have hardly made Crossjay's acquaintance
before he comes to a parting of the ways—a moral
crisis, which we watch with some anxiety. Because
we are studying a lesson set by a master, the temptation is one we are not at all prepared for, and yet it
is a very common one, and perhaps more 'golden lads
and girls' are spoiled through this than through any
other cause. Here we have it in a nutshell. Willoughby, we know, declined to receive the boy into
his house, but, all the same, took upon him the airs of
a patron—naturally, inevitably. It is good to see him
with young Crossjay. A casual observer would think
him perfect with the boy—'amused, indulgent, almost
frolicsome.' He has ever a joke and a jibe for him,
catches him by the elbows and gives him a leap in

the air, laughs at his idleness and mischief, is altogether in fine contrast with Mr Whitford's 'tutorly sharpness.' "He had the English father's tone of a liberal allowance for boys' tastes and pranks, and he ministered to the partiality of the genus for pocket-money." And, again, he was in contrast to Vernon Whitford: "he did not play the schoolmaster like bookworms who get poor little lads in their grasp." Willoughby poses, and his pose is admirable, one which all who have the bringing up of youth are tempted to affect; and still more those, be they fathers or schoolmasters, who wash their hands of responsibility and play to a gallery in the good-natured ways they adopt towards the young folk. It is surprising that Crossjay was not taken in; he liked it all, 'tis human nature so to do; he would run to his patron, take jumps, jokes, and tips with genuine delight,—"half-a-crown generally, but he had had a sovereign,"—and yet—was it always that question of his father being sent back to walk ten miles in the rain, or was it that he was constantly reminded of this treatment of his father by other slight circumstances which he hardly knew he observed? The latter seems to be the way in which we remember or forget the failings of those about us; faults are forgiven and forgotten until we are reminded of them by some new evidence of the same defect. But Willoughby would have been too much for the boy if his friends had not come to his aid. Crossjay wanted to be a gentleman; to shirk work, to play, ride, and generally to take life easily. He could not do these things and go into the Navy; and Willoughby, simply for the glorification of having one more hanger-on, deliberately chose that the boy should not work, but

should depend upon him for all his chance prefer-
ments and pleasures. The title of the novel tells us
why: was he not *The Egoist*, and therefore were not
all his actions and intentions designed for his own
magnification? Crossjay, we know, went to the
crammer at last and was saved; but only at the cost
of a veritable earthquake at Patterne Hall, a *boule-
versement* of all the views of all the persons who
revolved about the Patterne gentleman. But the
lesson remains for us.

There are many ways of playing the egoist with
the young people about us, but this of 'the English
father's tone of a liberal allowance for boys' tastes
and pranks' is distinctly the most fatal. For the
sake of popularity we make our appeal to a boy's
lower nature; and because he has that lower nature
also our appeal is very seldom in vain. If we trust
him as a creature who is to be won by tips and toffee,
we find him as we treat him, and in the end it will
be our turn as well as his to reap as we sowed.
Egotism is a subtle snare, hard to be aware of; but
the single eye will save us. If we regard children for
themselves and as themselves, without any reflex
thought as to what we do for them, what they think
of us, what other people think of what we are to the
children, and so on through the endless chain of
self-involved motives; if we look out upon the
children, and not in upon ourselves, we shall see them
as they are—with the great possibilities proper to
them as persons, and with the fearful hazards which
it is our part to steer them through.

But we all have need of instruction in the fine art
of bringing up children, and are therefore grateful to
the philosopher to whom we owe 'young Crossjay.'

V

BETTER-THAN-MY-NEIGHBOUR

Two persons meet in the porch of the King Archon; the one brings a suit, and the other appears to answer to a very serious charge. We know the impeached man and the charge brought against him. Socrates was charged by Meletus, a young man who was little known, with corrupting the youth of the city, and with inventing new gods and denying the existence of old ones. He says that Meletus shows a good deal of character in the charge he makes; and, " I fancy that he must be a wise man; and seeing that I am the reverse of a wise man, he has found me out. . . . Of all our political men, he is the only one who seems to me to begin in the right way with the cultivation of virtue in youth."

But Euthyphro, the other speaker, who has come to bring a suit, declines this explanation, and thinks that Socrates is to be brought before the court as a Neologian, such as he is himself. Socrates considers that danger lies, not in being thought wise, but in the attempt to impart wisdom to others,—" I have a benevolent habit of pouring out myself to everybody, and would even pay for a listener, and I am afraid

that the Athenians may think me too talkative."
Then the dialogue goes on :—

"*Soc.* And what is your suit, Euthyphro? are you the pursuer
or the defendant?

Euth. I am the pursuer.

Soc. Of whom?

Euth. You will think me mad when I tell you.

Soc. Why, has the fugitive wings?

Euth. Nay, he is not very volatile at his time of life.

Soc. Who is he?

Euth. My father.

Soc. Your father! my good man?

Euth. Yes.

Soc. And of what is he accused?

Euth. Of murder, Socrates.

Soc. By the powers, Euthyphro! how little does the common
herd know of the nature of right and truth. A man must be
an extraordinary man, and have made great strides in wisdom,
before he could have seen his way to bring such an action.

Euth. Indeed, Socrates, he must.

Soc. I suppose that the man whom your father murdered was
one of your relatives—clearly he was; for if he had been a
stranger you would never have thought of prosecuting him.

Euth. I am amused, Socrates, at your making a distinction
between one who is a relation and one who is not a relation; for
surely the pollution is the same in either case if you knowingly
associate with the murderer, when you ought to clear yourself
and him by proceeding against him."[1]

Then the case is stated more fully. The dead man
" worked for us as a field labourer on our farm in
Naxos," and in a fit of drunken passion slew a fellow-
servant. " My father bound him hand and foot and
threw him into a ditch" to await inquiry into the
case. Meanwhile the man, being neglected, died.
" And my father and family are angry with me for
taking the part of the murderer and prosecuting my

[1] *Cf.* Jowett's translation.

father.   They say that he did not kill him; and that
if he did, the dead man was but a murderer, and I
ought not to take any notice, for that a son is impious
who prosecutes his father.   Which shows, Socrates,
how little they know what the gods think about piety
and impiety."

"*Soc.* And what is piety, and what is impiety?

Euth. Piety is doing as I am doing; that is to say, prosecuting anyone who is guilty of murder, sacrilege, or of any similar
crime—whether he be your father or mother, or whoever he
may be—that makes no difference; and not to prosecute them
is impiety."

Euthyphro is with us to-day, a familiar figure,
mentioned in every newspaper, talked over at every
table, having disciples in pretty nearly every house.
We may know him as Pro-Pigtails (*Punch*), or Pro-
pease; he may go without a hat or disport himself in
sandals,—things innocent enough,—but he has this in
common with his prototype: he may not indict his
father, but every Euthyphrodite is ready with—
'What is piety? you ask.   To do as I do,' whether he
malign his country or feed upon nuts.   By the way, he
generally does both.

We complain that the Euthyphrodite is narrow,
one-sided, illiberal, unnatural, undutiful: he is unreasonable, we say, silly, a fool.   But he does not
regard us.   Piety, he says, is doing as I am doing,
and it is piety because it is pleasing to the gods.   If
you be another Socrates you propose yourself to him
as a disciple, with wily tact, that he may give you
an opportunity to confute the fallacies he unfolds.
But it is of no use.   'Another time, Socrates; for I
am in a hurry, and must go now.'

We call him a *crank*, and he gets many disciples

because anybody who is cocksure brings relief to the hesitancy of the general mind. For himself, he is not to be convinced. However outrageous his conduct, whether he light the fires of persecution, make himself an exception to common law, say 'Corban' of the dues he owes to country or kin, or limit himself to such small pieties as 'I *always* wear' this or that; 'buy my tea' at so-and-so's, or 'spend the summer' here or there (the piety lying in the *always*), he has an infallible creed.

We, like Socrates, if we may presume to say so, are tolerant of the 'crank': 'he is not a bad fellow,' we say, 'but he has a bee in his bonnet'; and when we do not take up his religion, he ministers to our vanity, for it is not unpleasant to feel superior to his oddities.

Where is the harm in him? we ask; if he prosecute his own father, he does it with really pious intention. Well, it is a pity that a narrow-minded, illiberal, unjust person should exist; and it is a very great pity that he should be free to propagate those pious doctrines of his,—for this reason, that every foolish little piety we accept as the whole duty of man makes us the less capable of just, liberal, and reverent thought; and we cannot be more in any situation than our own conception of what that situation requires. However likeable he may be, the crank is not a harmless person. He is bad for himself and bad for other people.

But Euthyphro is not open to conviction. The whole field of his mind is occupied by his own fallacious reasoning: there is no getting at him later, so we must catch him before he becomes a tiresome person, and, in order to do so, must find out what there is in him (and in us) that goes to the making of a crank.

An incident is told in *Lavengro* full of instruction on this point. We remember how Preacher Williams, who went about, with his wife Winifred, doing good, was subject to fits of spiritual despair, which came upon him especially of a Saturday because he was going to preach the next day. *'Pechod Yspryyd Glan'* (which is the Welsh for 'the sin against the Holy Ghost'), he would be heard to cry in a paroxysm of grief and terror; and 'Lavengro,' who overheard this, asked him to tell the story of his life. It appeared that when he was a child of seven he had wilfully and intentionally said certain awful words (we are not told what they were), and this was the unpardonable sin. His sweet wife was right when she told him that pride was, in truth, his sin; but 'Lavengro' made the matter plain to him. "'You said that after you had committed this same sin of yours you were in the habit, at school, of looking upon your schoolfellows with a kind of gloomy superiority, considering yourself a lone, monstrous being, who had committed a sin far above the daring of any of them. Are you sure that many of your schoolfellows were not looking upon you and the others with much the same eyes with which you were looking upon them? . . . . All I mean to say is, they had probably secrets of their own, and who knows that the secret sin of more than one of them was not the very sin which caused you so much misery?'

"'Dost thou imagine, then,' said Peter, 'the sin against the Holy Ghost to be so common an occurrence?'

"'As you have described it,' said I, 'of very common

occurrence, especially amongst children, who are indeed the only beings likely to commit it.' "

Here we have the root of the matter indicated. The desire to be exceptional is in us all, and some of us prefer a bad eminence to none. Pride takes all sorts of unexpected action; and when it leads us to rest our right to distinction on some oddity proper to us, we are on the way to mania.

The thing that strikes us about the Euthyphrodite is the strength of his convictions. He may or may not consciously seek distinction that way, the question does not occur either to us or him, but the passionate energy with which he holds and propagates what seems to us some trifling article of faith is what characterises him, and distinguishes him from the *prig*, a person with whom he may turn out to have some things in common. He takes his own absolute conviction to be synonymous with absolute truth. We have seen how it was with Euthyphro. There was no least chink in his mind to let in light. We do not go so far, but most of us owe our failures to the fact that we will not be convinced against our convictions; and the more ardent we are, the more we err if these should be mistaken.

For this reason it is well we should make children perceive at a very early age that a man's reason is the servant of his own will, and is not necessarily an independent authority within him in the service of truth. This is one of the by-lessons of history which quite a young child is able to understand,—how a good man can, as we say, persuade himself that wrong opinions and wrong actions are reasonable and right. Not that he *does* persuade himself, but that his reason appears to act in an independent way, and brings forward arguments in favour of a conclusion which he has already unconsciously accepted.

This is a piece of self-knowledge upon which every child should be brought up if we would not have him at the mercy of *chance* convictions. Perceiving this, he would see for himself the object of his education; and young people would be eager to acquire knowledge were they brought to perceive that wide knowledge of men and events is a necessary foundation for convictions which shall be *just* as well as *reasonable*.

This is one reason why children should have a wide and generous curriculum. We try to put them off with a parcel of ready-made opinions, principles, convictions, and are astonished that these do not stick to them; but such things each of us has to get by his own labour. It is only a person of liberal mind whose convictions are to be trusted, because they are the ripe fruit of his knowledge.

But, after all, the crank (it is possible to write with impunity of cranks and prigs, because the characters do not precisely fit anyone), is a person who errs by excess. It is not always that he does not know, but that he allows one aspect of a subject to fill his mind. Euthyphro knew as well as anyone the love and reverence due to a parent, but he allowed this single conception,—of justice, without regard to persons, as pleasing to the gods,—to occupy his mind exclusively.

And this is how we bring up cranks. We magnify a single good quality or a single conviction until there is no room for anything else. We probably fail to get in either the virtue or the conviction, but we *do* get in the notion that some one aspect of truth is the

whole truth. This mental attitude accounts for the
extraordinary fitfulness of our opinions and efforts
with regard to education. Now, the country is to be
brought up upon nature-lore, and now upon handicrafts; now upon science, and then upon art; we *will*
not understand that knowledge is food; and therefore we believe that the whole of education may be
accomplished by means of a single subject.

The time may come when we shall consider in the
ordering of our lives the Aristotelian doctrine of the
Mean, not because the Mean is safe and comfortable,
but because excess is injustice, and no one may allow
himself to be carried away by a single idea. Those
who enlist for offensive attack upon some fortress of
iniquity—intemperance, unchastity, ignorance, god-
lessness—are, of course, occupied before all things
with the duty of their calling : a fighting soldier is
not required to fulfil all the claims made upon the
peaceable citizen. For the rest of us, excess is weakness; the ill-balanced character is harmful to society;
and I venture to think that the zealous propagation
of a single virtue in our schools, that of temperance
or thrift, for example, to the omission or neglect
of other teaching, may well do harm to the national
character. We know how the inculcation of thrift has
operated in France. Let us teach these (temperance
and thrift) by all means; but also, and equally, diligence, candour, kindness, all the graces that go to
make up love and justice, all the habits that ensue in
intelligence.

To repeat what I have already insisted upon to
weariness, we must teach children a definite, ordered
philosophy of life. It is all in the Bible? Yes, but
our teaching of the Bible is no longer of the full,

exhaustive, progressive kind that should issue in a balanced character.

The school curriculum should be an exemplification of the doctrine of the Mean as regards both studies and students, and should not be allowed to depend for its success upon the extremes of emulation or ambition. We have seen that the desire for distinction which makes the conventional person come out first in sports or examinations, converts the more erratic into what we call a crank. But, indeed, he has not had fair play—neither the one nor the other boy. Many motives must be allowed due action, and many interests must make their appeal, if we would have a sane and serviceable outgoing person. We are all creatures of infinite variety. It is a wonder to some of us how the fashionable woman sustains the London season: 'excitement,' we say, and dismiss the subject; but many a lady goes through the toils of the season with ease and pleasure who is not in the least excited by any of its events, just as many a man of affairs has a bewildering number of matters to attend to, but finds the day, as Goethe did, 'infinitely long,' and is able to get them all in.

Child or man, we spend half our time in being bored; and we are bored because our thoughts wander from the thing in hand—we are inattentive. When for a moment we do brace ourselves to an act of attention, the invigorating effect of such act is surprising. We are alive; and it is so good to be alive that we seek the fitful stimulus of excitement—to be the more listless after than before, because we have been stimulated and not invigorated. Being bored becomes a habit; we secretly look forward with longing to the end of every occupation or amusement, and are ready to take up with any 'crank' that promises distraction and fuller living, for however short a time. When we have used up that interest, another may occur.

That we cannot find life enough for our living is perhaps one of these 'shoots of everlastingnesse' (not always 'bright') which remind us that we are the 'children of an infinite hope.' But we may not check these growing pains by any means which stunt our growth; and, to begin with the children, we may do something to keep them from getting into the habit of being bored. As it is, the best children pay attention probably for about one-third of a given lesson; for the rest of the time they are at the mercy of volatile thoughts, and at the end they are fagged, not so much by the lesson as by the throng of vagrant fancies which has played upon their inattentive minds.

How, if we tried the same quantity of work in one-third of the time with the interest which induces fixed attention? This would enable us to reduce working-hours by one-third, and at the same time to get in a good many more subjects, having regard to a child's real need for knowledge of many kinds: the children would not be bored, they would discover the delightfulness of knowledge, and we should all benefit, for we might hope that, instead of shutting up our books when we leave school or college, each of us, under ninety say, would have his days varied and the springs of life renewed by periods of definite study: we should all be students, the working-man as well as the man of leisure. The writer knew a man of ninety who then began to study Spanish. We know how our late Queen began the study of Hindustani at seventy, and we all know of work of great value accomplished by aged persons.

But this highly varied intellectual work must not have the passing character of an amusement (is not this the danger of lectures?). Continuation and progression must mark every study, so that each day we go on from where we left off, and know that we are covering fresh ground. Perhaps some day we shall come to perceive that moral and spiritual progression are also for us, not by way of distinction, but for us in common with all men, and because we are human beings.

Much and varied knowledge, the habit of study (begun early and continued through life), some acquaintance with the principles of an ordered moral life, some knowledge of economic science, should help in the making of well-ordered, well-balanced persons, capable of living without weariness, and without a disordered desire for notice from other people. But if, by giving them knowledge, motive power, and work, it is possible to keep the bright impulsive children from becoming erratic persons, what about the slower and less generous natures who are apt, under culture, to develop into prigs?

This letter from a boy's master to his father indicates the sort of thing :—

"Masters sometimes growl because bad boys are sent to them : am I unreasonable in complaining that Herbert is a deal too good? I have always felt it difficult to define a prig, most people find it so, but I begin to feel that the thing is developing under my eyes. Such an early growth should be easily checked. Have you any suggestions to give me?

"Herbert does everything well; is punctual, and if

late, has excellent reasons for being so ; he is absolutely
never in the wrong ; he is industrious, does his ' preps,'
takes his turn in construing, even does his French
exercises (!), has an orderly desk, tidy note-books, a
decent necktie—what is there he does not do ? He
is strong in this new nature-study, turns out a decent
set of verses, makes a decent score at cricket.
' Why grumble ? ' you will say ? ' Haven't I sent you
a model, dutiful schoolboy, if he is a bit conceited ? '
He is not exactly conceited, and he is not dutiful.
What he does is just to let all those virtues shine by
comparison with the rest of the boys who lack them,
many of whom are really more interesting and original
than this Admirable Crichton. He just surrounds
himself with an atmosphere of righteousness, in
which ordinary mortals can't breathe. He is most
aggravating when great people and great things are
being talked about. It is proper then to be humble,
and he puts on the air of an Uriah Heep. If I
snub him, he is silent and stubborn. He is always
too busy doing his duty to be of any use to the small
boys ;" etc.

This sort of virtuous child is apt to be a home-
product. We are not told how long Herbert had
been at school, but should judge that the school
was small and for young boys. Also, we should
imagine that the boy's father, and perhaps his mother
were persons genuinely interested in education, who
set ideals before their children. We gather, too, that
the boy has little originality, although he turns out
decent verses.

Here we have the young prig fully accounted for ;
and at a time when parents and teachers are taking
education very seriously, we must remember that he

is a likely outcome of this very zeal. Such another wave of educational thought reached England in the eighteenth century, and we have 'Mr Barlow's' admirable pupils, Miss Edgeworth's *Frank*, and all the nicely-labelled scales of virtues and vices. The child in a family with perhaps the least in him sees that his parents commend certain things—a well-cleaned bicycle, for example—and that they reprove his brothers and sisters for being late, or untidy, or careless. He is perhaps half-conscious of inferiority to the rest in many things, so he builds up an ideal of various virtues which are easily within his reach, and presents that product which we call a 'prig.' He is a very difficult person to treat. It is not easy to say to him that his virtues are a bore; that nobody cares a pin about them; and as for snubbing him, to snub a person full of conscious virtue is to awaken a slow fire of resentment, not likely soon to go out. Perhaps education should be with us (in our family life) like religion—to be acted, but not to be talked about. The danger of offering material for a false ideal is a very real one. The child with plenty of stuff in him will slip the yoke now and then, and make jokes about the ideal which, although he does not know it, is shaping him; but the good child of slow intelligence 'acquires merit,' picks up the virtues that come in his way, and makes a caddis-worm case of them, an unattached integument instead of a growth from within. It is hard to get at him, because there are no depths to be sounded; even 'the sharp ingredient of a bad success' does not affect him much—he has no measure for the badness. We must recollect that his desire for distinction is as great as that of his more original brother; but, with the cuteness of a small mind, he chooses to excel in being good rather than in being odd.

But this, too, is only a phase of the uneasiness of human nature. It is encouraging to reflect that a sense of deficiency may be at the bottom of it; and for the sake of this weaker brother we must be careful not to put too big a premium of praise on the little conventional virtues, as easy as they are necessary: in our readings and talk, qualities of heart and head must be emphasised, rather than all the good little virtues contained, so to speak, in our own skin. We may even be obliging and helpful, just out of virtue: really it should be possible to make children see that self-contained virtue bores other people, that kindness and service is of value only as it comes out of love, that industry and perseverance are good only when they are the outcome of duty, that there is no worth in the diligent doing of lessons unless we love knowledge. Our danger in dealing with children of this type is that we should lose sight of our own ideal, and accept the display of virtues which are certainly convenient.

It is to be hoped that Herbert will go, by and by, to a big school. Boys do not tolerate the Better-than-my-neighbour order of virtues. Goodness, for them, must be spontaneous, and not laboured; must be unconscious too; they scent a prig from afar, and have ways of their own for taking it out of him.

The prig and the crank appear to have one thing in common—the desire to be remarkable, distinguished in one way or another; this universal desire is a natural provision for the feeding of the mind, as hunger is for that of the body; but we may not bring

up boys and girls to depend upon a moral tuck-shop.
There are other things to live for besides the getting
of praise and the shirking of blame, and every child
is open to the greater considerations.

The more sincerely we face the problems of education, the more shy we become of any cut-and-dried
treatment of human nature.   We have an increasing
sense that a person is infinite, capable of so many
joys, such aspirations, such labours, such distresses—
and uneasiness like that of the restless sea!   How
shall we get tenderness enough to deal with child or
youth? is a question ever present with us.   We know
that his distress and his uneasiness are 'growing pains,'
but we know, too, that he is not always able to bear
them, and finds ways to ease his aching at the cost of
his growth.

Is there no peace?   Goethe, we have seen, found a
curious peace which lasted him all his life in the perception that " we are His people and the sheep of His
pasture," which he got out of his study of the early
books of the Bible.

The writer is familiar with a German watering-place
much frequented by Polish Jews of the poorer sort,
sent thither probably by benevolent brethren of their
race.   These men are by no means phlegmatic; groups
of three or four will engage in talk for hours at a
spell, enviably earnest talk, impersonal, one would
gather, from the faces of the speakers, and not like
the chatter about baths and symptoms to be heard in
passing other groups of talkers.   We may take it for
granted that they are not notable for the conventional
virtues.   But the curious thing about all these men,
whether of the ruddy or dark type, is their tranquillity of aspect; their faces are like those of little

children, simple, interested, untroubled, and very free from lines of anxiety. Is it that, like Goethe, they are aware of themselves only as "sheep of His pasture," and for the rest, take life as it comes?

This peace comes to all simple, natural persons who have faith in God—as to the great German poet, —for faith is the only key to that science of the proportion of things which enables us to take ourselves simply as part of the general scheme, sure of being duly nourished and ordered, and under no compulsion to make life too strenuous. "My peace shall flow like a river" has been said; and this is what we forget, that the peace of God is an active principle, — ever-flowing, ever-going, ever-nourishing, ever-fertilising, — and not a passive state, a quiet creek, where we may stagnate at our ease.

"My peace I leave unto you" conveys a legacy to children as well as to their elders. They appropriate this peace while they are quite young, and live in gladness and at ease; but we disturb them too soon. We throw them back upon their own endeavours; convict them of naughtiness, but do not convince them of goodness; make them uneasy and unhappy, so that they wince under our touch; and fail to open to them free paths to goodness and knowledge.

That children should have the peace of God as a necessary condition of growth is a practical question. If we believe it is their right, not to be acquired by merit nor lost by demerit, we shall take less upon ourselves, and understand that it is not we who pasture the young souls. The managing mother, who interferes with every hour and every occupation of her child's life, all because it is her duty, would tend to disappear. She would see, with some amusement, why it is that the rather lazy, self-indulgent mother is often blessed with very good children. She, too, will let her children be, not because she is lazy, but being dutiful, she sees that—give children opportunity and elbow-room, and they are likely to become natural persons, neither cranks nor prigs. And here is a hope for society; children so brought up are hardly likely to become managing persons in their turn, inclined to intrude upon the lives of others, and be rather intolerable in whatever relation.

No doubt children are deeply grateful to managing parents, and we are all lazy enough to be thankful to persons who undertake our lives for us: but these well-meaning persons encroach; we are required to act for ourselves, think for ourselves, and let other persons do the same.

It is our puritan way to take too much upon us for ourselves and others: we must 'acquire merit' and they must acquire merit; and the feeding in quiet pastures, the being led beside still waters, we take to be the reward of peculiar merit, and do not see that it is a natural state and condition, proper to everyone who will claim it. If we saw this, we should be less obtrusive in our dealings with children; we should study to be quiet, only seeing to it that our inactivity is *masterly*.

Wordsworth sums it all up in a few lines of profound insight, and adds the noble suggestion that, given elbow-room and the freedom of opportunity, we have within us natural powers whose due activity will of itself correct our failings. We may come to see that

this is some part of God's way of forgiving us our
sins :—

> "'Tis known
> That when we stand upon our native soil,
> Unelbowed by such objects as oppress
> Our active powers, those powers themselves become
> Strong to subvert our noxious qualities.
> They sweep distemper from the busy day,
> And make the chalice of the big round year
> Run o'er with gladness ; whence the Being moves
> In beauty through the world ; and all who see
> Bless him, rejoicing in his neighbourhood."

VI

A MODERN EDUCATOR

THOMAS GODOLPHIN ROOPER

I CANNOT better conclude this volume than by adding a grateful if unworthy appreciation of a great Educator, whose sympathy and criticism stimulated, whose life and thought inspired me during about twenty years of educational work. Even so slight a notice of one who served his country with devotion may be stimulating to the reader; but I hope we shall soon have ampler materials for judging of this unusual life.

The Parents' Union sustained an immeasurable loss in the death of Mr Thomas Godolphin Rooper on the 20th of May 1903. From the first inception of the idea he was with us. He was a member of the first committee, which (in 1887) held many meetings in Bradford, where he was Inspector of Schools, to discuss the ways and means of launching such a Society; and he went straight to the principles of the Union, and embraced them with great warmth and insight.

His power of appreciation, in the fullest sense of the word, the outcome of a fine and highly cultivated mind, of wide reading and a wide knowledge of affairs, enabled him to weigh delicately and justly the possibilities and performances of the Union. He considered, for example, "that the Parents' Union is the most important society for stimulating discussion" (on educational matters). Also, I believe he thought that in proportion as parents brought themselves to take an active part in educational thought and educational schemes would schools become altogether living and serviceable. The discriminating quality, which enabled Mr Rooper to appreciate justly and hope steadfastly both as regards this Union and an immense number of other educational efforts and outputs, made him also a keen critic. All who worked with him had the assurance that if there were a defect he would see it, and would help to mend it.

In the matters of encouragement and of just criticism his value appears to have been profoundly felt by the Board of Education, by other members of the Inspectorate, by the teachers in his district, and by many and curiously various educational bodies and associations. But we of the Parents' Union seem to have worked a new vein in that so rich mind and generous nature. One would say that he had a singular power of self-effacement, except that there appeared to be no self to efface. "It is all in the day's work," he would say to his nurses when they sympathised with his weariness in the last sad days; and the saying was a key to his life. He appeared to find no necessity for self-expression or for self-advancement; the work, and he there to do it, appeared to limit his outlook. It is here, I think, the Society in question has reason to rejoice in having drawn from him some graceful and scholarly output of his cultivated mind. He probably would never have written for the sake of literary expression, but we have obtained from him, from time to time, lectures which make up almost the whole of two volumes of essays,[1] full of wisdom, literary charm, and profoundly philosophic teaching. The secretary of a Branch would invite him to lecture; he always appeared to think such an invitation an honour, and the address he wrote for the occasion, while touching on some question of the hour, would rifle his treasures of wisdom, scholarship, and wide reading. The essay on "Reverence, or the Ideal in Education," will occur to some readers. This sort of phrase we find in it: "Without great thoughts there are no great deeds"; "the true spirit of patriotism is . . . . such an appreciation of his country's greatness as leads a man to be humble, modest, ready to sacrifice himself as an insignificant portion for the good of the whole community." I must digress here, to notice how the sterling character of Mr Rooper's thought proceeded from the fact that it was the outcome of his life. " I feel like a soldier who has given his life for his country," he said, smilingly, towards the end, and it is curious how the fact has been recognised. It has been well said of him that "he died a martyr to the cause of education."

Another purely delightful essay is entitled "Lyonesse: Education at Home *versus* Education at a Public School." 'Lyonesse' is his name for the romantic land of public-school life, buried beneath the waves of this troublesome world, but by no

[1] *School and Home Life* (A. Brown & Sons, London), and *Educational Studies and Addresses* (Blackie & Sons).

means forgotten. 'Lyonesse,' no doubt, also, because Harrow, his school, was founded by one Lyon. Has anything more charming been written on this subject, revealing the pieties and loyalties of the public-school man, things which abide with him to the end? Indeed, one wonders if anywhere but in a great English public school and in one of our old universities could a character of such modesty, culture, and capacity be produced as we have to lament in Mr Rooper. He was a Balliol man, a fervent disciple of Jowett, to whom his loyalty was unbounded, and to him, may be, he partly owed his insight as regards the true issues of life. From him, too, came his, shall we say, Balliol way of leaving a question open—of stating both sides and every side. I think he hated dogmatism and declamation, and his quiet, tentative way of throwing out ideas and suggestions was apt to be misleading to audiences not on the look-out for Attic salt and philosophic acumen.

Perhaps an instructed reader of his essays might readily find in them the springs of thought and purpose which moved his life. Was Lord Colling-wood his special hero? The essay on his 'Theory and Practice of Education' is written with what appears to me the sympathy we feel for a *life* which has helped to make us what we are. Speaking of the three great admirals —Jervis, Nelson, and Colling-wood — he says: "It is hardly possible even to speak of these three men without our language and thoughts rising to an elevation above the common and ordinary level of social intercourse." Surely in this sentence we have a key to the fighting ardour which brought about the untimely end we mourn. But then, Collingwood too was an educationalist :

"It was his character and superior education, and study of education, and its kindred study of occupation in daily life, which made possible to Collingwood such an unparalleled achievement" (to keep eight hundred men on the high seas for twenty-two months, and to keep them in health and happiness).

Indeed, what he says of Collingwood is so word for word the testimony those who knew him would bear of Mr Rooper that I cannot help quoting further:— "For it was not merely his ceaseless military (read 'educational') occupation that wore him out. His correspondence was immense, and so highly esteemed was his judgment that he was consulted from all quarters and on all occasions, and on a great variety of questions. . . . He was by nature and education a man of cultivated and refined taste, and of great simplicity of character. He united great intellectual power with great amiability, and these two gifts are rarely united in a man. His occupations at home were reading, especially works on history, from which it was his habit to compose well-written abridgments. His recreations were drawing, and cultivating his garden at Morpeth. . . . 'My wits,' he writes, 'are ever at work to keep my people employed, both for health's sake and to save them from mischief. We have lately been making musical instruments, and have now a very good band. Every moonlight night the sailors dance, and there seems as much mirth and festivity as if we were in Wapping itself.'

"Lord Collingwood was a saint, but he was a human, not a Puritan. Occupation of the right kind was the keynote of his educational system, and it seems the safest and most practical for all engaged in Education."

In this essay on Lord Collingwood we get several keys to Mr Rooper's own life: for instance, the wide reading, especially in works on history, the love of a garden, and above all the stress laid on occupation in daily life. The National Handwork Union found in him a staunch supporter, as did its publication, 'Hand and Eye.' He delighted to turn out a perfect wooden spoon on his Sloyd bench, and was most keen to learn leather-work by watching the students at the House of Education. His zealous work in connection with school gardens and his report on Continental school gardens are well known.

We get another touch of Mr Rooper's genial wisdom and of his many-sided character in his charming essay on 'Gaiety in Education,' and still another in his essay on 'Don Quixote'; and in his praise of chivalry, even reckless chivalry, a further peep into the moving springs of a life is afforded to us.

One more essay I must mention, which he sent for publication a few weeks before the end, on 'Robinson Crusoe in Education.' No other writer that I know of has seen in this delightful tale another 'Pilgrim's Progress':—"But the island hermit is not alone in the spirit. He had thoughts which led him, now undisturbed by the slow stain of the world, to a more elevated frame of mind than he could find in society.

"Knowledge and truth and virtue were his theme, and thoughts the most dear to him were lofty hopes of Divine liberty.

"Robinson Crusoe saves from the wreck a Bible, which his sad life on the island leads him to appreciate. Just as Defoe describes his hero as cut off from social and political life, so he thinks of him as free from ecclesiastical controversy. As Crusoe bit by bit fights Nature and subdues her, so his spirit wins her way to religion by aid of the Bible without human intervention. . . . If you overlook this passage you cannot understand the drift of Robinson Crusoe." Here we get a glimpse into a region of thought which the writer was apt to keep jealously guarded. He abhorred cant—educational, social, religious; but those who knew him best, and were continually about him, knew that he too, like Collingwood, was "a saint."

Delightful as these lectures were to his audiences, the lecturer found perhaps an equal pleasure in giving them. On his annual visits to the College at Ambleside, Mr Rooper had always gleeful — there is no other word—reminiscences of Parents' Union meetings which he had addressed at various places. He was incapable of pettiness or ungentle criticism; and whether his audiences were small and dull, large and intellectual, or large and fashionable, he always seemed to take the same gleeful delight that such an audience (of whichever sort) should gather for the consideration of an educational topic. Indeed, the Parents' Union was always a fresh wonder to him, an extraordinary realisation of the ideal. Perhaps the same sense of gratulation, almost self-gratulation, was shown in the news he brought of students whom he had found at work here and there. In their work, too, he seemed to find the element of surprise that comes upon us in the realisation of the ideal. "Hope," says Dante, "is the mark of all the souls whom God has made His friends"; and he projected, as it were without words, hope, confidence, aspiration and humility into the young people whose work he came to criticise.

Mr Rooper was by no means lavish of praise, and

was almost austere in criticism, but the students felt rather than heard that their spirit was congenial to him and their work satisfactory. His thoroughness was remarkable: he would begin at about 8.30 and go on till 1 o'clock without pause—hear each of the mistresses lecture, and each of the second year's students give a lesson chosen from three sets of notes. The charming thing to both mistresses and students was his keen, inquiring, and personal interest in the subject taught. He had a way of leaving the household more in love with knowledge than before—now galls, now weaving, now local geography would excite his curious interest; now a passage in a French or German author, now Italian or mathematics; but he had always the happy way of making a teacher feel, whether her class were making buns or working problems, that the subject was excessively interesting in itself and for itself. We were all struck by an instance of his thoroughness worth recording.

The notes of lessons presented for his choice by the students have always covered an unusually wide range of subjects, in languages, handicrafts, art, science, and what not, but it occurred to him that he had not heard them give piano lessons, and piano lessons were crowded into the busy day. In the afternoon he would examine the various handicrafts of the students with keen interest and knowledge; then there were drills to be seen, various books to be looked at, and in the evening the students generally entertained themselves and him with some sort of impromptu acting—now and then a charade, in which that awful personage, the Inspector, would see himself taken off with rather graceful audacity. It was good to see his gleeful amusement on these occasions.

He knew people and affairs everywhere, and so was often able to have a good deal of conversation with the students on matters they knew; and certainly he took pleasure in contact with women of some culture who were preparing for that great work of education which he had so deeply at heart; their enthusiasm and their simple manners pleased him. For their part, the students held their Inspector in great reverence as well as cordial regard: they saw that he knew and that he cared. Once or twice, in his generous zeal for education, he came to us, I believe at great inconvenience, to give lessons before the students on subjects in which he knew he could help them. On one of these occasions a student was giving a rather dull history lesson before him; he took up the subject, and such an unfolding of associations, graphic pictures, living interests, perhaps we had none of us heard before. This lesson was hardly a model for general imitation, for I think there are few persons in the country who could have opened such a storehouse.

He used to cause a good deal of entertainment at table by referring with gravity to the time "when I was a governess." He really had, after he left college, undertaken the children of his friends, Dr and Mrs Butler, during some interregnum, an experience which he greatly enjoyed; and that and his five years' tutorship of the present Duke of Bedford gave him a special interest in the education of children brought up at home, and therefore in the work of the House of Education.

It is difficult to speak of Mr Rooper's delightful and stimulating conversation, and of his genial interest in everything. We have lost a great man, and at a moment apparently when his achievements, his gifts and his knowledge should have been of special value to the nation he served. "To me personally the loss is irreparable," writes one of his many friends ; and perhaps seldom have such sorrowful words found a wider echo. His extraordinary devotion as a brother is known to many. But to all who mourn him he has left, not only the legacy of his life amongst us, but of three sayings, spoken when he was very near the end : "hope"; then, after a long interval, "press forward"; and later, "help from Him." Whether spoken consciously, to his sisters, or unconsciously, the messages are those of his life. The blood of the martyrs is the seed of the Church. May we all "hope," "press forward," and look for "help from Him."

I cannot close this inadequate notice of a great, good man better than by quoting a few phrases from an essay on *The Grammarian's Funeral*—with the motto " Great Men do mean what they say," by Mr Rooper :—

"His whole life was a long ascent, in the course of which there was no level ground."

"He lived to magnify the mind."

"Left play for work, grappled with the world, bent on escaping the common life."

"He had laid out his plan for his lifetime."

"A great work will require a lifetime, and its payment will never be received this side the grave."

So let us—

"Leave him still loftier than the world suspects,
    Living and dying." [1]

[1] This *In Memoriam* article appeared in the *Parents' Review* (the organ of the Parents' Union) shortly after Mr Rooper's death. The more intimate references I was allowed to quote from letters written by Miss Rooper and Miss Agnes Rooper.

Appendix

APPENDIX

Pastor Agnorum: A Schoolmaster's Afterthoughts, by J. Huntley Skrine, Warden of Glenalmond (Longmans, 5s. net). We have in *Pastor Agnorum* another very delightful and stimulating book about education; not a number of collected papers this time, but a carefully ordered work. It is addressed to schoolmasters, Headmasters for the most part, by no means an easy class to approach from the rostrum; but Mr Skrine writes with so scholarly an ease and grace, sprinkles his matter so cunningly with the Attic salt of his wit, that we venture to predict that even his hard sayings will be genially received by the appreciative audience he has in view. But the rest of us are not to be left out in the interest of masters. This is a book for us all—fathers, mothers, teachers—whoever is interested in the bringing up, not only of boys, but of girls also. The "shepherd's" calling, he tells us, is "to nourish, rule, and lead," and he must learn his method by the study of the Incarnation. From the life of the *Pastor Pastorum* he must learn to teach with authority, that is, he must know and feel what he

---

[1] It is with diffidence that the writer ventures to reprint anything so fugitive as these short notices of books, which have appeared from time to time in the *Parents' Review*. On the other hand, it may be well to keep certain useful books more permanently in mind, and also, each notice gives an opportunity to bring out, often in the author's words, some instruction of value.

teaches, but must seek, not to reproduce himself, but to produce the pupil's self. He must teach "not without a parable," school lessons must be a parable of the art of living well; humane letters, science lessons, mathematics can be such parables. He must be a preacher of the gospel to the poor, that is, he must teach, not some of his boys, but all, only he must also "give to him that hath." As a ruler, he must deduce the government of school from the ideas of chivalry. The secrets of chivalry are (1) *Truth*, which must be taught without convention or class narrowness, (2) *Freedom*, which needs to be interpreted, (3) *Courtesy*, which must be popularised, (4) *Hardihood*, which should not be only of the body, (5) *Chastity and Woman-worship*, (6) *Religion*, (7) *Brotherliness*, without exclusiveness or partiality. The richness and unusualness of this book may be judged of from the fact that, so far, we have been quoting solely from the table of contents. Seven chapters are devoted to the consideration of the shepherd as the life of the school, inspirer, teacher. Then follows the consideration of the fold. *Our Round Table* sets forth how chivalry can become the bond of Head and Colleagues. This is a singularly ennobling and purifying chapter and throws much light upon what is often a difficult relation, and here, especially, we admire the wit and charm which make hard things good to be listened to. The chapter on *Some Knights of the Round Table*, which gives us racy pictures of several types of master, and that on *The Parent as a Neglected Factor*, are capital reading. The subtlety with which the author justifies that old-fashioned institution, the Family, and even ventures to hold up its casual ways for the consideration, if not the imitation, of the schoolmaster, is an example of how the salt of wit may flavour discernment. The book is a witty and even worldly-wise apologia for Christianity, for the high chivalry of Christianity among masters and scholars; and we earnestly commend it to those other pastors who have but a few sheep to tend in that little fold which they call home. Reverence, insight and common-sense must needs grow from the seed-thoughts the author has dropped.

School and Home Life, by T. G. Rooper, M.A., H.M.I., Balliol College, Oxford (A. Brown & Sons, London, 6s.). "I have tried to study the education of children from the age of three onwards to their coming of age; and this, I think, few have had the chance of doing both practically and theoretically. Most teachers specialise on one period, in the nursery, the 'private' school, on the 'public' school, or the university, because they have only the experience of one such period. The relation of one stage to the next has been too much neglected, with the result that in many young persons there are two or three distinct characters." We have ventured (without permission) to quote the above from a private letter from the author of *School and Home Life*, because we feel that the passage throws much light on the method and scope of the work before us. The casual reader might, without such a guide, say, "Oh, but the work does not deal with education at any particular stage, or even with the education of one sex or the other," and might suppose the charming classical English in which the essays are written to be the vehicle of a literary production, and that only. But parents will find here a mine of suggestions on each of the phases of educational work with which they are concerned, including the bringing up of boys and girls from three (or one!) to one-and-twenty. Perhaps the special characteristic of the work is the author's power of initiating ideas. You read one of the essays, feel that all the thoughts are your own thoughts, and that nothing new is being said; that the "art of putting" is so happy that you are carried over the ground unawares. You digest the essay, consider it in its bearings on your own children, and behold, you find you have imbibed a number of new ideas, practical, vital, full of interest and hope. This would be something were the ideas those of a mere theorist on education; but we have in Mr Rooper an educational expert, at home in the literature, both English and foreign, of each subject on which he touches, an adept in practical education, and, at the same time, an original thinker who passes the materials he receives through the illuminating medium of his own mind. Probably no man in England has initiated so many and so many successful new departures in education; and not the least claim on our gratitude is that, from the very first inception of the Parents' National Educational Union, Mr Rooper has unwaveringly and actively supported the movement. Many of the lectures have been delivered to Parents' Union audiences, and those of us who have heard some of these lectures are likely to keep the impression of them at the bottom of all our educational thought. This is absolutely a book for parents and teachers, not to be borrowed, but possessed, to be at hand ready for reference at the moment.

Thoughts on Education, by Mandel Creighton, D.D. (Longmans, 5s. net). Dr Creighton's *Thoughts on Education* is a possession. They do not, as Mrs Creighton remarks in her preface, propose any system of education; indeed systems failed to interest him; he was too true an educator to care for anything but the practice and principles of education. These papers have been gathered under difficulties. Many of them exist only in newspaper reports, but, such as they are, they embody the insight of the historical mind, the enthusiasm of the educator, and the serious fervour of the Christian Bishop. They deal with such questions as *The Child and the Education Question*; *Examinations*; *The Training of the Schoolboy*; *The Art of Teaching*; *The Hope of the Teacher*; *The Use of Books*;—in fact, these thirty papers cover a wide field of thought, and touch upon questions that exercise most of us. It is not too much to say that in each paper there are sentences of epigrammatic force and terseness which present the subject in a new aspect and leave nothing more to be said. From the inspiring address to Sunday School teachers on *The Hope of the Teacher* we get, "That our daughters may be as corner-stones polished—there is no picture here of useless grace ; quiet solidity of character receives its due adornment, and while it supports the fabric, gladdens the passer-by." And this from *Apollos : A Model for Sunday School Teachers* :—"You must try and make them feel that Christ is knocking at the door of each of their little hearts, and you must realise with reverent awe that it is your work to help the little trembling fingers to undo the bolt and lift the latch to admit that gracious and majestic visitant." We must add two or three sentences from *The Art of Teaching* (which will commend themselves especially to members of the Union) :—"As regards teaching itself, however, I believe it to be an incommunicable art, a gift which may best be defined as the power of showing others some reason why they should learn. . . . That is just what the good teacher does ; he brings knowledge and his pupil into a vital relationship ; and the object of teaching is to establish that relationship on an intelligible basis. . . . The acceptance of knowledge is an internal process which no external process can achieve. . . . A child is much more idealistic than a grown-up person, and readily responds to an ideal impulse. . . . Remember that memory is a power which does not need to be especially developed. It is the most worthless of our mental powers, and a true teacher should always try and prevent his pupils from relying on it." 'This volume comes to us as a welcome memorial of the late Bishop of London.

Vittorino da Feltre and other Humanist Educators, by W. H. Woodward (Cambridge University Press, 6s.). This volume is something more than an interesting study in the by-ways of history. True, it treats of the schoolmasters— especially of perhaps the most famous of them, Vittorino himself—of that most fascinating period, the early days of the Renaissance, the revival of learning. But the real value of the work to us is that it shows on what liberal lines the humanist schoolmaster dealt with the questions which are debatable ground to-day. The radical fault of our English thought and opinion on the subject of education seems to be that we have somehow lost the sense of historical perspective. At each new idea, which we believe we have ourselves conceived, we cry—" We are the people " ; " Never was education like unto ours." And here, towards the end of the fourteenth and early in the fifteenth centuries, we have every one of our vexed questions answered with liberality and philosophic conviction to which we have not attained. Should girls have equal advantages with boys? Vittorino taught girls and boys together. Is early education important? He laid himself out for children of five years old. Should lessons be pleasant? *La Giocosa* not only named but described his school. Should there be a mixture of classes in a school? He taught children whom he educated out of his large charity with the children of princes. Do we desire a wide and liberal curriculum? This was what he accomplished—Latin and Greek, Arithmetic, Geometry, Algebra, Natural Philosophy, Euclid, Astronomy, Natural History, Music, Choral Singing, Dancing, all Games for the training and exercise of the body, and a good deal besides. Plutarch was made much use of as an educational instrument, being employed with the Bible to teach morals. Does it distress many a mother that her son should wade through the pages of classic authors too apt to be unchaste ? Such authors were not admitted into the curriculum of Vittorino. Do we pride ourselves on the higher education of women? This is an old story in Italian education, where women were advanced to professorial chairs even in universities for men. Are we beginning to expect that parents should be serious students of the philosophy of education? This was a matter of course for the fifteenth-century parent, to whom the schoolmaster looked for intelligent co-operation. We owe a great debt to Mr Woodward for focussing our loose thoughts on the subject of the Renaissance in Italy. Persons who wish to have just and liberal views of education, not limited by the last output of the last English writer on the subject, will do well to give this volume a careful and studious perusal.

Educational Studies and Addresses, by T. G. Rooper, H.M.I. (Blackie and Son). This volume of Educational Essays by Mr Rooper is singularly refreshing. The range of the Essays is considerable. We have the treatment of mentally deficient children in the very enlightening and encouraging article on the great French educationalist, Séguin, who studied education as it were at the fountain-head by discovering the possibilities of defective children. Séguin's great discovery was that the normal intellect depends upon the interaction and proper co-ordination of various parts of the nervous system,—"Now in a normal child the various parts of the nervous organism work so rapidly and promptly that it is almost impossible to follow the process of co-ordination. It is indeed quick as thought. In the cretinous child, owing to want of co-ordination, different movements can be studied before they are combined into a whole. The method of training such children consists in doing for them artificially what in the ordinary child is done naturally."

The lecture which follows, upon Manual Training, is an application of this principle to the normal as well as the defective child. The author deplores the fact that the home has ceased to be a miniature technical school; and certainly no English person who saw the unique exhibition at Stockholm some years ago could fail to envy a people who showed so much art feeling, industry, and capacity, such genuine love of work. Again, in natural sequence, follows the essay on Obedience; for the physical possibility of obedience also depends upon the interaction and proper co-ordination of various parts of the nervous system. This is the *rationale* of military discipline. This military discipline the author accepts as the physical basis of obedience; but, he contends, obedience must be moral and rational before it is really human. The working out of this thesis is exceedingly interesting and suggestive; all the more so because, as is his custom, the author adds modern instances to his wise saws. He begins with Agnes Grey, the unfortunate governess portrayed by Acton Bell, and concludes the essay with a reference to the great speech of the late Lord Russell of Killowen, made before the American Bar in 1896, when the vast audience—many of them lawyers—were so impressed with the beauty and dignity of law that they rose to their feet at the end of the speech and cheered vociferously for a quarter of an hour. The next essay, *Lord Collingwood's Theory and Practice of Education*, works out the theme in that most delightful form of a practical experiment. Few people will read this essay without added reverence for a great man, increased pride in a country that has produced a Collingwood, and clearer and more forceful notions of how to bring up one's children and how to rule in one's little domain. Personally we feel that this sort of object-lesson in education is worth more than many manuals of teaching and many studies in psychology. We cannot dwell on the charming essay on *Gaiety in Education*, nor on that on *Individualism in Education*, nor on those on the teaching of special subjects, nor on the especially charming essay on *Miguel de Cervantes Saavedra*. But the thoughtful reader will find in this volume much food for reflection; and, always, the pleasant sense of tempered judgment, great experience, and the recognition that education is not an air-tight compartment of life, but is a part of life itself, open to all the winds that blow and to a thousand changing lights from literature, philosophy, art,—the things and thoughts which we care about.

Religious Teaching in Secondary Schools, by the Rev. Geo. Bell, M.A. (Macmillan & Co., 3s. 6d.). The former Headmaster of Marlborough has done most important service in these "Suggestions to Teachers and Parents for Lessons on the Old and New Testaments, Early Church History, Christian Evidences, etc." Only those who have to do with young people know the steadily increasing ignorance on all matters connected with our faith which they manifest, whether they have been brought up at home or at school. The cause of this lack of preparation for the religious life does not, we are convinced, lie in the carelessness whether of parents or of teachers, but is due to a sort of uneasy conscientiousness; a sense that they are not qualified to deal with Biblical criticism in its present stage; they do not know what to allow or what to refute, and the shortest way on the whole seems to be to let the subject alone. But negligence on this score is alike perilous and culpable; and a grave, moderate, practical treatment of the question by an author qualified both as a scholar and as a schoolmaster is an incalculable boon. The opening chapter on the difficulties that beset the teacher of religious knowledge is very helpful. Mr Bell shirks no difficulty, and he writes always with fervour, reverence, and unshaken faith. We cannot better indicate the aim of this work than by quoting a passage: "'The true value of religious education is to supply children with that faith in man's destination for a spiritual life, which nothing can give them except a belief that the universe is under the guidance of a Divine all-powerful Spirit. Without such belief man drops into a utilitarian secularist. We need, then, to use specially for education such parts of the Bible as display the highest qualities of human character developing under the influence of a pure faith, and thus foster the germs of spiritual heroism and earnest devotion.'[1] But in this, as in other subjects, teaching must be graduated according to capacity. In the religious teaching of young children, as in other subjects, their quickness and freshness of memory will be turned to account by making them learn facts and details suited to their intelligence; but the

[1] *Spectator*, February 1896.

primary aim will be to select and use facts and details as means of quickening and cultivating the germs of religious and moral feeling towards God, love, reverence, trust towards man, such emotions as are stirred by the biographies of the Bible. The purity and equanimity of Joseph, the piety and wisdom of Samuel, the manly faith and religious earnestness of David, the heroism of Stephen, the unselfish zeal of Paul, and, far above all, the ensample of Jesus' most holy life, attract the fresh sympathies of the young, and teaching must indeed be dull which fails to draw from such sources that which stirs emotion and lifts the heart. And in the early years this will be the main object and result of religious teaching; the reason is not much exercised, the higher ideas and truths of religion—sin, atonement, judgment, heaven, eternity—are as yet almost unintelligible, dimly foreshadowed by familiar types or analogies; the difficult problems of freewill, predestination, inspiration, have not as yet taken shape in the mind; the battle-cries of sects, transubstantiation, infallibility of Pope, or Church, or Bible, are unheard of or meaningless. . . . . There is, however, very serious practical difficulty in deciding at what stage in education, and by what methods and agencies, the teacher should begin to supplement instruction in the letter of Bible history and doctrine by a gradual unfolding of the principal arguments and objections that will ultimately have to be faced. There are two questions of first importance on which such supplementary teaching seems to be necessary:—(1) the historical truth and degree of inspiration of the various parts of the Bible, especially the Old Testament; (2) the evidences of the Christian religion, *i.e.* those facts and arguments which convince an educated Christian that his faith is intellectually and spiritually more tenable than any of the rival theories of belief or unbelief that prevail in modern society." The chapters which follow are no mere disquisitions, but contain carefully ordered practical advice as to what to teach and how to teach it; with, for example, a scheme of selections from the Old Testament, or again, topics for lessons suggested by the early chapters of Genesis. The author makes frequent reference to Mr C. G. Montefiore's invaluable *Bible for Home Reading*. The chapters on the "Inspiration of the Old Testament," the "Composite Character of the Books of the Old Testament," the "Resurrection of Jesus Christ," "Miracles," and the "Difficulties of Constructive Unbelief," will be found exceedingly helpful. Indeed, we have seldom met with so much guiding and stimulating counsel in so small a volume.

Special Reports on Educational Subjects, Vol. VIII.: Education in Scandinavia, Switzerland, Holland, Hungary, etc. (3s. 2d.). Mr Sadler in these extraordinarily instructive reports is providing the country with an educational library of unique value. The essays on education in Norway and Sweden are especially interesting, and the new law for secondary schools in Norway contains important suggestions. The article which attracts us most is that upon Children's Workshops in Sweden; the *Arbetsstugor* appear to us to do more than indicate *the* right way of teaching handwork to the children of the working-classes. They strike at the root of a fallacy which tells against educational progress; that is, that educational results are in exact proportion to the elaborateness and costliness of appliances, buildings, etc. In the Arbetsstugor the children work in an ordinary cottage—no more and no less comfortable than a workman's dwelling. The head of every Arbetsstuga is a lady, who, as a rule, gives her time freely to the work. Practical craftsmen are engaged when necessary to work under her direction. Boys and girls attend the Arbetsstuga separately every other day for two consecutive hours; the number of children attending one such school varies from fifty to two hundred. Ten to twelve form a class. Small rooms will do for a class, because of the excellent method of ventilation employed. The work taught is of various kinds: chip and bast plaiting and needlework for the youngest children (7-9 years); for the elder pupils (10-14) fret-sawing, brush-making, weaving, netting, carpentry, boot-mending. "Thus the children have made different kinds of objects. They have plaited hats, made slippers, chairs, baskets of many kinds, tables, shelves, baking troughs, mended shoes, made waistcoats with the button-holes, pantaloons, children's dresses and aprons; they have woven mats, petticoats, aprons; they have made iron and steel instruments, hammers and other tools, rakes, spades, small iron beds, sledges, etc." The work is disposed of at an annual sale, and the sales more than cover the expenses of fresh materials. The children are rewarded by a meal, either dinner or supper, and in these meals not only health and economy, but the tastes of the children are regarded. The children get to love work, and to beg to have some to do at home. The paper on *The Teaching of Arithmetic*, by Mr A. Sonnenschein, is a most helpful contribution, and not less so is that on *The Teaching of Latin*, by Dr E. Sonnenschein. But the whole volume is too full of wise thought and suggestive practice for us to do it justice in a short notice.

Special Reports upon Educational Subjects—Supplement to Vol. 8. *Report on the School Training and Early Employment of Lancashire Children* (Eyre & Spottiswoode, 3d.). To quote from the prefatory note: "The following Report, prepared by Mr E. T. Campagnac and Mr C. E. B. Russell, deals with a question of great interest and importance at the present moment: namely, how best to fit boys who are educated in primary schools for their life's work, and how to better their present haphazard method of obtaining employment." This supplement is melancholy reading. The result of the evidence given by working-class youths, teachers, inspectors, employers, and other authorities with whom the young people of the working-classes come in contact when they go out as wage earners, amounts to a

strong indictment against our system of elementary education. The boys and girls turned out of the schools, even those who have passed through all their standards with credit, are glaringly deficient in intelligence, initiative, and perception. They have no interests, they do not think, and they do not care to read. More than one employer states that he would rather pick up a street gamin for work in his office or shop than the boy who has distinguished himself in passing through the sixth or seventh standard. It is hoped by the Board of Education that the publication of this Report at this time "may be of service to local educational authorities in considering what steps can be taken for securing better and more permanent results from the large sums now spent upon our elementary schools." We profoundly hope that it may, and commend the study of the authors' judicious and stimulating remarks to all teachers. Here is a passage whose insight should commend it to intelligent persons :—
"It may, of course, be said that work is work, and play is play, that the habit of attention is not to be easily acquired, and that labour is necessary to enjoyment. . . . This is true, but it is not a high view either of work or of its reward ; and it may well be doubted whether any work which is done in this spirit is of much value, either to the man who does it or to his fellows. But as regards intellectual work, the doctrine is false and misleading, and it is peculiarly dangerous when it is applied to the work of a school. Discipline must be kept and labour must be exacted, but there should be no radical distinction between discipline and happiness, between labour and enjoyment ; and we believe it is because, somehow, this distinction has been established that an antipathy to books and to reading has grown up in the minds of so many children." We have cried aloud our panacea in the market-place, and no one heeds; but it is cheering and hopeful to come upon so authoritative a condemnation of the defects we lament.

Special Reports on Educational Subjects : Education in

Germany (Eyre and Spottiswoode, 2s. 7d.). This excessively interesting volume opens with an important essay, a considerable work in itself, on *The Unrest in Secondary Education in Germany and Elsewhere*, by the Editor, Mr M. E. Sadler. This essay is encouraging reading to all who recognise "Education" as a living force rather than a more or less mechanical routine. The Board of Education commissioned Mr Sadler to visit the Paris Exibition of 1900 in order to report upon the educational section. The first thing that struck him was that "education is not a thing by itself, but one aspect of national life." It is this recognition which marks the whole essay, and is perhaps the key to the unusual discernment and breadth of view with which the subject is treated. There has never been so deep an interest shown in education, we are told, as there is to-day, but the nations differ in their aims in this matter. Here is a passage which at the same time encourages and condemns ourselves. "Some are in the habit of identifying 'education' with what is taught in schools, and, therefore, of regarding a tidily organised school system as necessarily the most fruitful kind of national education. Others have preserved a healthier sense of the truth that education is but one aspect of life, and, therefore, as varied and as long as life itself, with the result that some of their children get a very much better education than others, and that, in the community taken as a whole, the average of intellectual attainments is low." The comparison between English and Continental secondary schools is searching and suggestive, but the gist of the whole is, that, that which we have, that in which we are great, is due to the free play allowed to individuality in English education. This admits of the action of an enormous force in the making of character. "We English have always believed that some of the highest kinds of learning are not necessarily printed in books, but may be embodied in institutions; that some of the noblest combinations of intellectual and spiritual power seek to revive, inspire, or create some form of corporate life." This is cheering so far, but we cannot escape the charge, brought home to us by this prophet of our own, that we are *intellectually* below other nations, our compeers, and far below what is possible to ourselves. The problem is how to level up our secondary education intellectually without loss of moral force or physical fibre. If we take the author's advice, two doors are closed to us—the perpetual examinations by which school-life is made an uneasy dream, with little or no waking profit, and for which we are held in some contempt by our Continental neighbours; and that other tempting escape, by which we run in and out to this foreign system and that, snatching at a patch here and a patch there to piece up our deficiencies. We must recognise that education is organic—the outgrowth of our nationality—and we can only take in new material of thought in proportion as we can assimilate it and it becomes part of ourselves. Among the nations, two are singled out by Mr Sadler as having characteristics which are a possession for the world, not to be endangered by rash strictures and hasty reforms. England, on the one hand, has the spirit engendered in its public schools. France, on the other hand, has that perfect instrument of thought—its literary language—the outcome of ages of education, in its secondary schools, upon literary traditions. In considering the schools of Germany, the author's view is that German thought and English thought are at opposite ends of the pole. Germany leans to the production of high attainments, England to the all-round development of character; and each country perceives that it has much to learn from the other. The rest of the volume contains deeply interesting reports of education in various parts of Germany, Primary and Secondary girls' schools and boys' schools, Realschulen, Commercial schools, Handelsschulen and what not; an examination of the provision for training teachers; and a very interesting article upon the measurement of mental fatigue in Germany, which discloses sad facts concerning 'overpressure.' It is well that the Head of the Empire is aware that the manhood of his people is being sapped in the schools. The whole volume is most interesting reading, and we commend it to teachers. Probably no step made in England in the promotion of education is more notable than the periodic production of these perfectly adequate yellow-books.

Ideals of Culture: Two Addresses to Students. By Edward A. Sonnenschein, Oxon (Swan Sonnenschein, & Co., 2s. 6d.).—Parents who have not made up their minds on the vexed question of classical or modern culture will find Professor Sonnenschein's two lectures pleasant and helpful reading. We have only room to quote his summing-up of the matter of his first lecture on *Science and Culture:* "Let me cast a brief glance upon the general aim and purport of what I have said. The prime essentials of culture are science and poetry; and they may be cultivated without spreading ourselves impartially over the whole field of knowledge, without ascetically denying our special bent. One branch of either of the great departments, nature and literature, may give us scope for both energies of soul; but the student of nature cannot be independent of the aid of poetry, unless, indeed, he is a poet himself. Further, in resigning claims to universal knowledge, we may remember that to command one department is to command many potentially, and even involves inquiry into and partial grasp of subjects lying outside it. Finally, life is long enough to admit of our making practical experience of our fellow-men, without which we ourselves are scarcely human."

The second essay, on *Ancient Greek Games*, is very interesting, and tends to show that "there are many points of kinship between Greece and England: not the least is the ideal, fostered alike by ancient philosophers and by English philosophers, and by English schools and universities, of physical and intellectual education going hand in hand." We cannot refrain from giving our readers the pleasure of reading of the games of the Greek child: "The rattle, the ball, the hoop, trundled by a crooked necked iron, the swing, occupied the same position in Greece as in our nurseries; the top is as old as Homer. Boys amused themselves with a kind of stilts and with toy carts, girls with the inevitable doll, made probably of wax or clay. It is pleasing to hear of children making their own toys. Aristophanes speaks of a precocious child that carved ships for himself, and made carts out of leather, and frogs out of pomegranate peel. Lucian says that when he got out of school he used to make oxen or horses, or even men, out of wax. Plato recommends that children should have mimic tools given them, in order to amuse themselves with carpentering. But it may be gathered that he did not approve of too many toys, which are apt to discourage originality; he rather praises the natural modes of amusement which children find out for themselves when they meet."

Ethics of Citizenship, by Professor J. Maccunn, M.A. (Maclehose, Glasgow). A singularly sane, many-sided, instructive volume, which most of us would be the better for reading in this age of many open questions. Parents, whatever be their political creed, one of whose chief duties is to bring up good citizens, would, we believe, find matter for careful consideration in Professor Maccunn's book. It is probable that the education of the future will recognise, as its guiding idea, Matthew Arnold's fine saying, that "The thing best worth living for is to be of use." Every man and woman will be a candidate for service beyond the range of his or her own family. The solidarity of the nation, anyway, if not that of the race, is being pressed home upon us, and already the more thoughtful among us suffer from uneasiness if we are not engaged in some kind of public duty. It is not a new thing, by any means, for many of us to take such public service in the cause of religion, but it is a new thing, and shows a wider, deeper conception of religion, that so many of us are now zealous to serve merely as citizens.

But the public has its choice of servants who will serve without wage. It has no call for the ignorant amateur, will none of him. If our children are to be prepared for public service, they must be indoctrinated with what Professor Maccunn calls the *Ethics of Citizenship*. "Oh, my Brother, my Brother, why cannot I shelter thee in my bosom and wipe away all tears from thine eyes?" says Carlyle; and here perhaps we have the note of the future for whatever party or creed. But mere blundering good-will will not serve us. We must be brought up in the principles and in the methods of wise co-operation.

A Survey of English Ethics, being the first chapter of Mr Lecky's "History of European Morals," edited by W. A. Hirst (Longmans, 3s. 6d.). We are exceedingly indebted to Mr Hirst for the idea of publishing in this handy form the first chapter of Mr Lecky's *History of European Morals.* Mr Hirst prefaces the volume by an introduction tracing the history of English ethics from Hobbes to John Stuart Mill. It cannot be denied that our English moralists have belonged for the most part to the utilitarian school, of which it is well said that "The history of the Utilitarian principle is the history of contribution to the stock of happiness; it is the history of what has been done from time to time to improve and perfect the operations of which enjoyment is the result." Again it is said of the Utilitarians and the philosophic radicals, "Efficiency was, in fact, their watchword. The object of efficiency, of a better system of government, morals, and legislation, was happiness." At the present moment the doctrine of the man in the street, and of the thinker who represents him, is distinctly utilitarian. In religion, morals, politics, and education, happiness is his aim; his altruistic aspirations are expressed in "the greatest happiness of the greatest number," and assuredly he labours for the aim he has in view. His benevolent and socialistic enterprises show fine results, all the more so because, as compared with the intuitive moralist, his results are readily put in evidence. In face of these obvious facts, it is startling to read Mr Lecky's statement that "the intuitive moralist (for reasons I shall hereafter explain) believes that the Utilitarian theory is profoundly immoral." This is startling, but it is also encouraging. There are still those among us who believe in the intuitive sense of obligation which we call duty; who believe that the hope of the race lies, not in the alleviation of its discontents, but in this, which they are assured is the fact—that every man has in his nature a notion of right which carries with it a feeling of obligation; that when circumstances call upon a man to express this sense of obligation (though it be at the peril of life or limb or property), that man is for the most part ready to seize such opportunity as offering a supreme good. This is the theme which Mr Lecky works out with singular lucidity and power, and at the same time with full and fair treatment of the Utilitarian position. We strongly advise the study of this "survey" as offering a key to many questions of the hour.

Knowledge, Duty, and Faith: a Study of Principles Ancient and Modern, by Sir Thos. Dyke Acland (Kegan, Paul & Co., 3s. 6d.). Sir Thomas Acland has done a very valuable and timely public service in the production of this volume. We say valuable, because he has reduced a subject of so much inherent difficulty as philosophy to the simplest possible forms of expression, to be "understanded" by people who know nothing of the language of the schools, but who are stirred by the natural human curiosity as to what man can know and what man should do. We say timely, because, since the mind of man began to think, it has occupied itself with the real and the ideal in, so to speak, rhythmic pulsations. For fully a generation the real has been strongly in the ascendant, and science has advanced by leaps and bounds, *pari passu* with materialistic thought. But, according to that law of rhythmic thinking which affects the race as truly as the individual, thought is again turning to the ideal. The limitations of the real, with its one possible outcome, that man himself is a *congeries* of regulated atoms—that there is nothing in the universe but atoms and regulating laws—this doctrine is oppressive to the spirit of man, and there is a strong rebound towards the Platonic conception of the Idea. Thoughtful people, who feel that they know nothing of the history of thought and nothing of the laws of thinking, will find here just the help they want—an introduction to the principles taught by typical thinkers, ancient and modern. Sir Thomas Acland's chapter on Aristotle seems to us especially useful and interesting, and still more so that upon Lotze, whom he describes as having spoken the last word on knowledge and faith and the relation between them. The author has that quality of temperance in thought and word which should distinguish the philosopher. We quote a passage illustrating this quality, and showing the practical value of the work in the conduct of life :—" If we are justified in accepting this doctrine, that the validity which belongs to ideas and to laws (of nature and mind) may be distinguished from the reality which belongs to things embodied as matters of experience, some important inferences may be drawn as to modern speculation.

"One suggestion is, that we must be very careful and self-restrained in drawing logical conclusions as to matters of fact from ideas in our minds, especially on moral and spiritual realities, the bearing or relations of which we may only imperfectly grasp by the intellect. We may feel confident that ideas or conceptions in our minds involve some preceding conditions, or some succeeding conclusions. But we cannot infer the reality of such conclusions—though they may correspond to our limited thoughts—especially when they take a negative form.

"On the other hand, while experience brings home to our minds a conviction of the reality of certain facts as known to us by their appearances or phenomena, and further teaches us that facts follow one another (as far as our experience goes) in a regular order, we shall do well to remember that no length of experience amounts to demonstration, still less to the disproof of spiritual convictions resting on grounds beyond our experience."

A chronological table of modern philosophers is a valuable appendix, and so is a list of books *at low prices*, meant for the help of the students in University Extension Classes, for whose use the volume is intended. We hail a book setting forth a scheme of knowledge, duty, and faith, so distinctly making for righteousness, and recognising the Divine as a fundamental necessity. To criticise the limitations of the work would be to ignore its objects and to forget the class of students for whom it was written. We repeat that the venerable author has done a lasting service for those who will come after him.

PRINTED BY NEILL AND CO., LTD., EDINBURGH.